CHRISTOPHER KENT is a member of the Department of History at the University of Saskatchewan.

A group of Oxford graduates, influenced by Arnold and later by Comte, formed the core of a generation of academic radicals who attempted to define the role of an educated élite in an emerging industrial mass democracy. This perceptive study of the English academic scene traces the emergence of Comtism in the university community and examines its expression in the ideas of Frederic Harrison and John Morley.

The social and political dimensions of Comte's ideology in England are commonly considered to have been obscured by the tendency to regard it as a sort of eccentric religious sect. This study demonstrates the subtlety with which Harrison applied positivist ideas to mid-Victorian politics and the generally underestimated influence of Comte in Morley's political thought. Both men looked to the frank élitism of Comte in an attempt to reconcile – in both thought and action – the political claims of 'brains and numbers.' It was, as the book shows, an attempt singularly appropriate to the requirements of an educated middle class. Set within the context of mid-Victorian academic radicalism, the appeal of Comtism becomes more clear.

This book brings together a complex of philosophical, political, and religious ideas. It reflects the Victorian intellectual's perspective on the process and problems of social change.

CHRISTOPHER KENT

Brains and Numbers: Elitism, Comtism, and Democracy in Mid-Victorian England

UNIVERSITY OF TORONTO PRESS
Toronto Buffalo London

© University of Toronto Press 1978
Toronto Buffalo London
Printed in Canada

Library of Congress Cataloging in Publication Data

Kent, Christopher, 1940 –
    Brains and numbers.

    Based on the author's thesis, University of Sussex.
    Bibliography: p.
    Includes index.
    1. England – Intellectual life – 19th century. 2. Comte, Auguste, 1798- 1857.
    3. Morley, John Morley, Viscount, 1838- 1923. 4. Harrison, Frederic, 1831–
    1923. I. Title.
    DA 533.K32   320.5   77-21722
    ISBN 0-8020-5360-2

To my parents

Acknowledgments

I wish to thank Lord Briggs, the supervisor of the thesis from which this book has grown, for his kind encouragement. Professor Martha S. Vogeler, whose biography of Frederic Harrison is eagerly awaited, has been a generous friend. Professors W.M. Simon, Walter Houghton, Elisabeth Wallace, Royden Harrison, D.A. Hamer, Mr A.F. Thompson, and the Reverend William C. MacVean have helped me in ways they have perhaps forgotten.

I wish I could name all the librarians at the Universities of Saskatchewan, Prince Edward Island, and Sussex, and at the London Library without whose courteous help I could not have written this book. Also, for their permission to use manuscript material in their custody, I am grateful to the librarians of Balliol College and Magdalen College, Oxford; University College, London; the Imperial College of Science and Technology and the Working Men's College, London; the British Library, the Bodleian Library, Lambeth Palace, the Bishopsgate Institute, the West Sussex County Record Office; La Maison d'Auguste Comte, Paris; the John M. Olin Library, Cornell University; the University of Birmingham, the Brotherton Library, University of Leeds; the University of London, and the British Library of Political and Economic Science.

The Canada Council helped me to finance my doctoral studies at the University of Sussex. The Social Science Research Council of Canada, using funds supplied by the Canada Council, the University of Saskatchewan, and the University of Toronto Press, using grants to it from the Andrew W. Mellon Foundation and the University of Toronto, have contributed to the publication costs of this book.

Contents

Preface

Radicalism is relative to time and place. Yesterday's radicalism may be today's orthodoxy, and tomorrow's reaction – it tends to travel in generations. And what is radical in a college commonroom may not be so at a trade union meeting (and vice versa). A century ago, when Oxford and Cambridge were still regarded as among the soundest pillars of the status quo, to be a university radical demanded no prodigies of vanguardism. It was enough to believe that 'the people' were not the enemies of intellectual values and that although they might increasingly be questioning the presumption of leadership by their social betters, they were becoming progressively more willing to give active consent to leadership by their intellectual betters. It was necessary only that the people be given the opportunity to express this willingness and that the intellectuals demonstrate their readiness to provide such leadership. The prime agency of this transaction would be public opinion, that great Victorian invention which promised at last to enable leaders and led to communicate with each other. This line of thought belongs to what Edward Shils has called the 'populistic tradition' of the intellectual – the readiness among many intellectuals to believe that the ordinary people, the uneducated and unintellectual, are a repository of intuitive wisdom and superior virtue (a notion that has gained greatly in strength since the French Revolution). As intellectuals have become increasingly secularized and divorced from the moral authority of institutional religion, they have sought other sources of moral legitimacy. One obvious source has been the people themselves – or 'the nation,' in the more organic formulation; hence the attraction of the idea of some natural affinity between 'brains and numbers.'[1]

This book is about a generation of university radicals who emerged from the intellectual establishment – the public schools and universities of Victorian England. Generation means here a group born within approximately a twenty-year span and shaped by a common education and by common social concerns in its politically formative years.[2] This particular generation was given coherence by a common concern about the duties of an intellectual élite in an industrializing and democratizing society. Since its members regarded themselves as part of that élite, their concern was very immediate. Yet they belonged to the establishment: they were educated to be its leaders and were quite happy to remain within it. They were not alienated intellectuals repudiating their assigned situations. Their radicalism consisted rather in their belief that the answer to England's social and political problems was to broaden the establishment itself – an essentially Coleridgean solution. (There was indeed a strong populistic current in Coleridge's organic idea of natural unity, particularly his belief in union between intellectuals and a people uniquely endowed with an intuitive understanding of political fundamentals.) The university radicals believed that the nation's established institutions must embrace the various excluded groups in English society, notably the dissenters and working classes, so as to give them a fuller sense of participation in the nation's life. Instilling this sense of membership in the nation was particularly important in the case of the working classes. Because the radicals tended to mythologize the working classes by attributing to them attitudes which confirmed their own social ideals, they believed that fuller working-class participation, such as through political enfranchisement, would strengthen rather than weaken the social fabric. Above all, they believed that their own authority as the nation's intellectual élite would be greatly enhanced by a broadening of the establishment, since they would function more effectively with the recognition and deference of a more unified society. Such a development was particularly desirable in a nation felt to be only too ready to disparage the importance of ideas and to deny the need of an increasingly complex society for coherent, authoritative, intellectual direction.

The first section of this book describes the intellectual milieu from which this élite emerged in the 1840s and 1850s, Oxford particularly. Here the movement for university reform was strongly influenced by followers of Thomas Arnold and Samuel Taylor Coleridge who were anxious to promote the nationalization of the old universities – to see them brought into the main stream where they could exert a decisive influence on the nation's affairs as national centres of intellectual authority. This meant ensuring that intellectual rather than social values were given priority in recruiting and educating the élite. It meant reform of the curriculum and teaching arrangements to reflect these priorities. And it also meant ensuring that adequate opportunities existed outside the university for the élite to exercise its talents, to wield its intellectual authority, and so bring the university to the nation. Fortunately the contemporary expansion of the press, civil service, and the professions seemed to offer appropriate opportunities.

The political and social circumstances of the 1850s and 1860s – the slack water of Palmerstonism, the lessening of social strains, the surging prosperity – provided an hospitable climate for the ambitions of these intellectuals. Their ideal was a society without class tensions, united in respect for the benevolent authority of gentlemen whose minds bore the assay mark of a first-class degree and a college fellowship won in open competition. They demonstrated their good faith by 'going to the people' on a number of issues during the 1850s and 1860s, and the people seemed to respond. Then, following the Reform Act of 1867, they put their creed to the test in the 1868 elections when a number of them stood for Parliament as popular candidates, standing above class interest. However, this episode of gentlemanly narodnikism, like so many populistic gestures made since by intellectuals, proved a disappointment.

The second section examines the Comtist movement in England during the 1850s and 1860s as a more systematic and explicit attempt to organize and extend the authority of the university élite. It is within this context that the often misunderstood appeal of Comtism in mid-Victorian England can best be understood. It was not the exotic aberration of a coterie of eccentrics but rather a comprehensive ideology remarkably harmonious with certain established English currents of thought and remarkably well suited to the needs of a middle-class intellectual élite. It not only legitimized their pretensions to intellectual authority but also provided a powerful ideological solvent for social irritants to those who were ready to entertain fairly radical notions of social change for essentially conservative ends – a sort of prospective conservatism rather than the more common retrospective variety. Comtism met the anxieties of classically-educated, amateur-oriented intellectuals by providing a scientifically sanctioned blueprint of the future which assured their continued relevance despite the increasing industrialization, specialization, and democratization of society. The nineteenth century produced no more explicit and comprehensive statement of intellectual populism. It could well be argued that the remarkable thing about Comtism was not that it attracted some support in England but that it did not attract much more.

The check administered to the notion of a political alliance of brains and numbers by the electoral disappointment of 1868 indicated a need for closer attention to the problem of the relationship between politics and the intellectual. The third section of this study therefore focusses on the efforts of two men, John Morley and Frederic Harrison, who alone among Victorian political thinkers attempted in their respective studies, *On Compromise* and *Order and Progress*, to resolve this problem by clearly defining the proper relationship between intellectual and political activity in a mass society. Both drew on Comte's theory of the separation of powers, which presented a clear division between the spheres of thought and action as the only way of defending the integrity of the intellectual against the compromising temptations of temporal power, while at the same time protecting the efficient functioning of temporal authority from the illegitimate ambitions of intellectuals. Comte's solution had a certain ruthless logic to it, but it entailed accepting the rest of his political theory which was an élitist substitute for democracy. Though Morley was attracted, he finally drew back from its inapplicability to existing circumstances and, after much agonizing, crossed the frontier into traditional political activity. Harrison, in contrast, found in this very inapplicability a shelter from the intellectual's dilemma.

It is to the discredit of neither man that they failed to resolve this perennial problem, yet part of their problem was the absence of a recognized profession for the intellectual (indeed the term itself was only just emerging). Like many of their contemporaries, Morley and Harrison sought such a profession in journalism – the great organ of public opinion through which they hoped to exercise intellectual leadership over the nation. Neither found it satisfactory, since it lacked an adequate institutional framework to meet their professional needs. And despite even the authoritarian efforts of Morley as an editor, it seemed impossible to reconcile journalism as a profession with the essentially amateur ethos of independence to which they were also strongly committed as gentlemen. The institution which in this century has come nearest to achieving this reconciliation is the university. It is significant that the secularization of the university, and its opening to a wider clientele, were among the earliest causes espoused by university radicals like Harrison and Morley. These were the preconditions for the emergence of the academic profession, which includes probably the majority of intellectuals in our own time and provides them with greater opportunities than ever to pursue the elusive union of brains and numbers.[3] As A.N.L. Munby has irreverently asked:

Remote and ineffectual Don,
Where have you gone? Where have you gone?
Don with Bentley, Don with Rolls,
Don organising Gallup Polls,
Don back from Russia, off to Rome
Don on the Third, the Light, the Home ...

PART ONE
ACADEMIC RADICALS: 1840-68

1

Elitism, the Clerisy, and University Reform at Oxford

'I hold it the disgrace and calamity of a professed statesman not to know and acknowledge that a permanent, nationalized learned order, a national clerisy of church is an essential element of a rightly constituted nation, and without which it wants the best security alike for its permanence and progression.'

Samuel Taylor Coleridge, *On The Constitution of Church and State*

'We must have more wisdom to govern us, we must be governed by the Wisest, we must have an Aristocracy of Talent! cry many. True, most true; but how to get it?'

Thomas Carlyle, *Past and Present*

'Élitism' is not a nineteenth-century word; one searches the *Oxford English Dictionary* for it in vain. But if it is a new word, it applies to a very old set of assumptions which only floated to the level of political consciousness as a result of the French Revolution – the source of so many 'isms.' That event first challenged seriously the dominant assumptions of political and economic inequality which underlay élitism by thrusting the alternative of equality into the realm of political and even economic possibility: the owl of Minerva had taken flight. The Revolution also challenged traditional élitist assumptions of political causation. What if it was the product of a great upsurge of mass discontent, as its most ardent apologists maintained? This was a fearsome prospect to ruling élites, and it is understandable that they should have favoured more comforting conspiratorial explanations which at least attributed its cause to a rival élite of disgruntled intellectuals rather than to spontaneous mass movements whose existence threatened the very possibility of élites.

The widespread belief that the French Revolution was the product of intellectual subversion called attention to the growing opportunities for influence afforded to intellectuals by urbanization, increasing literacy, and other phenomena of modernization, and to the need for the state to maintain or increase its authority over them. It was in response to the French Revolution that Coleridge, its most profound English critic, gave sharper definition and a new name to that traditional but hitherto unarticulated English type of intellectual élite, the clerisy. Coleridge's clerisy are servants of the state through the national church. Indeed, they are the national church by definition: 'The clerisy of the nation, or national church, in its primary acceptation and original intention comprehended the learned of all denominations; – the sages and professors of law and jurisprudence; of medicine and physiology; of music ... of the physical sciences ... in short of all the so-called liberal arts and sciences, the possession and application of which constitute the civilization of a country.' The Coleridgean church being an institution whose concerns transcend matters of dogma to embrace the entire cultural life of the nation, the clerisy are therefore priests in the widest sense – ministers of culture to the nation.[1]

It is important to recognize the crucial distinctions between Coleridge's clerisy and that more modern type of intellectual élite, the intelligentsia, for the continuing orientation of English intellectuals towards the clerisy ideal largely accounts for the persistent absence of a true intelligentsia in England. By proposing an officially recognized 'permanent, nationalized learned order' of intellectuals Coleridge intentionally deprived them of the function of completely independent criticism which is the ideal of the classic intelligentsia (in its original Russian sense). The clerisy is by intent a conservative body, traditional and hierarchical in its institutions which are supported and given authority and independence by the state, while the intelligentsia is a sort of permanent opposition, determinedly secular and self-consciously apart from the established hierarchy. Coleridge's explicit development of the clerisy idea, an idea rooted in the historic traditions of the national establishment, was largely inspired by the French Revolution's terrible warning against the dangers of disaffected and unrooted men of intelligence driven by a sense of exclusion to challenge the social and political order. Thus he made provision for including all the educated in his national clerisy, so that their abilities might be directed into acceptable channels and their ambitions provided for within the ample and secure bosom of the establishment.[2]

The narrow, negative function of the clerisy as a means of neutralizing the dangerous potential of intellectuals should not be over-emphasized, however, nor its subservience to the state exaggerated. For Coleridge, independence was an important attribute of the clerisy; such independence would be guaranteed by the permanent, unalienable endowment, the 'Nationalty,' supporting such national institutions as the church and the university. Thus the college fellowship or the church living are forms of landed property giving their holders that stake in the nation which ensures independence and responsibility. Coleridge of course envisaged most of the clerisy as coming from the upper classes and thus bringing to it their own independence and self-respect as gentlemen. Upon the rest, however, membership in the clerisy would itself confer the status of gentleman. Yet the clerisy was intended to transcend mere class interest, and its loyalty to lie not with the state narrowly conceived but with the nation, the organic social whole. Nor was it simply to serve as apologist for the status quo but to temper both morally and culturally the antagonistic forces of 'permanence' and 'progression' – represented by the landed and commercial interests respectively – at work in society, and thus to act as an agent of harmony commanding the allegiance of all.

Although Coleridge's public reputation did not prosper after his death, his sensitive and often remarkably far-seeing social and political ideas were sedulously preserved and propagated by a small but strategically placed band of Coleridgeans of whom the best remembered are Thomas and Matthew Arnold and F.D. Maurice. Like many currents in nineteenth-century English thought, Coleridge's influence flowed chiefly through the universities. Thomas Arnold also made Rugby school a primary focal point of Coleridge's ideas – particularly his élitism and his emphasis on cultural homogeneity. The earnest, hothouse élitism of Thomas Arnold's juvenile republic has often been described, but it is significant that Arnold was deeply committed to the education of a *national* élite in which the dissenting and commercial middle classes should take their rightful place. It is significant that Rugby was essentially non-aristocratic and drew on the professional and merchant classes more than did the other major public schools. It was a chief aim of Arnold and his disciples, the best known being his son, to bring these classes out of their cultural isolation and into the main stream of national life and to prepare them for the responsibilities of fuller citizenship (conferred by the 1832 Reform Act) which demanded commitment to the nation rather than the sect.[3]

The Coleridge-Arnold-Rugby connection became prominent at Oxford from the late 1830s when the university was preoccupied by the burning issue of Tractarianism, on which Thomas Arnold became John Henry Newman's leading opponent. 'Everybody in Oxford who does not believe in either Newman or Arnold cares for nothing but Greek verbs,' reported one enthusiastic Arnoldian in 1843. Arnold's position supported a liberal and latitudinarian church – the so-called Broad Church – which might embrace even Dissenters by playing down contentious points of doctrine and stressing instead the Coleridgean ideal of nationality and unity. Many of Arnold's disciples as they came up to the university conscientiously ('priggishly,' some said) propagated this viewpoint regarding themselves as 'the leaven in the lump.' By the 1840s and 1850s Rugbeians had established a remarkable intellectual and moral ascendancy among the more serious and socially conscious undergraduates and formed the backbone of a university reform party that was emerging among the dons. They dominated the Oxford Union and were prominent in intellectual societies like the famous Decade, to which such future luminaries as Matthew Arnold, Arthur Hugh Clough, A.P. Stanley, Richard Congreve, Benjamin Jowett, John Conington, Goldwin Smith, John Duke Coleridge, and Chichester Fortescue belonged.[4]

One social issue that particularly concerned the Rugbeians, at a time when Oxford still preserved the full panoply of social privileges and distinctions, was the Gentleman Question. Aristocratic 'tufts' wore their gold tasselled caps, visible signs of superior station, while lowly servitors like Tom Brown's friend Hardy eked out a shabby undergraduate existence by performing menial duties. Rugby radicals were critical of the aristocracy of birth and the debased, pseudo-mediaeval cult of the gentleman which valued idleness and waste and bred snobbery by dwelling obsessively on outward appearances. They called instead for a new aristocracy of talent and achievement more in conformity with the social and economic realities of an industrial society, and a 'new economy of manners' for the gentleman which would recognize and incorporate the best values of the industrial and commercial middle classes. Perhaps the most articulate spokesman for this cause at Oxford in the 1840s was the poet Clough (whose father, a younger son of old gentry stock, had been compelled to enter trade as a Liverpool cotton merchant and had gone bankrupt). Oxford radicals made pilgrimages to Manchester, capital of the new England, to peer into the nation's future and marvel at the simple and unaffected manners of manufacturing families 'with 10 or 12,000 a year, dining at 2, and with nothing but maid-servants.'[5]

The rhetoric for this radicalism was supplied by Thomas Carlyle, whose writings fired the imagination of many young Oxford men at this time. Carlyle's social views had a good deal in common with Coleridge's, but his visceral, headlong prose gave greater immediacy and a wider circulation to the élitist, organicist critique of society than did the more tentative and cerebral writings of Coleridge. Rugbeians were particularly eager to be enchanted by Carlylean tales of the heroism of industry, for Thomas Arnold had firmly impressed upon them the importance of the new world of industrialism. 'Carlylese,' with its delphic neologisms and inversions, became the jargon of the university avant garde (the 'thaumaturgic heroism of the conquerors of cotton' was the mid-nineteenth-century equivalent of the contemporary 'reification of bourgeois hegemony'), and at the Oxford Union Carlyle was the subject of numerous debates. His ideal of a service élite, an aristocracy of talent working in the great world, whetted the hungry social consciences of young Oxford radicals. One weakness of Coleridge as a social prophet was his diffidence towards industrialization; here Carlyle's idealized captains of industry more than redressed the balance. A synthesis is depicted in Ford Madox Brown's famous painting 'Work,' in which the two men who stand together to the right of the painting and view the efforts of the manual labourers with obvious approval are those two 'labourers of the brain,' Thomas Carlyle and the eminent Coleridgean, F.D. Maurice. Significantly, on the wall facing them is a notice proclaiming Maurice's Working Men's College, where many Arnoldians became teachers after leaving the university and coming to London to pursue their careers. Here they could discharge their duties as members of the clerisy by spreading culture and furthering social harmony. If few Oxford gentlemen could direct the working classes as captains of industry, they could at least direct their education at Maurice's College.[6]

But how well was the university preparing its students to take their places in the contemporary world? Was it educating the sort of élite required by the times? Such questions increasingly concerned the more advanced thinkers at Oxford in the 1840s. The limited old curriculum was an obvious focus for such concerns. Benjamin Jowett complained of the eternal grind of 'simply converting Butler into Aristotle, and Aristotle into Butler, and making them both mean pretty much what we believed before.' By 1853 he had succeeded in making Plato's *Republic* a Greats text and henceforward that Platonic allegory the Noble Lie, with its classic reconciliation of élitism and egalitarianism, became part of the intellectual furniture of the 'men of gold' sent out by Jowett's Balliol to govern the Empire. An even more important development was the introduction in 1850 of a new School, Law and Modern History, which increasingly came to be regarded as a particularly appropriate preparation for the expanding employment opportunities of the civil service. Its foundation was largely the work of Arnold's disciples, who shared his high estimation of the value of history as practical training for 'the great work of government, the highest earthly desire of the ripened mind.' Arnold's brief tenure of the Regius Professorship of Modern History at Oxford (1841–2), during which his lectures were crowded with avid listeners, had done much to spark interest in a subject long virtually ignored at the universities and at most public schools. His disciples became the major force in history teaching in mid-Victorian Oxford.[7]

Arnold taught that history was a science, its study disclosing the laws which governed the growth of nations, like the growth of men, through the stages from infancy to manhood. Such a view of history had obvious educational advantages since it made possible instructive comparisons between nations and across time. The manhood of Classical Greece chronicled by Thucydides was comparable with England entering its maturity in the nineteenth century – 'modern' history meant for Arnold the history of any nation at its period of fullest development. Thus the science of history provided students with 'rules or formulae' applicable not only to past events but to the present as well. One such rule was the prevalence of class conflict as nations passed from one stage to the next. Related to this was the tendency towards immiseration and the widening of the gap between rich and poor. Change was inevitable; it could not successfully be resisted but it could be controlled and its impact moderated. The task of a clerisy initiated in the laws of history was to bridge the gap between the classes and to prepare the way for change – such as the inevitable coming of democracy, ensuring that it came at the right time. Arnold believed that England in his own time was passing through a particularly critical transitional stage in her development, and succeeded in instilling in many of his students some of his own intense and conscientious concern with current politics.[8]

Another of Arnold's rules of history was the critical role of revolutions in the development of nations. Guizot's history of the English Revolution and Mignet's study of the French Revolution were Rugby texts. Arnold himself welcomed the 'most blessed revolution' of 1830 in France, and in 1848 his former students greeted the proliferating European revolutions with even greater enthusiasm. All had of course read Carlyle's *French Revolution*, which Arnold praised highly. Thomas Hughes and John Conington were active in Maurice's Christian Socialist movement. 'Citoyen' Clough became a connoisseur of revolution, visiting first Paris, where his letters show acute insight into the ideological splits which shattered the Parisian revolution, and then Rome where he witnessed the death of Mazzini's republic (his poem *Amours de Voyage* brilliantly evokes the Roman revolution and the dilemma of the sympathetic but ineffectual English intellectual who looks on, unable to bring himself to participate). Preceding him to Paris in April 1848 was a party of Oxonians including A.P. Stanley (who had won a prize at Rugby for an essay on 'Sicily and its Revolutions'), Benjamin Jowett, F.T. Palgrave, and Robert Morier – all eager to penetrate the mysteries of revolution by interviewing its participants. They visited Michelet, mythologist of the revolutionary 'People,' who turned the conversation to the impending Chartist demonstration of 10 April in London, from which he expected much. 'It will be of little consequence,' was Jowett's knowing comment; 'Ireland will be our revolution,' was Stanley's.[9]

The revolutions of 1848 brought home vividly to such minds the lesson of Arnold, Carlyle, and Comte (who was also being read by the more advanced at Oxford) that they were living in an age of revolution. Neither Napoleon's 'whiff of grapeshot' nor Wellington's 'thin red line' had stopped the true revolution – that of ideas – from which not even England could isolate itself. As Matthew Arnold remarked eleven years later in his largely forgotten pamphlet, *England and the Italian Question*, the 'ancient world of force' had given way to the 'modern world of ideas'; foremost among these were 'the ideas of 1789.' Only those statesmen who recognized this fact could hope to govern the idea-moved masses in an age of incipient democracy. But where were the English statesmen who recognized this, Arnold asked? The lesson drawn in England from the first French Revolution had been that politics and ideas were somehow dangerously antithetical and a flight from ideology into pragmatism was the response. By the 1840s an articulate generation of young university men, strongly influenced by Arnold and Coleridge, was beginning to speak out against this national characteristic of political anti-intellectualism and was looking to the university as a possible force for overcoming it.[10]

Mark Pattison, a leading Oxford reformer, detected anti-intellectualism in practically every area of national life. England, he argued, was blundering along without order or authority in its institutions, without system or principle in law, trade, or government, trusting in a vaunted pragmatism which was no longer adequate to the complexities of the mid-nineteenth-century world. Such a nation stood in particular need of intellectual direction from the university. Unfortunately, however, the university seemed all too inclined to confirm this national prejudice against ideas. Able young academics, especially the Arnoldians, were very sensitive to the currents of continental scholarship; but, as Pattison remarked, 'German' was a term of abuse among many insular academics who plumed themselves on being 'practical.' 'Their only claim to the title is never to have looked at a demonstration or a theory,' he observed acidly. These younger university men also deplored the university's prevalent isolation, intellectual and social, from the 'proper organ' of the 'national mind'; yet it was noteworthy that two of the most important intellectual forces among young Oxford, Mill and Carlyle, came from outside the university.[11]

The inadequacies of the university were attracting increasing attention from critics outside its walls as well at this time. To the more utilitarian critics the backwardness of the curriculum was most evident in the neglect of natural science: its study declined notably at Oxford between 1830 and 1850 and, despite the founding of a School of Natural Science in 1850, continued to be little regarded. Pointed comparisons were made with the more relevant courses offered at the newly-founded University College, London ('Stinkomalee' as it was contemptuously dubbed by Oxonians). Such criticisms came frequently from Dissenting interests, which were of course excluded from Oxford matriculation by religious tests (at Cambridge they were excluded only from the degree). Indeed, the universities were above all vulnerable to external critics on their claim to be 'national' institutions, and were attacked for the inefficient, extravagant, and exclusive manner in which they used the national endowment that supported them.

The popular middle-class radical cry of 'Disestablishment and Disendowment' might easily be turned on them. Earlier in the century the public schools had been seriously threatened from this quarter but had successfully responded with the great internal regeneration of the 1830s and 1840s in which Thomas Arnold was the leading figure. These reforms not only stemmed the tide of criticism but enabled the mid-Victorian public schools to win over middle-class opinion. As one would expect Thomas Arnold was an early advocate of opening the old universities to Dissenters, for it was an obvious way of making good their claims as national institutions also.[12]

Pressure for university reform began to build up within Oxford in the late 1840s, as the fading of the Tractarian controversy freed intellectual energies for new concerns. The very appointment in 1850 of a Royal Commission to enquire into the condition of Oxford was a triumph for the reformers, and their evidence gave its *Report* (1852) a strongly liberal tone. Arnoldians were very prominent as members of the commission (A.P. Stanley was appointed secretary, Goldwin Smith assistant secretary), as a pressure group within the university, and as publicists of the reform cause outside it. In the ensuing decade of reform they forced the conservative elements onto the defensive and made themselves for a time the dominant interest in university politics and government. The reformers did not agree among themselves on all points, however, and had no unanimous concerted programme. Their unity consisted essentially in their common ambition to 'nationalize' the university, to restore it to the nation by making it better suited for providing a national élite, a clerisy. As élitists they had at least three questions to answer: where was the élite to be recruited? how was it to be educated? and what was to sanction its authority? Framed in practical terms, the first question related to defining the university's clientele, the second to providing appropriate teaching arrangements, and the third to ensuring suitable employment of university graduates. The second question, not surprisingly among academics, was the most contentious.[13]

The professorial system seemed to many reformers the best means of expanding the curriculum, extending the reach, and improving the quality of university teaching. Professorships were of course long established in the universities but had come to be considered largely as sinecures, venerable relics of mediaevalism. Professorial instruction had been replaced almost entirely by the tutorial method, centred in the individual college. Advocates of professorships claimed that their rehabilitation and expansion offered a lever for all sorts of desirable reforms. Since many colleges, particularly the smaller ones, had few members actually engaged in teaching, and these were usually classicists, they could not provide instruction to students who wished to pursue studies outside the traditional classical curriculum – in the new schools of science or history, for instance. An expanded professoriat could provide non-collegiate university lectures in those subjects where the colleges were weakest. Professorial teaching also offered a means for opening Oxford to poorer students by reducing the cost of university education. This entailed schemes for permitting students to live outside the colleges in boarding houses while receiving instruction through the public lectures of university professors in the Scottish and continental fashion. A third benefit expected of professorial teaching was a general improvement in scholarship, for the appointed professors would be the most learned men in their fields, mature scholars able not only to transmit their vast knowledge but to further it by research and study unburdened by constant undergraduate tuition. A related benefit was that the prospect of elevation to such prestigious and appropriately remunerative professorships would greatly enhance the attraction of university teaching as a career for able young men. [14]

Reformers were not wholly agreed on the question of professorships, however. The liberal Pattison vigorously defended the tutorial system by pointing to the United States with its 'poverty of thought' and France with its 'chaos of speculative politics' as awful warnings against basing education on 'the facile process of lecture hearing.' He felt the tutorial system was the proper method for educating 'a cultivated clerisy,' and envisaged a division of roles, with the new professors chiefly fulfilling the university's other duty – scholarly research. Benjamin Jowett, in contrast, spoke for those who were less fearful of the extension of professorial teaching; he hoped it would restore intellectual order at the university. Jowett argued that the unsettled state of opinions at Oxford during the Tractarian controversy had been largely due to the absence of authoritative intellectual oracles to dispel the confusion. This want would be filled by an eminent professoriat who would also restore the university to its rightful position as the intellectual authority for the nation. [15]

The apparent ambitions of the more extreme advocates of professorial expansion aroused suspicion among many college tutors, however. The spectre of centralization and the consequent threat to college autonomy led them to organize against the spectre of a university-wide dictatorship of the professoriat along Germanic lines. As a result the professorial approach to university reform had to be largely abandoned and a more decentralized approach through the colleges adopted. The attention of reformers concentrated on that uniquely English academic institution, the college fellowship. Here, perhaps, was the key to university reform. The problem was that the precise function of fellowships was becoming increasingly unclear. Their original purpose was to endow and support the clerical profession, by tradition the nation's chief learned profession. Thus the conditions governing their tenure were largely religious, tied to subscription to the Church of England, celibacy, and eventual ordination. But many reformers now argued that the fellowships were properly meant to be a national endowment of intellectual culture and that their monopolization by the church, however appropriate in the middle ages, had become anomalous and anachronistic. Pattison argued that college fellows should constitute a 'professional class of learned and scientific men,' a phrase recalling Coleridge's 'permanent nationalized learned order.' The word 'professional' identified the crux of the dilemma, however, for the fellowships were the keystones of the amateur ideal of gentlemanly independence which permeated the ancient universities.[16]

The amateur status bestowed by the security of the fellowship – the freedom and independence ensured to its holders – was quite out of harmony with the academic functions of the university and unconducive to professionalism in teaching. Fellowships carried no obligation to teach and in 1852 Oxford, with 540 college fellowships, had only some seventy efficient college tutors (total undergraduate enrolment at this time was about 1500). Post-1852 college reforms reduced the number of fellowships to 350, which still left a considerable surplus of non-teaching fellows. Those who did teach were usually extremely young, many staying on only a few years before leaving the university for other fields; thus turnover was very high. One reason for this was the call of marriage, celibacy being generally a condition of fellowship tenure until the 1870s. Another was poor promotion prospects: there was a shortage of higher positions in the ill-defined academic hierarchy and mortality was the chief determinant of their availability. Under such circumstances university teaching did not offer an attractive career for the ambitious intellectual.[17]

A fellowship was thus both an endowment to teach at the university and an encouragement to try other professions. For there were alternatives: the bar was a traditional temptation for the ambitious young fellow; journalism was claiming an increasing number, as were the expanding public schools which paid well (a senior classics master could earn over £1400 a year at Rugby in 1864). There was also private coaching at the university, which was becoming more common as competition increased among students for the financial rewards of success in examinations; an energetic coach with a good record for firsts could do very well financially. (Paradoxically, private coaching flourished because of the very amateurism of formal instruction at the universities.) In exercising these and other options the possession of a fellowship could be a crucial consideration. As long as the holder remained unmarried, or for a reasonable term (some fellowships had a fixed term), he could count on a basic income averaging about £200 a year – a cushion of financial security which softened the hazards of venturing out of the snug harbour of academe.[18]

As a result of this mobility, undergraduate education was left largely to young fellows whose vocation was not necessarily scholarship or education. The teachers were often little older than the students, had similar background and interests, frequently moved in the same social circles, and were active in the same societies such as the Union. One observer commented on the absence at the university of an intermediate class between the transitory young dons and the old ones who had not been bold enough to 'push into the adventures of life.' There was a generation gap, but it divided the teachers rather than separating students from teachers. Meanwhile, more colleges were opening their hitherto exclusive fellowships to university-wide competition based on intellectual ability, in order to raise their prestige and attract able undergraduates. As a consequence, despite the reduced number of fellowships, the opportunities for gaining them had in fact increased – for the talented. Yet this simply brought into the colleges fellows all the more able (to pass exams, at least) and therefore more likely to find attractive employment outside the university.[19]

Because enrolment was declining in the 1850s (the turning-point of this trend was 1862), the colleges responded by creating new undergraduate scholarships with funds released by the reduction in fellowships in order to attract a greater number of talented youths. Leslie Stephen noted sardonically that 'the price of good undergraduates has risen fearfully' as a result of the spirited bidding of the colleges. But the increased prize money did not open the universities to the poorer students; rather it placed bounties on the privileged preparatory education to which the poor had no access. Worse still, Mark Pattison feared, it aroused the ambitions of young men who had the intelligence but lacked the scholarly vocation, luring them into the university and away from their proper destinations in commercial life. Fellowships were being treated as pensions, awarded as prizes for examination success instead of as a means to promote the furtherance of knowledge.[20]

The academic milieu created by these conditions was perhaps stimulating to the young, ambitious, and talented. But pedagogic amateurism encouraged by the system of fellowships, combined with the increasingly competitive atmosphere, produced an educational formula with obvious limitations. Since many of the tutors were young honours and prize men with fresh memories of their exams, they naturally urged their students along the same road that they had so recently, and successfully, travelled. Critics remarked that a tutor fresh from his finals could hardly be expected to have much knowledge beyond the bounds of the required texts, and the large number of hours of teaching per week which each tutor undertook left little time for independent study. For exam purposes there was a well-defined body of knowledge to be transferred from teacher to student, and the tutor had neither opportunities nor encouragement to deepen his own learning. This hermetic method, a sophisticated version of Lancaster's and Bell's monitorial system, was conducive to intellectual complacency both in teacher and subject. Thus C.H. Pearson, an Oxford student of the 1850s, criticized the 'superficial completeness' of Oxford philosophy teaching which he attributed to the 'skill with which clever men, constantly grinding at it, had reduced it into form.' The teaching of history, though less pretentious, was much sounder thanks to Arnold, he felt. However undergraduate studies even in classics were becoming increasingly sensitive to contemporary intellectual trends: Mills' *Logic* and *Principles of Political Economy* were said to have become essential reading by the 1850s for those who aspired to a first. Mark Pattison sourly noted the results of this growing emphasis on relevance: Oxford undergraduates were being taught to write with a dogmatism proportional to their ignorance on important contemporary matters – the notorious art of the leader writer. Tutors were urging students to model their essays on the *Spectator* and *Saturday Review*, leading intellectual weeklies largely written by clever university men. (Pattison was himself an editor of the avant garde *Westminster Review*.) There was indeed a growing intimacy between the university and the periodical press, yet this could be defended as a valuable channel through which the authority of the university could be brought more effectively to bear on the nation, thus helping to answer the other questions posed by élitist reform.[21]

To sustain its claim to being the nation's 'intellectual capital,' in Pattison's phrase, the university had to draw upon the nation as a whole – which meant opening its gates more widely. The exclusion of Dissenters was all the less justifiable after the Religious Census of 1851 had authoritatively confirmed their numbers and importance, and, indeed, religious tests for the Oxford BA were abolished by Parliament in 1854. But there still remained virtual social and financial tests: a university education was the traditional prerogative of the gentleman, costing on average £1000. Reformers did not agree on the extent to which these informal but real barriers should be lowered. Some advocated special accommodation for poorer students in private halls or lodging houses to enable them to gain a university education at minimal cost.

But Goldwin Smith, the Regius Professor of Modern History, thought it absurd and archaic to resurrect the mediaeval ideal and assume that in the middle of the nineteenth century swarms of middle and lower class youths would uproot themselves and occupy uncomfortable Oxford lodgings merely to hear a few professors when they could get much the same thing more easily through books, periodicals, and public lectures. After all, one of the great advantages of the mid-Victorian publishing boom, particularly in periodicals, was that it gave Oxford the ear of the people without inflicting their physical presence on the university. It could thus both speak to the nation at large and educate in the more traditional way a small élite. Smith conceived of the university fulfilling a social as well as an intellectual role, the essence of which lay in the college community – something the lodging house could never reproduce. Thus a liberal education was inevitably expensive and had to remain largely the prerogative of wealth. But there were many rich Dissenters who could well afford to send their sons to Oxford, where they would be made into gentlemen and brought within the cultural establishment. Arthur Hugh Clough argued that this expense was a wholesome check, since it discouraged those who were falling in society, such as unsuccessful professional men anxious to send their sons to university lest they lose caste as gentlemen. To maintain artificially an impoverished upper class was 'contrary to the genius of England,' he declared. The university should reflect social realities and register the arrival of new social élites. But to open the universities too widely might 'destroy the subtle superiority which it is the object to communicate.'[22]

This socially restricted view of the university was called the 'gentlemanly heresy' by those reformers who did not share it, such as Thorold Rogers, professor of political economy at Oxford. Rogers was disturbed by the contrast between the nation's rising population and Oxford's declining enrolment in the 1850s, which seemed to indicate that the university was losing its importance to the nation. His remedy was to reduce the cost of a university education to nearer a hundred pounds by encouraging lodging houses and public lectures so as to create an independent, non-collegiate class of students. These he believed would be largely Dissenters, who would be uncomfortable in the 'narrow and limited society' of the colleges but whose presence would bring into the university a breath of the real world and rescue the 'gentlemen' from their cloistered existence. His concern was thus the reverse of Goldwin Smith's. Rogers was a prominent member of the Oxford Local Examinations Delegacy, established in 1857 to draw up and administer the system of local, voluntary exams for schools which, it was hoped, would establish a reputable and nationally accepted standard of secondary education in England (among its originators were J.L. Brereton, a former pupil of Arnold's at Rugby, and Frederick Temple, headmaster of Rugby). Rogers welcomed this scheme as another means of restoring the university's national influence. By introducing some measure of order and coherence into the notorious tangle of voluntaryism that characterized English secondary education, it could extend its leadership from the university level even to those who did not intend to enter the university.[23]

Examinations were the great Victorian device for reconciling equality and élitism, and in the 1850s university reformers were becoming very conscious of the opportunities they offered the university to command certain strategic heights of national life. At Oxford and Cambridge the art of examining undergraduates had been developed since the turn of the century to a very high pitch. The scientist

Francis Galton confidently claimed that a senior wrangler at Cambridge who in his finals gained thirty-two times the marks of the lowest honours candidate obviously had thirty-two times his ability. A young Oxford man, G.C. Brodrick, argued that given adequate time and skilled examiners there was 'hardly a quality required in the transaction of business, whether vigour, readiness, address, judgement, accuracy, power of combination, memory, invention, presence of mind, or what may be called intellectual generalship, that cannot be weighted in an examination.' He therefore proposed yearly or half-yearly government-administered examinations which could be taken by an applicant specifically to determine his 'intellectual standing ... with reference to the qualities which are most valuable in practical life.' The result would be a public degree, first class, second, third, or pass, recorded for future reference should candidates subsequently seek government employment. In the brave new world of competitive exams the university might become the nation's intellectual assay office, setting its mint mark on the population through examinations. This was already beginning with the newly instituted civil service exams, the majority of whose examiners were university (mainly Oxford) graduates. And as for Brodrick, a Balliol double first, president of the Union, Arnold prizeman, fellow of Merton, barrister, civil service examiner, and *Times* leader writer – he was a perfect specimen of the mid-Victorian university élite which looked forward confidently to positions of influence and authority in the nation.[24]

The cult of exams had its critics among reformers, however. Pattison feared that the universities were becoming so absorbed in perfecting the mechanics of examination that subject matter was becoming increasingly a subordinate consideration – examinability being the chief criterion for its choice. Dons were thus acting more as umpires than scholars. It was also objected that examinations rewarded second-rate minds, producing a breed of mechanical examination-passers. Two respected French observers, Montalembert and Tocqueville, remarked that the extension of education and the encouragement of competitive exams in England would artificially stimulate the expectations of humble youths, deflecting them from their normal paths. The pressure of their demands for employment would inevitably lead to expansion of the government bureaucracy, which would not however be able to keep pace with demand – hence the eventual development in England of a potentially dangerous unemployed intellectual proletariat such as was believed to exist in the over-bureaucratized states of France and Germany. Another consequence would be the usurpation of English government and administration by a mediocre functionary group recruited from the lower classes. But optimistic young university men like Bernard Cracroft scornfully dismissed the warnings of these demoralized foreign aristocrats: the vigorous ruling classes in England would gladly accept the challenge of competition, for 'the higher class is more intelligent than that below, or civilization is but a name.'[25]

We thus arrive at the third major question of university reform – finding suitable employment for the university's élite. The reform of the civil service was not only contemporary to but closely linked with the university reform movement, through men like Jowett and Temple whose influence on the Northcote-Trevelyan Report of 1853 was very considerable. These two men had already established a strategic Balliol presence in a major area of civil service growth, the Education Department, and Jowett was quick to appreciate the opportunities for greater university influence in a reformed and competitively recruited civil service – not just by examining but by providing candidates for the higher positions.[26]

The activities of the civil service, and the civil servant, were much in the public mind at this time. The great social reform legislation of the 1830s and 1840s, most notably the New Poor Law and Factory acts, demanded a growing administrative apparatus for their enforcement which bred fears of centralization and bureaucratic dictatorship in many minds. This 'heroic age' of reform called forth a generation of civil servants of appropriately heroic proportions, men like James Kay-Shuttleworth, Edwin Chadwick, and Rowland Hill, – agitators and interventionists, zealous in promoting the particular causes for which their very appointments marked major victories. The heroic age ended, however, in the late 1840s when, as Henry Parris has remarked, the defeat of Chadwick's and Kay-Shuttleworth's centralizing ambitions were a decisive check to the trend towards government interventionism. It was a critical moment for the redefinition of the function and style of civil servants. Their legitimate spheres of activity and influence were still ill-defined, as Chadwick's propagandist activities demonstrated; political and administrative activities were rather confused. The hierarchical position and social status of the civil servant were also indeterminate – that Chadwick, Kay-Shuttleworth, and Hill had not the social provenance of gentility was one of the major obstacles they faced in their work. However, traditional recruitment by patronage was also coming under increasing criticism, which found its focal point in the Crimean War mismanagement. Here was a clear opportunity for university men to step in and create a proper gentleman's profession in the civil service, to regularize and codify relationships between politicians and civil servants, and to create an appropriate style and mode of operation through their shared social and educational background with the politicians.[27]

A major problem of civil service reform was the tension between two different conceptions of the civil servant – on the one hand the bureaucratic conception of the dependent career specialist, efficient and expert within a confined area, and on the other the clerisy ideal of the independent gentleman amateur, the liberally educated generalist capable of applying his comprehensive viewpoint to a variety of activities untrammelled by bureaucratic routine and less vulnerable to political pressures by virtue of his occupational mobility. The solution to this problem, the answer to the pessimists who foresaw the domination of the civil

service by examination-induced mediocrity, was of course the formal establishment within the civil service of a two-tier division, corresponding to these different conceptions, with recruitment of the upper division reflecting the clerisy ideal
and the lower containing the routinized, specialized bureaucrats. The university
man naturally inclined towards the former. The emerging mandarinate offered
status, power, and a sound income (upwards of £300 a year to start in the first
division openings). The civil service commissioners appealed directly to the university man, requiring 'no particular course of special studies'; their ideal con-
formed with that of the university – the well-rounded amateur. The India Civil
Service was particularly attractive; as G.O. Trevelyan irreverently observed, it offered a young graduate authority 'as great as that arrogated by the most sublime
of Dr. Arnold's praepostors during his first term in university.' It was even suggested by Pattison and Thorold Rogers that the possession of a university degree
might be made a requirement for holding senior civil service posts, as in Prussia,
though such bold suggestions raised in most minds the spectre of excessive intimacy between university and governments such as had led to the loss of university
independence on the continent. The English universities were rightly proud of
their independent and self-governing status. They would shape the civil service
rather than vice versa.[28]

University reformers were also anxious to ensure the allegiance to the clerisy
ideal of the new professions whose proliferation was characteristic of later Victorian society. This was difficult because professions such as accounting, archi-
tecture, or engineering, in emphasizing the division and refinement of technical
skills required by an industrial society, differed markedly from the traditional liberal professions such as the church or law, with their commitment to general culture and their ethic (however attenuated) of service to the community. Yet reformers hoped that a common liberal education, preferably provided by the university but at least approved by it (through the ubiquitous exam), would be recognized by the new professions as a necessary prerequisite for professional training so that the proliferating specialities would not become non-communicating.
Jowett was even ready to entertain the possibility that the university might offer
introductory courses in professional specialities to be taken at the end of the undergraduate programme so as to smooth the transition to professional education
and strengthen the university's contact with the professions.[29]

The law attracted particular attention from university reformers not only because the bar was the traditional and increasingly popular secular profession for
university graduates but also because the haphazard method by which barristers
were trained seemed increasingly inappropriate to the strategic importance of the
profession in the national life. The absence of any coherent study of general principles in English legal education was felt to be reflected in the irregularity and un-

certainty of court decisions (in a system relying heavily on judicial precedent) and in the evident inadequacies of Parliament's response to the increasingly complex legislative needs of society. Here again smug pragmatism seemed to be the order of the day. University reformers, many of them barristers, were in the van of the growing feeling that England's ramshackle legal system demanded the reforming attention of systematic legal scholarship such as the university was best suited to provide. The division of the School of Law and Modern History into separate schools in 1872 was one consequence of that demand.[30]

But the obvious profession for the clerisy was the academic profession itself; so at least it seems in retrospect. The university reforms of the 1850s, particularly the opening of many college fellowships to competition on merit, opened a debate between those who wished to see the fellowships made the exclusive endowment of an academic profession and those who regarded them, in part at least, as a reward for intellectual talent and an endowment enabling clever young university men to establish themselves in other professions. The former view, supported by such men as Mark Pattison and his Cambridge ally, Henry Sidgwick, ultimately prevailed. University enrolments began to climb from the late 1860s, reflecting the growing success of the universities in winning the allegiance of the middle class (this was assisted by the further secularization of the universities, such as abolition of tests for MAs). The professorships were markedly strengthened at the expense of colleges in the second wave of reform in the 1870s. And particularly significant to the academic profession, celibate tenure for fellowships was ended. Marriage, no longer the sole prerogative of senescent college heads, swept into Oxford with all to its characteristic pressures towards occupational stability.

However, the alternative or 'Balliol view' of fellowships regarded them as a means of creating a small but independent intellectual element distributed through English society. Belonging neither to the landed aristocracy nor the commercial plutocracy, yet possessing cultural, social, and even political influence by virtue of their endowment, such an élite was clearly central to the Coleridgean conception of the clerisy. Holders of fellowships were thus the university's accredited representatives in the world at large. The Balliol view enjoyed its heyday during the mid-Victorian decades – a golden age of academic amateurism. Henry Sidgwick complained that most fellowships were held by 'thriving schoolmasters, school inspectors, rising journalists, barristers full of briefs, and barristers who never look for briefs.' But to G.C. Brodrick, the quintessential prize fellowship holder, it was a source of satisfaction that 'at least a quarter' of the articles appearing in the leading reviews were written by fellows or ex-fellows from Oxford or Cambridge. Here was evidence that fellowships were fulfilling their purpose: through them the university was addressing the nation.[31]

The climate of mid-Victorian England was peculiarly favourable to the élitist ideals of university reformers. The relative social calm was auspicious for rational analyses and for the prescriptions of an intellectual élite confident of its capacity to guide the increasingly complex social organism of nineteenth-century England. Moreover, this was a period of political ambiguity. Between the Corn Law crisis of 1846 and the 1868 general election, while the great Victorian Liberal party was taking shape and the Tory party was being reshaped, the centre of initiative for political and social change seemed less clearly located than usual. Palmerstonian politics were rather diffident in the domestic sphere and the disarray of the parties made opportunities for individual political action appear greater than usual during this 'Indian summer of the Private Member.' But there was also growing awareness of alternative areas of political initiative outside Westminster – an obvious example was the Anti-Corn Law League with its remarkable campaign tactics, its up-to-the-minute techniques of publicity and organization. Improved communications – railway, telegraph, the post – greatly increased facilities for mobilizing public opinion on major national issues.

Public opinion, that Victorian talisman, was coming into its own. The convergence of high-speed printing technology and cheap paper with the abolition of 'taxes on knowledge' had set off a publishing boom which made the press the obvious means of summoning this mysterious but powerful entity. Through the agency of journalism one voice could be multiplied many thousandfold, as Carlyle and others never tired of proclaiming and as *The Times* impressively demonstrated. That 'firm believer in the public press,' Barchester's Rev. Obadiah Slope, was not alone in regarding it as 'the great arranger and distributor of all future British terrestrial affairs whatever.' The appeal of popular opinion to those who sought leverage outside the traditional areas of political activity was immense. The pristine vagueness of the term made it a great semantic solvent of class barriers and, in an intellectual élite with populistic notions of transcending these barriers and appealing to the nation, it could foster large hopes. Such was the climate that encouraged the generous ambitions of a generation of self-confident university men, eagerly seeking a national constituency.

2

Seeking the Nation, 1848–67

Of all the decades in our history, a wise man would choose the 1850s
to be young in.

G.M. Young, *Victorian England*

I conceive that it is a very great advantage to an Englishman to have received at
least a part of his education – the last, if not the first – in a regular English way ...
A comparison of the Radicals who have been to college with those who have
been brought up at haphazard would illustrate this remark.

F.D. Maurice, *Letters*

In the closely-knit, celibate, and youthful community of mid-nineteenth-century
Oxford, enthusiasms passed easily from teachers to students. The academic generations were close and the opportunities for influence numerous. Because many
of the university radicals of the 1840s became tutors or coaches, they were able
to create a following among their students for the causes they supported. Richard
Congreve, Goldwin Smith, and John Conington, all Arnoldians, radicals, and
members of the Decade, were the most stimulating of them, according to the
abundant testimony of their students. A characteristic vehicle of their influence
was the long vacation party organized for chosen undergraduates, like that described in Clough's poem *The Bothie of Tober na Vuolich:* these were occasions
of particular intellectual intimacy conducive to discipleship.[1]

Their students in the 1850s formed a fairly distinctive and coherent group and
proved worthy successors to the talented generation who taught them. In emula-
tion of the Decade, they created the Essay Society, which attracted many of Oxford's advanced undergraduates. As with the Decade, Rugbeians were again in the

ascendant. Here the future Comtists Frederic Harrison, E.S. Beesly, J.H. Bridges, and Godfrey Lushington, the future statesmen James Bryce, G.J. Goschen, C.H. Pearson, and C.S. Parker, and the future academic notables A.V. Dicey, G.C. Brodrick, T.W. Jex-Blake, and J.F. Bright met to resolve the nation's social and political problems. Even after leaving Oxford they continued to meet regularly to monitor the fulfilment of their youthful aspirations: when Goschen was elected to Parliament in 1863 he earnestly spoke of it as 'a wonderful chance ... above all to do credit to the Essay Society and my friends.' Goschen, with Pearson, Parker, and another statesman-to-be, Mountstuart Grant Duff, also belonged to the even more exclusive Tugend Bund, where they solemnly swore allegiance to a covenant of virtue proclaiming their 'sense of the duties entailed upon the educated classes ... in a transitional period like the present, between an old order and a new,' and their concern to turn to good account 'the irresolute energy and sincere though indifferent desire to do good which no one acquainted with the Universities can fail to recognize as characteristic of many of our contemporaries there.' Beesly, Bridges, and Harrison, inspired by their tutor Congreve, formed the Wadham College Confederacy where they devoted themselves to deep discussions of social regeneration and laid plans for future concerted action after graduation. Bryce and Dicey also belonged to the illustrious, Balliol-based Old Mortality Society with the philosopher T.H. Green and such future literary eminences as Walter Pater, John Addington Symonds, and Algernon Swinburne.[2]

Further knitting together this generation of undergraduates was the Oxford Union, which enjoyed a particularly brilliant phase in the 1850s when nearly half its officers were members of the Essay Society and advanced views were frequently heard in debates on such subjects as socialism, universal suffrage, regicide, divorce, life peerages, educational franchises, and the extension of civil service exams. As if to leave permanent, visible evidence of this avant garde generation, the Union moved into its ultra-Ruskinian new debating hall and commissioned the exuberant pre-Raphaelite wall paintings of Rossetti, Morris, and Burne-Jones (unfortunately impermanent, and shortly to become invisible) under the presidencies of C.H. Pearson and C.S.C. Bowen, both Essay Society members.[3]

Oxford's growing interest in the world outside was of course greatly facilitated by the advent of the railway in 1844. This, in combination with the post-university reform multiplication of prize fellowships, meant that the increasing number of fellows who lived in London practicing law or journalism, finding a footing in politics, or rising in the civil service could more easily maintain contact with their colleges or come up to participate in Union debates. The world was coming to Oxford, as the young historian J.R. Green observed: 'The great ambition of modern Dons is to turn Oxford into a suburb of town. The non-resident Fellow forms the link between society and Alma Mater. Troops of lions and lionesses, poetesses and novelists, Comtists and cardinals, flutter down on Saturday to return Monday morning.' Foremost among the lion hunters was Jowett; Balliol entertained a stream of important visitors who might be of use to the careers of its undergraduates. Colleges cultivated their contacts with care in the competitive post-reform climate. All this activity put Oxford much more closely in touch with the pulse of national life. Moreover, from 1847 onward Oxford again had as one of its two MPs a man who was at the centre of the nation's affairs. William Gladstone had been elected in that year, and prominent among his supporters were the young Oxford reformers, led by Clough and others. Though still a Tory, Gladstone justified their confidence by his diligence in drawing up and guiding through Parliament the Oxford University bill of 1854, in the midst of the Crimean War.[4]

English political life in the 1850s and early 1860s was marked by an unusual preoccupation with foreign affairs. This was due in part to the relative quiescence of domestic issues, promoted by prosperity and Palmerstonian priorities. Oxford radicals shared this national preoccupation for it offered particularly suitable common ground on which to test their claims to influence over the national mind. Their youthful idealism was drawn particularly to the causes of the various oppressed nations whose exiled leaders fled to England after each abortive national uprising. 'In the great Revolutionary Horologe,' Carlyle declared, 'one might mark the years and epochs by the successive kinds of exiles that walk London streets.' The revolutions of 1848 deposited yet another wave of continental refugees on England's shores. After a brief self-congratulatory lionization from the English, most tended to be forgotten, but the Italians were notably successful in keeping themselves and their cause in the public eye. The prolific and ubiquitous Mazzini voiced the aspirations of Italy in glowing humanitarian generalizations which appealed to all levels of English society. Aurelio Saffi, one of the triumvirate of the abortive Roman republic of 1848, married the daughter of an MP and was appointed to Oxford's Taylor Institution where he became the university's revolutionary-in-residence and an inspiration to academic radicals. Many of these had political connections in London and were fairly close to émigré circles. In 1849, for instance, Congreve was writing to John Bright to persuade him to turn the now idle machinery of the Anti-Corn Law League to propagandizing for Lewis Kossuth and the Hungarian nationalist cause. Others wrote on behalf of downtrodden nations like the Poles for the Liberal press.[5]

Foreign affairs were a unifying force among reformers during these years. For the emotional there was vicarious gratification (often seasoned with patriotic complacency) to be enjoyed from partisanship of continental liberty, while the more fastidious could gratify their sympathies free from guilt about non-involvement. Particularly welcome were indications of popular sympathy with foreign movements, such as the mobbing of the notorious Austrian General Haynau by draymen when he visited London in 1850 or the enthusiastic popular welcome given Kossuth and later Garibaldi. Sympathy for oppressed nationalities promised to reunite middle-class and working-class radicalisms which had drifted dangerously apart in the 1840s. Reformers of all classes could at least agree on the desirability of revolution for foreign nations, if not for England. For the university radicals questions of foreign policy had the additional virtue of being potentially national issues, involving the entire community and transcending barriers of class, sect, and geography – issues with a wide moral dimension in which narrower interests might be submerged.

The Italian independence movement commanded the allegiance of the politically advanced university generation of the 1850s, for it had a particular claim on the classically educated, just as Greek independence had for university men three decades earlier. Swinburne, an idolater of Mazzini, had visions of doing for Italy what Byron had done for Greece, while James Bryce had to be restrained by the Dean of Trinity from joining Garibaldi's Thousand. More prosaically, in 1856 T.H. Green had moved in the Oxford Union that it was England's duty to throw the Austrians out of Italy 'at point of sword' if necessary. Saffi was of course present at the debate to encourage Green's supporters. In 1859 Frederic Harrison, by now a young London barrister with few briefs and much leisure, attempted to organize his Essay Society friends to form a small volunteer newspaper staff to write pamphlets, lobby MPs, and feed copy to working-class newspapers like *Lloyd's* which would enable them to 'reach the masses' and mobilize public opinion on behalf of the Italian cause. Matthew Arnold's *England and the Italian Question*, published in the same year, illustrates the same faith in the peculiar mass appeal of foreign politics. Arnold cited the sympathy of the French people toward the Italian cause as evidence of the particular sensitivity of the common people to 'considerations of a higher order' in politics and praised Louis Napoleon for his grasp of this essential fact of modern political life, as attested by his decision to intervene on Italy's behalf in the Franco-Austrian war of 1859. The failure of the English government to act similarly was evidence of its lack of sympathy with these popular ideas and its inability to recognize their growing power. Though Arnold later retreated from the radical, populistic implications of this pamphlet, such a view of the working classes as being particularly idea conscious flattered the ambitions of the young intellectuals who saw themselves as their national guides in the realm of ideas.[6]

The British upper class demonstrated even more dramatically its inability to recognize the tendency of the times by its attitude and by government policy towards the American Civil War. University radicals definitely broke with their own social order in upholding the North. In the Oxford Union T.H. Green angrily condemned the prevalent upper-class assumption that only the Southerners were gentlemen and that the Northern cause meant no more than the selfishness of money-grubbing ruffians. He was an early admirer of Lincoln, whose rough features and manners were at this time being ridiculed in *Punch* and elsewhere as the epitome of Yankee vulgarity. G.C. Brodrick, now a *Times* leader-writer, was kept from writing on American affairs because of his pro-Northern sympathies. However, Goldwin Smith, Thorold Rogers, and Thomas Hughes were energetic and outspoken propagandists for the North on the platform and in the press, appealing to the nation against the government and respectable opinion. Smith even journeyed to America to confirm that morality was on the Union side, as did the young radical Cambridge don, Leslie Stephen. Participation in this agitation brought university men into contact with middle-class, non-conformist radicals through the Emancipation Societies formed in Manchester and London, a salutary experience in widening their social sphere and extending their acquaintance with the Nation. Even more gratifying, however, was the evidence of working-class support for their cause. Though recent research has called into doubt the traditional view of the English working class as solid supporters of the North, what is significant here is that this view was widely held by university radicals, whose working-class contacts were not wholly representative. The steady allegiance of the Lancashire cotton co-operatives, despite the cotton famine brought about by the Union blockade of Confederate trade, seemed to demonstrate a degree of altruism which exceeded the hopes of even the most sanguine believers in working-class idealism. When Frederic Harrison first visited Lancashire in 1861 he remarked that 'the finest examples of the working class remind me very much of my Italian friends; they have that same union of sensibility and practical sagacity so separate amongst other classes.' Returning in 1863 with Godfrey Lushington in the depths of the cotton famine his admiration was confirmed by the 'hearty strength of endurance and fellowship of fine feeling' he found there.[7]

Vindicated by the outcome of the Civil War, the same university radicals took a leading role in the even more bitter Governor Eyre controversy of 1866-8. Their consciences sharpened by the American slavery issue, they were quick to condemn Eyre's brutal suppression of the Jamaican Negro peasant insurrection of 1865. Thus they became leading participants in a classic *cause célèbre*, in which a large proportion of the Victorian intellectual community stood up to be counted, either defending Eyre as a hero and patriot who acted decisively to defend civilization at a critical moment or condemning him as a murderer who flouted both law and morality by directing a reign of terror against an oppressed people. Thomas Carlyle's fulminations against the 'rose-pink' sentimental liberals who cossetted the indolent but untamed 'Quashee' formed a rallying-point for Eyre's more eminent defenders which included Ruskin, Tennyson, Kingsley, and Dickens

- by no means blind reactionaries but honest doubters of the optimistic mid-Victorian creed of progress. On this side also was the bulk of respectable opinion. Once again radical university men found themselves more in sympathy with the non-conformist conscience than the conscience of the establishment, and the alliance formed on the Civil War issue was renewed. Frederic Harrison, Godfrey Lushington, C.S. Roundell, E.S. Beesly, Thomas Hughes, and Goldwin Smith among others joined such non-university intellectuals as John Stuart Mill and T.H. Huxley and middle-class radical Dissenters like John Bright, Edward Miall, T.B. Potter, and Samuel Morley in the ultimately unsuccessful criminal prosecution of Eyre. Working-class support was less evident this time, but the coincidence of the Eyre agitation with the growing working-class movement for parliamentary reform was highly significant. The two issues fitted together dramatically: the fate of Jamaica's insubordinate Negroes lent grim point to English workingmen's claim to the vote and deepened the unease of those who opposed that claim. The foreign issue came directly home to the emerging major domestic issue of mid-Victorian England.[8]

As an undergraduate in the 1850s A.V. Dicey had firmly believed that three things were necessary to bring about the 'regeneration of the world' - the abolition of American slavery, the unification of Italy, and the fall of Louis Napoleon. Needless to say, the realization of these ideals brought instead disillusionment. There was something unsatisfactory about vicarious participation in the struggles of other peoples, however noble the cause. The illusion of influence, for one thing, was difficult to sustain; events went their way and heroes failed to conform to the models and strategies of the library. Most of the episodic foreign agitations in which university radicals participated in the 1850s and 1860s had a certain surrogate quality about them, as if they were substitutes for coherent and connected activity in the sphere of domestic policy. A major factor in this dispersed activism was the absence of any organized national radical party to which the academic radicals might have attached themselves. This absence was not just a feature of Palmerstonian years of political fluidity; it was a permanent feature of nineteenth-century politics chiefly attributable to the lack of leadership capable of encompassing the wide spectrum of radical concerns and coalescing emotional affinities into a unified political force. Poor health or physical disability were endemic among potential radical leaders from Lord Durham to Henry Fawcett. Reluctance to lead was another problem; both Cobden and Bright lacked the ambition to forge a radical party. The cult of purity which militated against the compromises necessary to party discipline was a part of this attitude, since the traditional radical tactics were a conscious repudiation of party and a distaste for responsibility.[9]

For university radicals with their Coleridgean faith in national consensus, there was something grating in the sectarian note too often sounded in English radicalism; the note of bourgeois complacency was also somewhat offensive to gentlemanly ears. But at the same time they were eager to sympathize with the man who best seemed to voice the aspirations of the people. This was John Bright who, despite his passion for Milton, was hardly a scholarly radical. Yet he attracted a considerable following amongst the advanced element at Oxford in the 1850s. When his passionate denunciations of the Crimean War had made him the object of widespread jingo hatred, E.S. Beesly's motion that Bright was 'an enlightened and patriotic statesman' was supported in the Oxford Union by a number of Essay Society members. In 1858, after the Manchester electorate had turned him out of Parliament for his anti-Palmerstonian views, T.H. Green moved that Bright's principles of foreign policy 'deserved the support of the nation.' (Both motions were defeated.) With Cobden largely occupied in his semi-official role as British ambassador for free trade, Bright was the national leader of radicalism, if only by default. He was attractive because of his unquestioned integrity. Important too was the fact that he looked, spoke, and acted like a tribune of the people – he was impressive as a physical and moral presence. To young men nurtured on Carlyle there was an heroic element in Bright as the archetypal Northern Manufacturer: 'In that grim brow, in that indomitable heart which *can* conquer cotton, do there not perhaps lie other ten-times nobler conquests?' Perhaps Bright was the answer to Carlyle's question.[10]

When Bright came forward in the spring of 1859 with a bill for parliamentary reform, Oxford radicals again rallied to his support. A motion in favour of the bill was moved at the Union, and G.C. Brodrick whipped in his Essay Society friends from London to attend the debate and speak for Bright. Meanwhile Frederic Harrison tried to organize them, especially budding *Times* leader writers like Brodrick and Lushington and disgruntled *Saturday Reviewers* like C.H. Pearson, to write a series of letters to the liberal *Daily News* supporting Bright and reform 'from the historical and philosophical side.' He also talked of starting a pro-Bright journal directed at the educated classes to overcome the strong hostility, encouraged particularly by the *Saturday Review* and *Times*, which was generally felt towards Bright in gentlemanly society. Another possibility was to address the masses with a series of cheap tracts. Harrison confided to his friend Beesly his characteristic view of the possibilities of such a project: 'We are not sufficiently of the people to do much, without puerile education, to agitate; but we could do a little to alarm the upper classes, and render them ridiculous.' Nothing apparently came of these suggestions, however.[11]

Bright reciprocated the hostility felt towards him in the upper reaches of society. He felt a deep-seated antagonism towards the whole social and educational milieu to which his unexpected allies, these young university gentlemen, belonged.

He was probably gratified to hear the radical young Oxford historian, Edward Freeman, who was seeking a seat in Parliament at this time, hail him in a pamphlet as his leader and praise his 'eloquence, earnestness and general powers' (even though Freeman's views on reform, which called for full manhood suffrage, were well in advance of Bright's), but he needed to be wooed by his Oxford admirers. The two dons who did this most effectively were Goldwin Smith and Thorold Rogers. Both were already friends of Cobden, who was related to Rogers by marriage; indeed Rogers, a clergyman, abandoned his religious vocation for political economy and politics largely under Cobden's influence. The other great bond between the two reformers and the two professors was their shared sympathy for the Northern cause in the American Civil War. Smith and Bright were particularly obsessed by it – America even filled Bright's dreams. On visiting Oxford Cobden and Bright were impressed to discover there not only a strong liberal circle but 'a charming tolerance' even among the more conservative. Bright, who had virtually no previous contact with the universities and had once dismissed Oxford as 'the home of dead languages and undying prejudice,' warmed to the hospitality of his Oxford friends and was soon telling his wife with honest pleasure of a 'sumptuous breakfast' at Wadham College. Accustomed to the scorn of gentlemen, the two reformers were no doubt flattered to find themselves so respectfully treated by gentlemen – of the highest intellectual calibre, moreover.[12]

The university radicals were particularly anxious to draw Cobden and Bright into a cause that was central to their creed – the further 'nationalizing' of the universities. Under the leadership of the 1850s generation the cause of university reform now centred on the abolition of the remaining religious tests for MAs and fellowships which still barred Dissenters from participation in university teaching or government. In the mid-1860s G.J. Goschen and J.D. Coleridge, of the Essay Society and the Decade respectively, presented bills in the House of Commons to effect this reform (finally carried in 1871). It seemed reasonable to hope that Cobden and Bright would lend their support since this was no mere matter of internal university politics but a 'broad and simple question of National justice,' as Smith told Cobden, adding that no one would take the issue seriously until he and Bright threw their influence into the movement. 'Your voices, compared with those of the young academicians ... are the sound of cannon announcing a battle to the rattle of small arms heralding a skirmish,' he urged. Although sympathetic, neither reformer took up the issue actively, both pleading ignorance. Cobden rather defensively explained: 'I have always felt that I held my position in the House among a body of men nine-tenths of whom in a literary sense are better educated than myself by talking only on subjects which my audience knew I had studied more if not better than themselves.'[13]

Nevertheless, the university reformers tried to recruit support among the dissenting middle classes of the North, and here their contacts developed in the Emancipation societies and the Governor Eyre agitation proved useful. Edward Miall, a Congregational minister and veteran radical campaigner, lent the support of the influential *Nonconformist* which he edited, since abolition of university tests could be viewed as the thin edge of disestablishment (though this was not the aim of the university men). In April 1866 they held a public meeting in the very shrine of middle-class radicalism – Manchester's Free Trade Hall – and attracted some leading dissenting politicians to the platform. Frederick Temple came up from Rugby to tell the audience: 'It is because I believe Oxford to be so excellent that I would have no Englishman excluded from the culture which she can give,' the culture which would provide 'that unity which surely ought to unite all classes of Englishmen.' G.C. Brodrick assured his listeners that while there might remain some bigotry among the older generation of Oxford graduates, the younger men who now did most of the actual teaching were 'as liberal and enlightened a body as are to be found in any learned community.' There were also testimonials from non-academic speakers, such as W. Graham, MP, who proclaimed that he would give 'half his worldly goods' for the advantage of 'an early education in the University of Oxford,' and T.B. Potter, MP, an old Rugbeian and successor to Cobden's seat at Rochdale, who stated that on Cobden's recommendation he had put down the names of all his sons for Oxford. But as Jacob Bright, MP (whose brother was not present), remarked, it appeared not so much that non-conformists were trying to find their way into the universities as that the university men were 'trying to take hold of England.'[14]

The university men found disappointingly little response in what they had believed to be the radical heart of England. The reasons for this disturbing gulf between the university and the North were a chief concern of T.H. Green and James Bryce, who were at this time conducting investigations in the Midlands and North as members of Lord Taunton's Royal Commission of inquiry into middle-class education. Green noted in his report the prevailing view among 'commercial men' that universities were places where young men stayed until they were twenty-three to learn at great expense habits that made them quite unfit for business or anything else. Bryce calculated that the proportion of university men from Lancashire was only one-third the national average. He also found very few university men teaching there: 'a painful sign of that severance between higher and lower education of the country.' Confirming Green's assessment, he remarked that reducing the usual age of entry to sixteen or seventeen and providing some professional training would be necessary before the middle classes could be won over to the university. Meanwhile, Grant Duff tactfully assured his constituents that they would be making 'an excellent investment ... to sink a little capital into sending a son to Oxford.'[15]

The correspondence of Cobden and Bright during these years indicates the extent to which university radicals tried to draw them into one or another of their concerns. Yet they did distinguish between the two men and it was Cobden, unfortunately to die in 1865, who was in many respects the more promising figure for their purposes. As A.V. Dicey later remarked, Cobden was more the innovator, being much less conservative than Bright. He was also 'essentially a thinker,' Dicey claimed, his political course being governed by ideas, above all by the idea – the ideology, indeed – of free trade. He was more cosmopolitan than the somewhat insular Bright (whose lack of interest in the struggling nationalities of Europe, especially Italy, disappointed his university admirers). And if he lacked Bright's Carlylean charisma, Cobden was 'more of a gentleman': as a member of the Church of England he was not hobbled by the siege mentality of non-conformist sectarianism in his attitude towards the establishment (Bright, of course, was a Quaker). Thus Thomas Hughes could address him as the man most likely to bring unity to the English nation, while Matthew Arnold paid him the compliment in 1864 of soliciting his support as the 'statesman of the middle classes' in the cause of improving middle-class education. Unlike so many middle class radicals, Cobden was not hostile to state intervention in education – a great recommendation in Arnold's eyes.[16]

If Cobden was a thinker, Bright was a 'feeler.' Speculation on social matters was uncongenial to him. He remarked disparagingly to his wife that Richard Congreve, who corresponded with him intermittently, was 'a thinker, rather than a believer in anything.' Elsewhere he peevishly remarked to Congreve that too much was expected of him, and when Congreve in 1866 urged him to take the lead in the reform cause, and opened some of his own ideas on the subject, Bright protested, 'I do not believe in far-reaching schemes in politics ... I cannot see far before me, and try to go only as far as I can see.' This was essentially the creed of an agitator. Bright was also not wholly satisfactory in his views on 'the people'; indeed, he was not a democrat, as he admitted himself. His famous use of the term 'residuum,' in a House of Commons speech in March 1867, to describe the class 'which would be better for themselves if they were not enfranchised,' clearly indicated his reservations about the lower classes of society.[17]

Cobden and Bright lacked the somewhat sentimental faith in the working classes that characterized many university men who, just as they tended to romanticize Bright, tended also to romanticize the working classes. The growing literature of social meliorism, especially the novels preaching class harmony written by Mrs Gaskell, Thomas Hughes, and Charles Kingsley which were widely read and discussed in the universities, encouraged this enthusiasm. Kingsley's *Yeast* and *Alton Locke* had a particularly strong impact in academic radical circles. Ardent young university men were moved to guilty benevolence by the scene in which Alton Locke, 'tailor and poet,' contemplates Cambridge by moon-light and bitterly accuses her of excluding 'the mass of intellectual working men' simply because of their poverty. As Fitzjames Stephen remarked, Alton Locke and his friends might be tailors but they are 'most unquestionably like gentlemen reduced to that occupation – are most undeniable likenesses of the genus English-man, species Cantabrigian, *tempore* 184–.' Yet the acquaintance of university radicals with the working classes went somewhat beyond mere novels. Some of them, including Pearson, Hughes, and Conington, were active in the Christian Socialist movement, and a large number, especially the acolytes of Lincoln's Inn (where F.D. Maurice was chaplain) taught at the Working Men's College – Harrison, C.S. Pearson, Grant Duff, C.S. Parker, Thomas Hughes, and Vernon and Godfrey Lushington among them. Then too the Volunteer movement of the 1860s was a point of contact with the working classes for university men. Gold-win Smith, for example, joined because he liked 'being mixed-up in the ranks with a different class from my own'; Matthew Arnold, Leslie Stephen, C.S. Parker, and Thomas Hughes were also Volunteers. All these were selective contacts, of course – artisans, co-operators, and trade union leaders, but this only confirmed the favourable images cherished by their admirers.[18]

Extending the franchise to the working classes was an obvious corollary to such attitudes. But Bright's proposed reform bill of 1859 was in fact remarkably exclu-sive, being frankly intended to increase the electoral strength of the urban middle class. As a consequence Bright's university admirers noticed among their working-class contacts a marked coolness towards him, a coolness which, however, went beyond differences over the franchise to such well-established matters as Bright's suspiciousness of trade unions and his hostility towards factory legislation. This was a disconcerting reminder of Bright's aggressive middle-class consciousness and of his inadequacies as a unifying national force in radical politics. Yet the general absence of strong national feeling for reform in the late 1850s was shared by many of the university radicals, though for different reasons. As on so many mat-ters, Carlyle struck a resonant note for them in his dismissal of Parliament as the 'national palaver,' a note echoed by Ruskin, Dickens, and many others in the mid-century years when the very validity of Parliament as a political institution came under scrutiny from many intellectuals. Thomas Hughes remarked in 1861 that the English, the most intensely political people of any nation, were wearying of parliamentary debates and asking 'whether the august assembly is not a much over-rated institution.' Reform, as outlined in the various abortive bills of the 1850s, was viewed as mere tinkering by those who felt that a new departure was needed. The by now legendary anti-corn law agitation was one very influential precedent for those who looked beyond Parliament for a more effective and, above all, efficient political mechanism. Frederic Harrison was among those who indulged in extra-parliamentary fantasies:

I will undertake to say that there exist fifty men in this country who, if they would only be got together and set in action, would settle and carry a sound system of national education in three years and in five clear up the questions which divide the employers and employed. If the government won't do anything, somebody must. The tendency now is towards spontaneous parliaments. In some few years the Government will be stranded from having nothing to do, and then the country will actually turn it over to the men who are doing something.[19]

The élitist implications of such thinking are obvious and the general theme had numerous variations. Thus Parliament was felt to be out of touch and ill-equipped to accommodate new political forces which were tending to bypass the established channels through which public issues had traditionally proceeded towards maturity. Spontaneous pressure groups emphasizing specific issues and relying on the effective mobilization of public opinion were moving to the fore, and the possibility of rapid and direct communication with the nation provided the key to this new political world. As Matthew Arnold put it, echoing Carlyle: 'At the present juncture the centre of movement is not in the House of Commons. It is in the fermenting mind of the nation; and his is for the next twenty years the real influence who can address himself to this.' University radicals could claim access to the 'mind of the nation' by virtue of their experience in the various causes and agitations of the 1850s and 1860s. More significantly still, many of them had moved into strategic positions in the periodical press, which was felt to be the *primum mobile* of public opinion. Cobden and Bright were themselves deeply interested in the possibilities of the press and were particularly obsessed with the extraordinary influence of the *Times*. But the university men were within the sacred precincts themselves, as leader writers.[20]

In 1865 Frederic Harrison and a number of his barrister-journalist friends formed the Century Club – in Harrison's words, 'a kind of Caucus to effect definite political, social and ecclesiastical reforms, without distinctions of class, or tastes, or moral habits.' It was a club with a political purpose, meeting two nights a week for earnest conversation, any member being free to address any other without introduction or acquaintance and with complete freedom of speech. The club included a large proportion of the advanced liberal intellectuals of London, its nucleus being members of the Oxford Essay Society and many of the other Oxford men we have hitherto met. The Cambridge contingent included Leslie Stephen, Henry Fawcett, Sir Charles Dilke, G.O. Trevelyan, Leonard Courtney, Lord Edmond Fitzmaurice, and Lord Amberley. T.B. Potter, W.E. Forster, and James

Stansfeld were among the non-establishment members, and the club even sought to recruit prominent working-class leaders like George Howell and Robert Applegarth to give it a completely classless quality, though unfortunately the latter two found the subscription too high. The Century included a remarkable number of 'higher journalists,' Saturday Reviewers, leader writers for the *Pall Mall Gazette* and *Daily News*, John Morley, editor of the *Fortnightly Review*, W.H. Hutton, editor of the *Spectator*, and at least five *Times* leader writers. High seriousness was the keynote of the club – 'there are no boys in the Century' commented a character in Laurence Oliphant's satirical novel *Picadilly*. Here the cause of the American Union was upheld, the strategy of the Eyre agitation planned, and the swiftly ripening issue of parliamentary reform discussed. Leslie Stephen later recalled meeting at the Century to discuss 'the Universe and the Reform movement of 1866-67; the volume *Essays in Reform* would give some notion of our general tone.'[21]

As late as May 1865 James Bryce reported from Manchester to E.A. Freeman that little was stirring there politically; the franchise question was generating scant interest and only 'social questions' commanded any attention amongst the radicals he met. In July he wrote further: 'One would think that there was nothing to be set right in the country from the languid way in which men talk of reform. Personally, I don't care much about extending the franchise. But might it not be the means to something considerable?' It was this 'something considerable' that roused the university radicals to new enthusiasm for reform in the mid-1860s. When the issue finally caught fire it had taken on a new tone and had at last achieved a national character under the joint auspices of the middle-class oriented Reform Union, a spiritual descendant of the Anti-Corn Law League, and the more working-class Reform League which had lineal connections with the Chartist movement. The co-operation between these organizations was itself significant. Though the cause still owed much to Bright for its moral resonance, it had moved ahead of him and was now developing the momentum of inevitability. There was a feeling, epitomized in Gladstone's famous 'Pale of the Constitution' speech of May 1864 that the people had been proven in the crucible of hard times and were at last ready. Some of the university men, such as Beesly, Rogers, and Smith, took part in the activities of the reform organizations, though most were heavily committed to their other causes. But when the progress of reform seemed threatened by the nervous reservations of the educated class, a number of them decided it was time for them to speak out and defend it on the highest national grounds. Appropriately, they did so in two volumes of essays.[22]

3

The Alliance of Brains and Numbers

The extreme advanced party is likely for the future to have on its side a great portion of the most highly cultivated intellect in the nation, and the contest will lie between brains and numbers on the one side, and wealth, rank, vested interest, possession in short, on the other.

John Morley, 1867

Come lads and lasses behold here
One better than laces and gold,
Than cakes and ale or your speeches fine,
A man that's as true as he's bold:
The people's Soldier in woe and weal
So shout, brave lads to your fill –
Hurrah for *Worth* and the *Brains* lads,
And a triple hurrah for Mill.

Westminster election song, 1868

Essays on Reform and *Questions for a Reformed Parliament* appeared early in 1867 at a time of political uncertainty. Palmerston's death more than a year previously had removed a major obstacle to reform, yet the government of Russell and Gladstone had been defeated in the spring of 1866 over its very moderate reform bill. The minority government of Derby and Disraeli that replaced it had now to deal with the matter, but who knew what would emerge from the divided counsels of Toryism? Mass demonstration in Hyde Park – the famous fallen railings and trampled flowerbeds – dramatically dispelled notions of working-class apathy towards reform but suggested that the country's hard-won social equilibrium might be at risk. An economic recession heightened tensions further. Many of the 'possessing classes,' made sensitive by the Governor Eyre controversy and by the coincidentally simultaneous upsurge of Fenian outrages (culminating in the Clerkenwell explosion which killed twelve people in December 1867), looked with renewed concern at the question of extending the vote to the working classes. Some, such as Carlyle and Matthew Arnold, drew back in dismay from the precipice that seemed to loom ahead.

But the man who had done most to lend intellectual respectability to the anti-reform cause was Robert Lowe, the brilliant renegade liberal ideologue whose speeches in 1864-5 played a major role in defeating the Russell-Gladstone reform bill. It was above all to answer this man that the reform essays were published, for, as one essayist remarked, Lowe's example fostered the notion that the cry for reform was the work of 'interested agitators and vulgar, uneducated men.' To counter this impression, to demonstrate 'the existence of a strong feeling in favour of reform on the part of the rising intellectual class ... one or two leading men among them proposed the idea of a "joint-stock" work in answer to Mr. Lowe's views.'[1] The names of the contributors reveal once again a large segment of the network of university radicals of the 1850s generation. The tables of contents carefully set forth their academic credentials, for in a sense they were speaking *ex cathedra*, as the clerisy: of the twenty-two contributors, eighteen were university graduates - eleven were fellows of Oxford colleges, three of Cambridge colleges. Nine were Essay Society members and at least ten were members of the Century Club. Eleven were barrister-higher journalists and all but two or three were active in journalism as leader writers, editors, or regular contributors; eight were Saturday Reviewers. Their average age was thirty-eight and all but seven were under forty.[2]

In a sense, one generation was speaking to another in these essays, and there was no doubt that Lowe was worth refuting. He had enjoyed a brilliant career at Oxford in the 1830s: he had starred in debates at the Union and had been a highly successful coach; he was a barrister, the senior *Times* leader writer, an administrator and politician - a paragon of the all-rounder ideal. Having lived in Australia and visited America, he could draw persuasively upon first-hand experience of democracy in describing the grave implications of reform. His arguments had to be answered. 'Whatever we learnt at Oxford,' Lowe had proclaimed in Parliament, 'we learnt that democracy was a form of government in which the poor, being many, governed the whole country, including the rich who were few, and for the benefit of the poor.' But this was not the lesson which Oxford had taught his young critics. Lowe was himself a convinced intellectual élitist (he had been a prime mover in introducing open competition into the India Civil Service), but a nervous, defensive élitist who saw intellect and culture threatened by the ignorant and selfish passions of the mob. His critics, however, on the basis of their rather different experiences with 'the people,' were confident that democracy would afford even greater authority to the intellectual élite, if that élite would only transcend class and embody truly national ideals. While systematically refuting Lowe's arguments, the essayists asserted in various ways this central tenet of their social and political creed.[3]

G.C. Brodrick began by dissecting the rhetoric of Lowe's argument to reveal the appeal to prejudice which underlay its apparent rationality and logic. It was appropriate that one *Times* leader writer should expose the rhetorical stratagems of another. Lowe had cleverly erected the differences between reform and anti-reform into an apparently irreconcilable ideological antagonism, appealing to visceral backbench hostility to the language and principles of the French Revolution. Thus for his own side of the case, the status quo, he appropriated and monopolized the approved utilitarian vocabulary of political common sense – 'expediency,' 'efficiency,' 'the public good'; to the other side he conceded 'doctrinaire,' 'sentimental,' and all 'the *a priori* rights of men which formed the terror and ridicule of the French Revolution.' Brodrick attempted to break this old semantic spell. Lowe heaped scorn upon the metaphorical phrases of the reformers – the franchise described as a 'debt' to the working class, or a 'reward' earned by their virtues. But, Brodrick asked, what was more metaphorical than 'the just balance of classes' to which Lowe appealed in defence of the existing arrangement? What, indeed, was a class but an 'artificial aggregate' consisting of as many or as few as whoever used the term might wish? Whenever reformers talked of the legal and moral rights of the unenfranchised, Lowe spoke contemptuously of *a priori* rights; but, as Brodrick reminded him, one could legitimately talk of 'rights' without assuming their *a priori* existence. Unintimidated by the semantic superstitions of fearful conservatives, Brodrick unflinchingly maintained that the paramount object of Parliament was to reflect the 'will of the people,' but in such a reasonable, gentlemanly, confident tone that one could never mistake him for a disciple of Rousseau.[4]

As men of classical education, Lowe's critics also had to answer the traditional objections to democracy based on historical precedent. This task fell to James Bryce, who neatly disarmed the dangerous precedents of democracy by revealing their flaws: the Grecian example was vitiated by slavery, the Roman by plutocracy, and as for revolutionary France, it warned not against the evils of democracy but the evils of a democratic society without a democratic government. Bryce also enlisted the aid of Plato and Aristotle, or at least denied their comfort to the anti-reformers. The censures of these philosophers were not in any manner levelled against democracy; they advocated aristocracy, the government by 'the wisest, justest and most pure-minded men,' founded on 'the respect and willing obedience of their fellow citizens.' That such an ideal, rule by the best, was entirely compatible with democracy, was central to the creed of the university radicals.[5]

The confidence of the people was the true pillar of leadership and the onus for jeopardizing this confidence was upon those who provoked the people by denying them their rights, forcing them to assert them by agitation; for in no other nation, Bryce affirmed, were the working classes so peacefully disposed as in England. In his essay, 'The Political Character of the Working Classes,' R.H. Hutton, a disciple of F.D. Maurice, confirmed this analysis. No other class of English society was 'so open to the influence of a few great ideas, and so willing to make sacrifices for those ideas,' he noted, praising their acute moral perception of such great issues as the American Civil War. He attributed this quality to a stronger sense of community which made them less selfish and more cosmopolitan than the higher classes. This could be seen in their indigenous institutions, such as the trade unions, which taught the 'radically true and noble ideas of the organized whole over the individuals that constitute it.' Rather than seeing them as instruments of class war, Hutton urged his readers to see how trade unions demonstrated the aptitude of the people for political discipline and the respect for 'collective life' which eminently suited them to be a part of the political nation. These collectivist instincts made them in fact much more amenable to leadership than the higher classes with their individualist ethos, for they were willing to allow their leaders a broader mandate and greater latitude in leading them. And contrary to the fears of anti-reformers, the men they chose to lead them were not demagogues. The elections of John Stuart Mill, Thomas Hughes, and Henry Fawcett (professor of political economy at Cambridge) for large and open constituencies in the 1865 general election offered striking evidence of popular deference to men of intellect, as Leslie Stephen pointed out in his essay.[6]

The American experience of democracy demanded the attention of the essayists since it was a chief argument of anti-reformers that the violence, vulgarity, and corruption of politics there caused men of ability to shun involvement in political activity. Leslie Stephen virtually conceded this point but claimed that the American example was inapplicable to England owing to greatly differing social and political circumstances; the United States was a young country, after all, where the basic demands of 'practical life' still led to a certain political and cultural crudity. However, the Civil War had created firm ties of friendship and respect between the North's intellectual partisans in England and the Boston Brahmins. An important link in this relationship was Henry Adams, who lived in London during the war as secretary to his father Charles Francis Adams, the American ambassador. Thomas Hughes had introduced him to the university radical set, many of whom after the war travelled to the United States to meet Ralph Waldo Emerson (long admired as the prophet of democratic optimism), Oliver Wendell Holmes, James Russell Lowell, and others, and became frequent contributors to Adams' *North American Review* and E.L. Godkin's influential *Nation* (whose readers would receive their interpretation of English political life from Goldwin Smith, Leslie Stephen, A.V. Dicey, and James Bryce successively until the end of the century). It was a most gratifying experience to discover in democratic America a cultured class of men so agreeably like themselves. Did not Henry Adams wish to become a 'philosophical statesman,' and to found 'a national school of young men like ourselves, or better, to start new influences not only in politics, but in literature, in law, in society, and throughout the whole social organism of the country – a national school of our own generation?' These were almost the very words and aspirations of his English counterparts.[7]

Of course Harvard was not America, these visitors realized, just as Oxford was not England; but there was hope of a growing identity between them. Goldwin Smith, who was enthusiastically welcomed when he visited the Northern states during the Civil War, travelled quite extensively and had found at all levels of American society evidence of a socially and intellectually healthier condition than in England. He saw the rich living without the empty and expensive pomp of their English counterparts, and was flattered to find even domestic servants (in Harvard households, at least) who seemed to be familiar with his own writings. He was impressed by the mingling of classes in the schools, which did not coarsen the children of the rich but rather seemed to refine the children of the poor, and by the universities which this nation of alleged 'dollar grinders' hastened to build practically everywhere – so impressed that within three years he was to resign his Oxford professorship to teach at the newly-founded Cornell University. On his return to England he wrote to Cobden: 'I have come back more Radical ... but less impatient, because more assured of the future.' Goldwin Smith had seen the Future, and it worked. Thus in his essay on the American experience he confidently dismissed the standard criticisms of American democracy by attributing its worst evils to the incubus of slavery and the nefarious influence of the southern planter aristocracy; both having been finally defeated, the United States was at least free to realize the ideal community. To Lowe's vivid characterization of democracy as a 'bare and level plain where every ant's nest is a mountain, and every thistle a forest tree,' Smith replied that individual superiority necessarily declined as general intelligence advanced, and that in America national greatness was replacing individual greatness. This in itself demonstrated that intellect was more valued in America than in England; intellect was in fact America's 'social peerage.'[8]

For the opponents of reform Australia offered an even more relevant warning than America, since its political institutions were nearer to the English model and its inhabitants more nearly 'flesh and blood' (it had not long since been a dumping ground for English convicts). Lowe's seven-years experience of Australian democracy was of primary importance to the formation of his own anti-reform creed. In Australia, he claimed, the franchise was so despised that people hardly care to 'pick it out of the gutter.' C.H. Pearson had visited Australia and was later to emigrate there and play an important role in politics and education. In his essay he tried to dispel the belief that Australian society was hostile to gentlemen of means and culture like himself and his readers. Thus Australia had its gentlemen's clubs; its railways even maintained three classes of accommodation, though the servants could be a bit difficult, he admitted, owing to the absence of any 'feudal relations between the classes.' But if the *nouveaux riches* often returned to England, because of the young colony's inability to provide those luxuries which were the privilege of wealth, the men of 'breeding and education' were quite happy there: 'My Oxford friends in particular,' Pearson remarked, 'were as good citizens as if they were native to the soil.'[9]

If one major purpose of the reform essays was to proclaim the compatibility of culture and democracy, the other was to disparage the representational theories with which opponents of reform defended the status quo. Lowe claimed that the existing political system was perfectly representative of the various classes and interest groups in society, and indeed worked very well. The essayists challenged this claim by outlining a number of major policy areas, namely the Irish question, trade union law, popular education, provision for the poor, army organization, and foreign policy, in which the unreformed Parliament had been unwilling or unable to act in the national interest. The chief reason for this, they maintained, was the domination of Parliament by the interests of one class – the landed class. The result, according to the Balliol historian W.L. Newman, was that the previous twenty years, 'while the continent has been working out in a masculine spirit the ideas sown in what we thought the fruitless agitations of 1848,' had been for England a period of political sterility. The Cambridge barrister-journalist Bernard Cracroft documented this landed dominance in a pioneering analysis of interest-group representation in the House of Commons which revealed at least 500 MPs to be connected with the landed interest.[10]

The essayists deprecated the idea of society as a nexus of conflicting and competing classes and interest groups. James Bryce explicitly defined the state as 'not an aggregation of classes, but a society of individual men, the good of each of whose members is the good of all.' He warned that the real danger facing England was the isolation of classes: 'Treating classes as hostile bodies and playing off one against the other' promoted such isolation. A.V. Dicey elaborated this point in his thoughtful essay, 'The Balance of Classes.' He repudiated the entire theory of class representation by showing the impossibility of defining monolithic social units such as 'the so-called middle class' capable of establishing and pursuing, *en masse*, specific interests. Like Bryce, however, Dicey saw that imposed definitions could create conditions, as evidenced by the stronger class feeling that existed among the working population than among the rest of the community simply because 'treated as a class they have fallen back upon their class feeling and have devoted their energies to class interests.' Existing political arrangements encouraged this situation by assuming that their interests were hostile and therefore excluding them. 'The present system,' Leslie Stephen asserted, ' ... alienates the working classes from the upper because it implies distrust of them.' The university radicals protested from a strongly Coleridgean standpoint the negation of the organic community implied in the self-validating, class-conscious concept of society defended by class-warriors such as Lowe. The interests of the nation could only be represented, and national unity itself preserved, by a more democratic franchise.[11]

The social situation of the university radicals obviously had a bearing on their conception of the political and social structure. To what class did they belong, and what were their class interests, in the terminology of Lowe? In his interesting study Harold Perkin has characterized the intellectual-professional group to which most of them belonged as the 'forgotten middle class,' maintaining that in their social analyses, based on the customary three-part class division – labouring lower class, commercial middle class, aristocratic upper class – they failed to determine their own place: 'they forgot themselves.' He illustrates his contention by noting the tendency of members of this group to identify with one or other of the three major classes, and often to act as articulate apologists for their adopted class and its conception of society. Yet the evidence suggests that the university radicals, far from 'forgetting themselves,' were very conscious of their collective existence and social position. Their hesitancy about defining their own class position was largely a function of their repugnance towards the assumptions of antagonism implied by rigid categories of social stratification. The consensus-oriented clerisy ideal afforded a much more appropriate conceptual framework for their activities and pretensions. When Matthew Arnold adopted the terms 'Barbarians, Philistines and Populace' to describe the three classes of English society with particular reference to their differing cultural attitudes, he purposefully left room within each class for a certain number of 'aliens' (the term is uncharacteristically negative) in whom the 'humane instinct' overcame the 'class instinct.' Such aliens were the potential sources of cultural authority and unity so lacking in English society. It is this Arnoldian variant of the clerisy ideal which best defines the position of the university radicals. It was appropriate to their professional ideal of service to the community that they should have wanted to establish a standpoint for themselves transcending the categories of class, for each class was their client to the extent that its claims upon the nation deserved their advocacy. We may therefore briefly consider their relationship with each of the traditional classes. [12]

Within the broad economic categories of Victorian England the university radicals belonged almost to a man to that middle class of which Matthew Arnold enjoyed proclaiming himself 'a feeble unit.' But they were also unquestionably gentlemen and were thus separated from the great majority of the middle class who were not by that great fault-line of English society which ignored mere wealth. Arnold was greatly concerned about this 'social injury' which fractured the middle class and was perpetuated by differences between the establishment-educated gentlemen and the Dissenting and commercial middle class educated at its inferior sectarian academies and shut in on its own limited cultural resources. The desire to heal this fracture was reflected in the university radicals' campaign for university reform and in their eagerness to seek support in Manchester and elsewhere for their causes. Yet one also detects signs of ambivalence in their attitudes towards the commercial middle class. James Bryce admitted that while one might admire their leaders from afar, 'near at hand the roughness and the dirt are seen.' Gentlemanly disdain for 'the disgusting vice of shopkeeping' was not easily overcome despite Thomas Arnold's and Carlyle's commendations of the energy and achievements of the commercial middle class. The essayist J.B. Kinnear expressed concern that 'the class of moderate means and high intelligence' (his own class) was being swamped and rendered powerless by the rising tide of 'ten pounders,' the urban commercial middle-class beneficiaries of 1832, and suggested that an enfranchised working class might become 'potent allies' of his own class in redressing this growing influence. His observation conveys a certain sense of rivalry and resentment, as if the gentlemen feared for their own relevance in an age of growing specialization and technological, scientific, and commercial achievement which the pushing middle classes appeared increasingly to dominate. [13]

Relations between the middle-class gentlemen and the aristocracy were another matter of concern to Matthew Arnold, who claimed that the same division which left them unnaturally isolated from the bulk of their own class also gave them a false sense of identity with the aristocracy. Middle-class gentlemen, such as the university radicals, shared the same tastes and accomplishments as the aristocracy because they shared the same 'lines of training' – the public schools, universities, and established professions. As a result, he argued, they became 'intellectually too deferential, too little apt to maintain entire independence where the prepossession of that class [the aristocracy] are concerned.' Arnold was acutely aware of this tendency in himself. To what extent do his remarks apply to the university radicals generally?

It must first be noted that Arnold, for the purposes of his argument, heightens the contrast between the aristocracy and the professional middle class by glossing over the historic fact that the professional middle class has traditionally recruited members from younger sons shed by the aristocracy and landed gentry. These family connections, even if fairly remote, constitute a more complex and binding tie than just education. It has been suggested that the case of the dispossessed and aggrieved younger son is a neglected factor in the phenomenon of gentry radicalism in English history: one can certainly cite a number of interesting nine-teenth-century examples of radical younger sons, such as Auberon Herbert, Lord Edmond Fitzmaurice, and Lord Randolph Churchill. An obvious source of this radicalism is evident in W.V. Harcourt's tart reply to the complaints of his elder brother about his lack of 'landed ideas': 'You have the land, and may leave the ideas to me.' The academic radicals had ideas about the land, though they may have lacked 'landed ideas.' Many of them had gentry connections, however distant; some of them, such as G.C. Brodrick, were younger sons and very critical of English land law, particularly primogeniture. W.L. Newman in his essay on the land laws argued the need for reform of the laws of entail to permit the break-up of large estates and allow landownership to become more widespread. This would prevent the 'schism of labour and capital' from spreading into agriculture and check the growth of an alienated agricultural proletariat. The conservatism of the continental peasantry was of course cited by Newman to demonstrate that the diffusion of landownership was very favourable to social stability.[14]

Even the educational connections between the aristocracy and the profession-al class are historically tied to the younger-son phenomenon since the public schools, universities, and Inns of Court initially won much of their aristocratic patronage and social prestige from the fact that they came increasingly to be viewed in the sixteenth and seventeenth centuries as appropriate spring boards in to the world for the younger son in need of a career. An important factor in the rising nineteenth century prestige of these institutions was the increasing tendency for the first-born as well to be exposed to this education as a matter of duty. The result was to augment mutual respect between birth and talent, a respect which was strengthened through such further contacts as politics, higher journalism, and metropolitan clubland. All of this served to promote the traditional attitude of the English aristocracy towards unattached talent, so different from traditional European attitudes which, it has often been argued, has helped to forestall the effective formation in England of a selfconscious body of alienated intellectuals, while serving to preserve the aristocracy itself. As Matthew Arnold put it: 'Every-thing which succeeds, they (the aristocracy) tend to welcome, to win over, to put on their side; genius may generally make, if it will, not bad terms with them.'[15]

The university radicals lived and worked among the social frontiers where this interaction took place, and certainly none of them shared the strong visceral opposition to the aristocracy of John Bright or the ideological opposition of the earlier philosophical radicals. The reform essays exude an implicit conviction of the continuing power and influence of the aristocracy and landed class in government, their implication being that the advent of democracy would not greatly alter this. They might be critical of parliamentary arrangements which gave an unfair preponderance to the landed class – thus Leslie Stephen could write scathingly of the dilettanti statesmen, lordlings privileged to enter Parliament at a youthful age through title or patronage, who abused their advantages of an early start in public life by becoming experts in the sterile arts of political manoeuvre rather than the fruitful arts of legislation. But the deference which they felt was so entrenched in English political life was important to them as well, since it provided the firm foundation for their own aspirations. They wished only to transfer its basis from social status to intellectual status, and hence were unwilling to attack or undermine it. [16]

The university radicals were not agents for the aristocracy or apologists for the aristocratic ideal except insofar as it served their own ambitions as a national élite. The class to which many of them were increasingly drawn in the 1850s and 1860s was the working class in which they thought they saw those qualities – cosmopolitanism, idea-consciousness, collective instincts, and amenability to leadership – which made them most suitable clients. Naturally there was in this a considerable element of wishful thinking, the projection of desirable virtues onto the *tabula rasa* of a still inarticulate and relatively unknown body. There was a tendency to see their own particular interests and preoccupations mirrored in the working classes. Thus the characteristic institution of the working class – the trade union – could be equated with the characteristic institution of their own order – the professional organization, as is apparent in the essays of Meredith Townsend (co-editor of the *Spectator*) and Godfrey Lushington. The House of Commons, Townsend complained, authorized unions of barristers and doctors, but not of labourers; while a doctor could prosecute and punish an unqualified competitor, a skilled mason attempting to restrain the unskilled mason who undersold him was liable to imprisonment. Trade unions, Lushington predicted, would soon become 'recognized social institutions' just like their middle-class equivalents, the Inns of Court, the Stock Exchange, or the College of Physicians. Such parallels were more persuasive at a time when the present-day, quintessentially middle-class individualist conception of professionalism had not yet wholly won the day. In the mid-Victorian years the idea that the more traditional corporate ideal of professionalism might provide an ethos and an organizational model to working men was not so far-fetched. (Indeed a latter-day Rugby radical who inherited a surprising amount of the Coleridgean-Arnoldian tradition, R.H. Tawney, could find the idea attractive even in this century.) [17]

It is at first sight remarkable that nowhere do the reform essays advocate minority representation. In his *Representative Government* (1861) John Stuart Mill had declared that he could see no other means of ensuring that Parliament would contain the 'very elite of the country ... the able men of independent thought' than the concentration of the votes of the more intelligent by some system of minority representation. The idea was much in the air during the 1850s and 1860s. All the abortive reform bills of the period, from Russell's in 1852 to Disraeli's in 1867, provided for special voting privileges such as multiple votes and special qualification franchises – 'fancy franchises,' Bright scornfully called them – as a means of extending the suffrage to those who were deemed particularly fit to exercise it and strengthening the suffrages of the fittest among those already enfranchised, while excluding or devaluing the unfit. Mill outlined some of the ways in which this might be done, such as plural votes for those who by occupation exercised 'superior functions' – the merchant, banker, professional man, and university graduate – and for those who had passed the university-administered middle-class exams (yet another task for the ubiquitous and omnicompetent examination). To ensure complete fairness he recommended voluntary exams open to all, regardless of education or circumstances, to determine whether they met the necessary standard of knowledge. For Mill, specialized franchises would offer positive and official encouragement of intellectual culture among the masses, as well as insurance against ignorant democracy. For the majority of supporters it was this latter, negative, and defensive aspect of minority representation that attracted them most. Given the apparent inevitability of democracy, an eventuality to which increasing numbers of thinking mid-Victorians were privately resigning themselves, and the lamentable inadequacy of English educational arrangements, some means of protection for good government seemed highly desirable. Mill, who was interested in improving the existing system and in extending the influence of the intellectual class quite apart from insurance against the future, also had schemes for utilizing life peerages towards this end: he presciently suggested that the 'speculative class' might be granted them – university professors, for instance.[18]

Minority representation attained its apotheosis in the complex scheme of Thomas Hare which gained prominence in the 1860s from the advocacy of Mill and Henry Fawcett. It utilized ballots on which voters could make multiple preference choices, which were to be centrally processed and transferable between constituencies to enable local minorities to group their strength on a national scale. Hare's intention was mainly to increase the influence of the intelligent and public-spirited voter, but many intellectuals were critical of his scheme, as they were of minority representation in general. Hare wished to thwart those well-entrenched and influential minorities who exercised an improper degree of influence under the existing system, but his scheme seemed to promise protection to sectarianism. Its operation would in effect offer bounties to crotcheteers. It was the essence of Millite thought that minority opinion should be protected from the 'tyranny of majorities,' since only through the clash of ideas, the 'noisy conflict of half-truths,' could the whole truth, and hence progress, emerge. Such was Mill's prestige that his views could not be dismissed lightly. Yet minority representation could itself be rejected on Millite principles; for as Thorold Rogers stated in his essay, the function of a minority was to try to impress its views on the majority by argument. If sincerely held, these views would be canvassed indefatigably in the forum of public opinion, and if correct they should ultimately triumph, becoming the views of the majority. But if these views were given representation as of right, the intellectually and morally salutary process of public debate would be arrested and stagnation would set in. Free trade in ideas would be curbed by the intellectual protectionism of minority representation. Moreover, there were technical objections to minority representation which might lend itself to large-scale manipulation (as Joseph Chamberlain's Birmingham Caucus was to demonstrate).[19]

More importantly, however, the whole principle of minority representation was repugnant to the assumptions and ideals of a clerisy – to the Coleridgean emphasis on national unity.* It was divisive both in assumption and in operation, for it assumed the desirability of interest groups, classes, and sects by affording them protection. Instead of promoting unity and enlarging the ground of consensus in the nation, it fostered awareness of differences and antagonisms. The prospect of multiplying minorities and the exacerbation of sectarian strife was most unpleasing to an aspiring national élite and the mistrustful, somewhat defensive note struck by many of the exponents of minority representation was alien to their confident assumptions.[20]

John Stuart Mill occupied an important place in the intellectual landscape of the university radicals. His *Principles of Political Economy*, the prime source book for his social and economic ideas, was expounded by the more advanced university tutors. In it Mill had portrayed an increasingly class-conscious working class no longer accepting an identity between their own and their employers' inter-

---

* Most of the reform essayists already possessed special minority representation through separate university representation, which the 1867–8 reform legislation extended to the University of London and the Scottish universities. In 1885, however, a motion for the abolition of university representation was unsuccessfully moved in Parliament by James Bryce, supported by Thorold Rogers, and encouraged by Sir Charles Dilke. It is significant that these university radicals of the 1860s were by this time representatives of large and strongly working-class London boroughs: Tower Hamlets, Southwark, and Chelsea, respectively.

ests, and rapidly moving away from an attitude of deference towards 'the authority and mere prestige of their superiors.' Mill's book contained some stern warnings against complacency but it was written in the troubled mid-1840s; the experience of the prosperous 1850s and 1860s seemed to have discredited his ap-
prehensions.[21]

Young Oxford did not fear the end of deference but was confidently looking
forward towards a more rational variety of deference – intellectual rather than
feudal. Nor did their ideal of a classless society suggest acceptance of Mill's diag-
nosis of increasing working-class consciousness. In answer to a letter from J.B.
Kinnear, Mill wrote: 'I cannot join you (glad as I should be to do so) in thinking
that the wage receiving class if universally enfranchised, would have no class feelings or class opinion as such.' And though Mill did grant 'the greater mental hon-
esty and amenability to reason of the better part of the working classes, compared
with the average of either the higher or the middle,' he was suspicious that this
was simply because they had not yet been 'corrupted by power.' It was not, however, in the writings of Mill the cautious philosopher of democracy that the university radicals found reinforcement for their views but in the experiences of Mill
the politician. [22]

Walter Bagehot regarded 1865 a particularly significant year in Victorian political life because it marked 'a change of the sort that generates all other changes
– a change of generation' – specifically, a decisive shift in political power to the
post-1832 generation. New breezes stirred the stagnant air of Westminster, dis-
pelling some of the doubts of impatient intellectuals about the relevance of Parliament. Already a few young men of intellect and advanced opinion were appearing in the House of Commons, such as Goschen, Grant Duff, Sir Wilfrid Lawson,
and G.J. Shaw Lefevre. The general election of 1865, even though it took place a
few months before Lord Palmerston's death in October, helped to generate a
mood of anticipation that when the old prime minister shortly left the scene, a
new era of politics would emerge.[23]

Few features of the 1865 elections contributed more to this mood than the
candidature of John Stuart Mill for Westminster. The stringent and uncomprom-
ising terms of his candidature and campaign attracted as much attention as did
his great intellectual repute. It was seen as an important test case, an opportunity
for the large metropolitan constituencies to redeem their character. Westminster
was a popular constituency, but like most of the London boroughs it was distinguished more for the expense of contesting it and for the inordinate electoral influence exercised by its publicans and narrow-minded parish vestrydom than for
the quality of its representatives. The *Pall Mall Gazette*, the newly-founded organ
of gentlemanly intellectual liberalism, suggested that Westminster could both
atone for its past errors and afford a striking refutation of the traditional con-

servative warnings against the dangers of popular constituencies by electing Mill. Nor was Westminster the only metropolitan constituency being contested in 1865 by a radical with high intellectual qualifications. In Lambeth, Thomas Hughes, and in Finsbury, W.T.M. Torrens, were also outsiders standing as candidates on principles of purity and merit and depending largely on voluntary effort and popular respect in the conduct of their campaigns. When all three candidates emerged victorious, the *Pall Mall Gazette* drew the moral of their success: 'The truth is that they [the metropolitan constituencies] are so big that they need a real appeal to the nobler feelings of the constituencies ... the secret of success is not local wealth and proprietary influence, which have been defeated both in Westminster and Lambeth, but an *entente cordiale* between the educated middle class and the more enterprising leaders in the great underlying masses of society.'[24]

The 1865 general election offered other propitious signs to those anxious for the intellectual improvement of Parliament. G.O. Trevelyan, J.D. Coleridge, Duncan McLaren, Lawrence Oliphant, and Henry Fawcett were five more able minds brought in on behalf of the advanced liberal cause. Professor Fawcett's election was particularly encouraging since he was elected in the open borough of Brighton, which had a fairly broad electorate. Thwarted in earlier attempts to enter Parliament for Southwark and Cambridge University, he had come down to contest Brighton in a by-election in 1864, narrowly missing election after a vigorous campaign in which he was actively supported by the Rev. Leslie Stephen, who produced almost single-handedly an election newspaper to promote the candidature of his Cambridge friend: 'It is a common bid for the support of the electors to say that the candidates are friends of the working classes. The working classes want no friends in public. They can always depend on someone to take the chair on their behalf at large meetings and to advocate their claims loudly during election contests. Mr. Fawcett has shown that his support of these classes, based upon an intellectual appreciation of their difficulties, is capable of withstanding severer tests.' So wrote Stephen in 1864, presenting Fawcett to the electorate. When he returned to contest it in 1865, he was the popular favourite and won easily. Fawcett delighted in the hustings and showed none of the coy intellectual's manner. Mill, by contrast, ostentatiously remained in his French retreat leaving all the work to his committees, claiming that he had not offered himself as a candidate but had merely indicated that he would acquiesce if elected. He would stand, but not run for election. Just before the poll, however, he was prevailed upon to visit the borough and make a few speeches. At one of them the famous incident took place concerning his statement that the English working classes were 'generally liars.' Challenged as to whether he had in fact written this, Mill replied simply, 'I did,' and was immediately greeted with a storm of applause from his working-class audience in appreciation of his frankness.[25]

The other major event of the 1865 elections was Gladstone's rejection by the University of Oxford (or at least by its non-resident electors; the academic members of the university, more liberal in their politics, had remained loyal to him). Gladstone had long fascinated university radicals with his high intelligence, ability, and seriousness; there seemed to be a kindred spirit lurking within him, however obscured by his tortuous conscience and mystifying ecclesiastical attitudes. He had been actively concerned in those areas of politics which most interested them in the 1850s, such as university reform and continental liberation movements. His position on the American Civil War was certainly not to his credit, but redemption came with his 'pale of the constitution' speech of 1864. If Gladstone's defeat brought shame upon the university, did it not perhaps have a brighter side? Goldwin Smith assessed the possibilities in a letter to his American friend, Charles Eliot Norton: 'The event has crowned him leader of the Liberal party when the interminable decrepitude of Palmerston shall at last come to an end. It seems natural and is assumed by everybody that his change to a more Liberal constituency will make him more Liberal; but those who are aware of the waywardness of his genius are inclined to doubt whether the natural effect will ensue. He is however a staunch economical reformer and really disposed to improve the condition of our working class.' The effects of Gladstone's 'unmuzzling' were immediate. Released from a constituency where by tradition he could say nothing during election campaigns, he was soon enjoying the full exercise of his newly discovered powers of communication with the people. Gladstone was expanding to meet the political specifications for national leadership and would shortly crystallize the elements of a national, classless, Liberal party which seemed almost to be awaiting his transforming touch.[26]

The general election of 1868 afforded university radicals an opportunity to put their faith in the people to the test. The circumstances seemed promising: the electorate had been doubled by the previous year's reform act and practically every seat was being contested. Moreover, both the national issue and the national leader that they had long sought were now before them, combined in the person of Gladstone himself. A number of them decided therefore to take the plunge and try for election. Five of the reform essayists entered the lists: Godfrey Lushington (Abingdon), G.C. Brodrick (Woodstock), J.B. Kinnear (Fifeshire), Sir George Young (Chippenham), and C.S. Parker (Perthshire). Other candidates from among 'the rising intellectual class' included C.S. Roundell (Clitheroe), C.H. Robarts (Mid-Sussex), E.A. Freeman (Mid-Somersetshire), F.A. Maxse (Southampton), Henry Yates Thompson (S.E. Lancashire), Viscount Amberley (S. Devon), George Osborne Morgan (Denbighshire), Auberon Herbert (Berkshire), Charles Dilke (Chelsea), and Lord Edmund Fitzmaurice (Calne). John Morley and A.O.

Rutson unsuccessfully sought nominations at Blackburn and York, respectively, while Frederic Harrison and Goldwin Smith refused profferred nominations, Harrison in accordance with his Comtist creed, Smith because he did not consider himself cut out for parliamentary life. Almost all these men were members of the Century Club. One other Oxford radical was apparently offered nomination for an Isle of Wight constituency. This was Algernon Swinburne who seriously considered acceptance but finally declined, it was claimed, 'on the express advice of Mazzini.'[27]

The 1868 campaign mobilized the politically advanced wing at the universities, and many who were not candidates themselves nevertheless joined in to assist their friends who were. Brodrick and Lushington, both *Times* leader writers, stood for boroughs close to Oxford, Brodrick defying the potent Marlborough interest by contesting the borough of Woodstock. T.H. Green addressed a meeting on his behalf consisting largely of tenants of the Blenheim estates – earnestly pointing out to them 'the effect of bad laws upon their conditions, and (a harder task) the possible good to be done to them by good laws.' He was gratified to report that 'They seemed to understand me better than I expected.' W.T. Sidgwick, the senior tutor of Merton, C.S. Roundell, and W.V. Harcourt were other leading university men who spoke in Brodrick's campaign. Narrowly defeated (502 to 481), Brodrick found consolation in the fact that his successful opponent had to be protected from the mob at every public appearance by a large escort of policemen, while he went unscathed and was greeted with enthusiasm on the hustings. At nearby Abingdon Godfrey Lushington stood as 'the working man's friend'; his claims to that title were expounded by the professor of geometry (Henry Smith, a fellow Rugbeian) and Professor Thorold Rogers. A.V. Dicey and James Bryce travelled down to Somerset to aid their friend Freeman in his exuberant campaign for a 'seat in the Witan of England' (this was his third attempt). 'Gladstone' and 'Democracy' were his watchwords. In a letter to Gladstone requesting a few lines of recommendation, Freeman recounted how he was cheered when he declared that the struggle was one of 'brains against acres.' Goldwin Smith postponed his departure for America to participate in the canvassing but declined a safe seat and 'munificent' financial support from Samuel Morley, a leading Liberal power-broker, saying it would be wrong to waste a seat on him at such a critical moment. Smith had by this time become a figure of considerable political importance. Disraeli paid him the tribute of personal denunciation in Parliament as a 'wild man' who without any personal knowledge or experience went around the country maligning its institutions. Though Disraeli tried to dismiss Smith as an ivory-tower academic, Smith's correspondence with George Howell, secretary of the Reform League, shows him to have been an astute and down-to-earth politician in his own right. Leslie Stephen bracketed him with Mill as the intellectual leader of political liberalism, and though it is difficult to assess the influence of either man, they were widely credited with it by the Tories. The *Saturday Review* rather fatuously chided Smith and Mill for inconsistency in claiming that the working man had a natural instinct for choosing the best men, and then presuming to recommend candidates to them.[28]

However, the results of the 1868 elections left the hoped-for-alliance of brains and numbers largely unconsummated. Of the reform essayists, only C.S. Parker was successful, and of the others mentioned, only Morgan, Dilke, and Fitzmaurice. T.H. Green remarked that most of his friends failed not because they were 'philosophers' but because, unknown and without local connections, they were contesting corrupt or virtually close constituencies on principles of electoral purity (Fitzmaurice alone had the force of influence on his side). There were other disappointments too, such as the defeat of Gladstone in South-West Lancashire, though Charles Dilke felt that this would further encourage his political evolution since he was 'much more likely to become a democratic leader now that he acts for a big town' (Gladstone was elected for Greenwich). The defeat of Mill was another heavy blow. Henry Fawcett remarked that the new Parliament would be 'intellectually inferior' to the last one, while John Morley called it a 'chamber of mediocrity,' noting that 'brains have been steadily ostracized.' (Morley finally got a nomination in Blackburn when both victors in the general election were unseated for corruption, but was defeated in the by-election). The promise of 1865 had apparently been false; post-second reform act politics promised to be even less accessible to the independent intellectual. Indeed, the problem of accessibility and the 'vocation of politics' were concerning a number of thoughtful commentators at the time, including Bagehot and Lord Robert Cecil. A reviewer in the *Quarterly* concurred with Morley, noting that there were scarcely fifty of the 'professional and intellectual class' in the new Commons. Perhaps journalism was, after all, the only way by which 'the really intellectual man' could influence public life. Such was Morley's feeling also – for the time being at least. Bagehot, noting the difficulties that faced young men of genius and talent trying to enter politics, looked back to the greater accessibility to such persons of the pre-1832 Parliament and suggested that the need for some 'intellectual equivalent' of the old nomination boroughs was demonstrated by the experience of the 'Oxford Liberals' in 1868: 'their egregious failure was one of the most striking events of that remarkable time.' The smart satirical weekly *Tomahawk* took a different view, however:

Ho! Listen worthy people,
Some facts while I relate
Of the General Election

Of 1868 ...
From study and from Workshop
Came forth ambitious souls
To canvass the electors
And carry all the polls.
'A Mighty Revolution
Has England seen', 'twas said,
'None should be sent to Parliament
But worked with hand or head.
None but the swart mechanic,
Or philosophic sage
Should sit and prate and legislate
For the Forthcoming Age ... '
But answered them the victors –
'You have yourselves to blame;
Do what you will by Act or Bill,
England remains the same,
And men of sense, and gentleman
Instinctively will choose,
O'er uninstructed demagogues
Or academic views.'[29]

The direction of political change was not entirely clear from the results of 1868. As T.H. Green suggested, there was something Quixotic in the university radicals' choice of constituencies – rural boroughs and counties where the impact of 1867 was slightest. After all, it was the big urban seats where the working man had greatest electoral strength which had returned Fawcett, Mill, and Hughes in 1865. Such amateur gestures were somewhat redolent of the golden age of the private member which certainly ended with the 1868 elections. The politics, organization, and discipline of the party were closing in, and those with political ambitions would have to come to terms with these developments. One clever young university man who seems to have appreciated this was Charles Dilke. Twenty-five years old, fresh from scholastic, athletic, and social triumphs at Cambridge (Trinity Hall, where Leslie Stephen and Henry Fawcett were Fellows), Dilke had already published his highly successful *Greater Britain* when in 1868 he contested the new London borough of Chelsea which had a strong artisan element in its electorate. By dint of hard campaigning and highly effective organization he came out at the top of the poll. There was no trace of political dilettantism in the ambitious Dilke; a gentleman, he was certainly no amateur. His success pointed the direction in which ambitious intellectuals would have to move if they wished to enter politics, as John Morley, James Bryce, and Thorold Rogers soon realized.[30]

The 1868 election results somewhat deflated the aspirations of university radicals artificially inflated during the anomalous Palmerstonian political pause of the previous two decades. Fresh from the universities which were stirring with new currents of élitism, they had stepped confidently out into the bright sunlight of the 'Victorian Noon-time' – in G.M. Young's words, 'this season of national euphoria ... released from its gnawing fear of social subversion.' The benign uncertainties of this time encouraged political fantasies; 1868 brought them to earth with a jolt. The idea of an alliance of brains and numbers was not abandoned altogether, but to two men at least – John Morley and Frederic Harrison – it seemed that a more rigorous and practical analysis of the possibilities, methods, and purposes of élitism were needed. Their attempts to achieve this will be examined in Part III.[31]

But first it is necessary to examine the development in England of the doctrines which provided the élitist rationale within which Morley and Harrison worked – the doctrines of Auguste Comte. Previous studies of Comtism in England have not captured its peculiarly English flavour. Its origins, intentions, attractions, and weaknesses are best understood within the context of populistic university radicalism which the first part of this book has attempted to describe. The chief English adherents of Comtism were university radicals who found in it a coherent and complete solution to the social and political problems that particularly concerned them.

PART TWO
COMTE IN AN ENGLISH SETTING

4

From Oxford to Comte

I have often thought that if I had gone to Oxford instead of Cambridge I should have been a positivist myself.

Leslie Stephen to Frederic Harrison, 1902

In most cases, the normal condition of a clever Englishman between the ages of twenty-two and thirty is a feeling of disaster about his work and his prospects, and a chronic anxiety for 'a sphere.' If he is a master at a public school he wastes a couple of hundred pounds at Lincoln's Inn or the Temple, in order to delude himself with the fond idea that he will one day exchange his desk in the fourth form room for the more stirring cases of forensic life. If he still hesitates to surrender the ease and security of a fellowship, he compounds with his intellect by writing for the *Saturday Review* and representing the liberal element in the government of his college. He takes to the law and discovers that there are interests in the human heart which even conveyancing will not satisfy; to the Church – no, he does not take to the Church; to literature, and finds himself in the plight of that gentleman who,

At thirty years of age,
Writes stately for *Blackwood's Magazine*
And thinks he sees three points in Hamlet's soul
As yet unseized by Germans.

G.O. Trevelyan, *The Competition Wallah*

In the first major notice of Comte in the English press the physicist Sir David Brewster, while commenting favourably on Comte's philosophy of science, remarked that Britain was to be congratulated on possessing 'institutions which prevent opinions like his from poisoning the springs of moral and religious instruction.' Thus he drew the distinction between two aspects of Comte's work, the largely descriptive philosophy of science and the much more prescriptive and controversial science of society, which subsequently divided positivists into two categories: the incomplete sympathizers who confined their allegiance mainly to the former doctrines as set down in the *Cours de philosophie positive* (1830-42) and the full disciples who also embraced the latter as articulated in the *Système de politique positive* (1851-4). In speaking of 'Comtism' and 'Comtists' I refer to these full disciples who came in England from precisely those institutions in which Brewster mistakenly placed his confidence, the universities.[1]

Comtism in England was essentially an Oxford movement, like those other religious and intellectual movements which stemmed from the influence of Oxford tutors such as Newman, T.H. Green, and Pater. The official English Comtist movement was the creation of Richard Congreve, fellow and tutor of Wadham College, and its leading supporters were university gentlemen – products of the national intellectual establishment. Herein lies a crucial distinction from the earlier group of partial sympathizers such as John Stuart Mill, Harriet Martineau, and G.H. Lewes who were chiefly of the dissenting intellectual *avant garde*. Because it is usually interpreted as primarily a secular religion, and its adherents as members of a sect, the nature of Comtism's appeal has tended to be obscured. The very fact that its full adherents were predominantly upper middle-class university graduates suggests a distinct resonance with the concerns of the mid-Victorian intellectual establishment.[2]

Congreve was educated at Rugby where he became one of Thomas Arnold's favourite pupils and one of the most virtuous and conscientious of the sixth-form praepostors of his miniature state. Like Clough, his friend and Rugby contemporary, Congreve developed a precocious sense of responsibility for the moral welfare of mankind which accompanied him throughout the rest of his life. At Oxford he took a first, was ordained into the Church of England, gained a fellowship, and quickly created a reputation as an influential and successful teacher and a leading light among the university radicals of the 1840s.

Comte's writings were attracting attention among the more advanced tutors at Oxford during the 1840s. Fulsome references to them in Mill's *System of Logic* (1843), shortly to become the 'Oxonian's Bible,' helped to make his name known. Frederick Temple lectured on Comte as early as 1844 at Balliol, while Clough started a subscription to aid the penurious philosopher and Jowett studied his works closely. Congreve was introduced to him by a fellow Decade member, J.F.B. Blackett (briefly a Whig-radical MP until his untimely death). Much of Comte's initial appeal lay in his historical theories, though he was no historian. To those who felt that they were living at a critical juncture in the history of mankind, Comte offered historical confirmation and explanation for this belief. Confusing and even alarming social, economic, and scientific developments were all systematically integrated and accounted for in terms of the onset of the positive stage of history, the last of three stages in mankind's intellectual development which had commenced with the French Revolution. Ideas ruled the world in Comte's historical theories; in this he resembled Coleridge and indeed the whole 'Liberal Anglican' historiography which was the dominant historical school among the Broad Church-oriented liberal intellectuals at Oxford. A strongly relativistic, idealistic, and presentist approach to history was an important common denominator between Comtism and this school. Comte's explanation of the cosmic significance of the French Revolution was a special attraction for Arnoldians, who were particularly sensitized to Comte's concerns, and at least in Congreve's case, it fitted in also with his admiration for Carlyle, whose *French Revolution* (1837) was required reading in advanced university circles.[3]

Congreve's first major publication, a series of lectures on Aristotle's *Politics* (1855), clearly demonstrates how Arnold and Carlyle could prepare the ground for Comte. Here Congreve followed Arnold's precepts in applying the lessons of ancient Greek politics to the present political situation of England during the Crimean War, while adopting the impatient authoritarian rhetoric of Carlyle to promote the technocratic, managerial politics of Comte as a solution to the country's problems. By this time Congreve had been studying Comte for nearly ten years and had twice visited him in Paris, for his conversion was a slow one. It is significant, however, that in 1853 Congreve could still claim that on all political, social, moral, and religious questions he was 'the legitimate development of Arnold,' and would have his sympathy if he were still alive. In 1854 he married and had to give up his fellowship. He moved to London and came closer to the complete acceptance of Comtism which was symbolized by his returning his priest's orders in 1857, when Comte appointed him head of the Comtist movement in Britain. Many of his Oxford friends, who deeply regretted his going 'out into the wilderness' of Comtism, blamed his apparent aberration on Arnold's propensity for propelling his favourites into Holy Orders. It would appear, however, that Congreve did not mistake his vocation but simply concluded after his long study of Comte that he had been ordained into the wrong church, and so passed from the Arnoldian Broad Church into the even broader Church of Humanity, thus affording another example of the errant spirituality which was common among Arnold's disciples.[4]

The roots of the Comtist discipleship under Congreve can be traced back to the three years, from 1845 to 1848, during which he was master of the lower fifth form at Rugby under Arnold's successor, A.C. Tait (the future Archbishop of Canterbury). Although his assumption of apostolic superiority as one of Arnold's favourites antagonized his colleagues, Congreve's masterful personality had a great impact on his pupils, among whom were four future Comtists: John Henry Bridges, Godfrey Lushington, J.B. Winstanley, and Francis Otter. On returning to Wadham College as tutor, Congreve extended his influence as his former pupils now came up to the university. His rooms were a centre for undergraduates, especially Rugbeians who came 'very dutifully to discuss points social, political or general' with him. But it was among his own college students that he found his most ardent admirers, Bridges (his favourite), E.S. Beesly, and Frederic Harrison who were later to join him as the nucleus of the organized Comtist movement. They imbibed Comte's ideas without apparently being aware of it, for Congreve did not mention his name. Harrison records that he first heard it from a former schoolfellow, Charles Cookson (another future Comtist), and remarked in a letter of 1855 to Beesly that he was reading Comte and was 'surprised to find how prepared I am for the main doctrine.' Congreve's awareness of his personal influence over former students is suggested by Godfrey Lushington's statement that when he was having 'religious difficulties' around 1856, Congreve wrote to him: 'there is no man I would rather take with me than you, but I would not lift a finger to persuade you.' (Lushington did not become a full Comtist until around 1870.) While still a tutor and a priest he scrupled at taking advantage of his position of authority by proselytizing openly amongst his students on behalf of Comtism.[5]

Among Congreve's followers it was J.H. Bridges, a 'passionate Coleridgean' as an undergraduate, who first embraced Comtism. Beesly was a rather slower convert; he and Bridges were both sons of evangelical clergymen; both underwent crises of faith while at university which left them anxious to find some surer creed. Frederic Harrison's letters and writings provide a clear picture of his own religious vicissitudes. Brought up in the tenets of pious but unstrenuous high churchmanship, he was first exposed to the Coleridgean Broad Church as a pupil at King's College School, part of King's College, London, where F.D. Maurice was professor of theology. At Oxford he diligently attended the university sermons where every MA in orders preached in turn, making one Sunday's orthodoxy the next Sunday's heresy. Buffeted by the wide spectrum of doctrines which the mid-Victorian Church of England encompassed, the bases of his inherited faith weakened and slowly collapsed. It was apparently a painless process; Harrison claimed that he 'never knew the agonies of scepticism accompanied by superstition.' He simply became 'a theist,' and from this interim position was drawn steadily towards the socialized, duty-oriented, anthropocentric creed of Comtism. Religious considerations are important in accounting for the attractions of Comtism, though they have perhaps received undue attention at the expense of its political and intellectual attractions. It is easy to forget that the intellectual claims and functions of religion were still much more comprehensive and that its categories and terminology embraced a far wider area of experience before the fragmentation and disciplinization of social science set in. It is of the very nature of Comte's creed that its various attractions are particularly difficult to separate, since his 'Religion of Humanity' was so broad – was in fact an ideology.[6]

Comte's remarkably comprehensive ideology was specifically directed at the three most central concerns of the nineteenth-century middle class – upholding morality, providing a means of controlling social change, and providing a sense of identity to the individual by defining his place within the community. Comte offered a new social organization, scientifically and historically justified, which promised to reconcile permanently the two hitherto conflicting ideals, order and progress. This new society was to be attained without revolution, by moral rather than political means – by education, in fact. Like Marx he accepted industrial society based on the scientific organization of labour, conceiving it to be ultimately beneficial and liberating for humanity: unlike Marx he believed in monopoly capitalism, considering it, in its 'moralized' form, the ultimate type of economic organization. Like Marx he rejected conventional religions: unlike Marx he believed that mankind needed organized religion, and therefore synthesized a rational, surrogate to fill this need. Like Marx he envisaged a classless society grounded in the proletariat: unlike Marx he believed that the dominant values of this society would be largely those of the middle class, for he stressed the sacredness of private property, of woman as wife and mother, and of the family as central pillars of the social order, though he was opposed to liberal individualism. Finally, like Marx he believed that his 'positive' society represented the terminal stage of an historically determined process, though for Comte the determining factors in this process were ideal rather than material.[7]

Comte's ideology had an even more specific appeal to those of the middle class who viewed themselves as its social and intellectual leaders, because of its explicit and comprehensive élitism. The reconciliation of order and progress would be effected by the dissolution of the lower middle class, whose ambitions he believed were the chief source of social disturbance, into the proletariat (Comte's own term). Unsettling aspirations to social mobility would be eliminated with the classes themselves. There would be only one class, the proletariat, governed by two auxiliary élites – the spiritual power exercising intellectual authority and the temporal power exercising administrative authority. Political strife would disappear with politics itself, since the two powers would be strictly separated into the realms of thought and action, each élite confining itself to its own sphere. Government would become a science, upon which there could be no more disagreement than amongst scientists on the laws of physics.

It is commonly assumed that because Comte claimed scientific authority for his entire system, his ideas were taken up most avidly by the scientifically-oriented, the incipient technocracy. One would expect, therefore, to find few of his followers among the more traditionally educated. This was true in France, for Comte was a lecturer and examiner at the École Polytechnique, the prestigious forcing house of France's managerial élites, which provided many of his disciples. In England this was not the case. Comte in fact had little reason to expect any disciples from England, since according to his theories her society was so far advanced in the wrong – that is, the individualist – direction that she would only very slowly achieve the positive stage; but he understandably expected that Cambridge, with its strong mathematical bias, would be the most likely source of any who might emerge. Yet as he remarked to Congreve, the great majority of his English admirers came from Oxford. This unexpected development, Comte decided, indicated the superiority of literary studies in stimulating the generalizing turn of mind ('l'esprit d'ensemble') most receptive to his doctrines, and the tendency of mathematical studies to stimulate the particularizing turn of mind ('l'esprit de détail') which was 'the principle scourge of the present century.'[8]

Comte in a very real sense provided scientific sanction for the amateur ideal, the cult of the 'all-rounder.' The aspirant to the Comtist priesthood was supposed to study medicine as part of his education, but only a few of his English followers (such as Congreve) actually did. They were on the whole a rather unscientific lot. Comte's own approach to science was itself 'unscientific,' being predominantly philosophical and pedagogical. He was ultra-rationalist and anti-empiricist in the Cartesian tradition. Comte's most famous theoretical contributions were the law of the three stages, the classification of the sciences, and the subjective synthesis. According to the first of these, human progress – the progress of the human mind – proceeds through three stages, from the theological to the metaphysical and finally to the positive, each stage being characterized by a particular mode of explaining phenomena. In the theological stage the human mind explains phenomena by attributing them to anthropomorphic gods. In the metaphysical stage the mind explains phenomena by invoking abstractions such as 'nature.' In the positive or scientific stage, however, the mind renounces ultimate causes and is satisfied systematically to observe phenomena and to establish the laws of sequence by which they are interrelated. The human mind does not make the transition from stage to stage as a totality, however. Depending on the complexity of the phenomena being explained, the mind can simultaneously adopt positive explanations of the simpler phenomena of astronomy, for instance, while still adhering to metaphysical explanations for the more complex phenomena of biology. Hence Comte's second major point, the classification of sciences into a hierarchy of complexity corresponding with the sequence in which they attained the positive stage. The highest, most complex science was that of society itself, for which

Comte coined the term 'sociology.' With the attainment by sociology of the positive stage, the subjective synthesis becomes possible. According to this latter concept all sciences now become in a sense subordinate to social science; or rather, all science becomes social science, becoming 'subjective' in the sense that it can now be made wholly subservient to the needs of man – man-centred. (Hence the peculiar value of studying medicine, the embodiment of the subjective synthesis.'[9]

One can appreciate the virtues of Comte's subjective synthesis in an age which has perfected the thermonuclear explosion and now flirts with the chemistry of gene mutation, and one can perhaps feel more sympathetic towards his denial of the autonomy and objectivity of science. One can also appreciate better, in an age when disciplines contort themselves unbecomingly in order to achieve recognition as sciences, Comte's acuteness in recognizing the ultimate impossibility of objectivity in even the purest of sciences. Science can only answer the questions man puts to it, and obviously, in the putting of the questions, subjectivity is ineradicable. The hostility towards Comte of the majority of nineteenth-century scientists is understandable, however. After all, their noble pretensions to objectivity and autonomy were only just being decisively asserted against organized religion after centuries of resistance, and now here was Comte claiming jurisdiction over them with a new church – 'Catholicism minus Christianity' as T.H. Huxley wittily described it. But scientists had even better reasons for their hostility. Comte was fairly well-read in certain sciences, and was a very able mathematician, but in arrogating to himself the prerogative of deciding what mattered and what did not, what questions science should attempt to answer and what questions it should leave alone, he was less than perspicacious. Had the strategy of scientific discovery been left to his dictation, scientific knowledge would be impoverished indeed. Comte anathematized the cellular theory in biology (because he detected in it a dangerous similarity to the retrograde 'metaphysical' Leibnizian monad); he condemned among other things sidereal astronomy and probability theory. He was hostile to experimental research generally because of its tendency to lead to awkward discoveries which could only result in further uncertainties and 'mental anarchy.' Comte's scientific creed has aptly been described as a form of 'radical agnosticism,' for he declared large tracts of reality off-limits to scientific speculation and research partly because he believed that the human mind was incapable of ever penetrating them and that it was therefore wasted energy to try to do so, but partly also from a vague fear that they might yield discoveries disturbing to the intellectual dogmas which he propounded with such apparent confidence.[10]

But what repelled the practising scientist could very well attract the nonscientist to Comte's doctrines. They appealed to the earnest layman because they were didactic and reductive, an aid to comprehension rather than to discovery. Behind the complacent facade of the Oxford classicist there might well be gnawing uncertainties about his relevance in an age when science was not only beginning to initiate new technological triumphs but was seriously eroding the traditional foundations of religion and morality. Comte offered to allay such doubts with a dogmatic, encyclopaedic system which offered the generalist mastery over science itself. The primacy of the science of society – the subjective synthesis – was reassuring. Armed with Comte's dogmas about what mattered and what did not, the disciple could confidently command the armies of science from his armchair. Frederic Harrison expressed very clearly the agnostic element in Comtism:

I am quite thinking science is a fleabite. I really think the positivist minimum of the sciences is nothing so formidable. We are still so under the slavery of the pedants as not to feel the positive liberty of contented ignorance. I suspect that positivism in science means in a sense – an enlightened ignorance. What you chiefly want is to know firmly and believe indomitably when you may rest proudly without knowledge. [11]

The religious appeal of Comtism was related to its scientific appeal; Comte, the scientific agnostic, offered an answer to religious agnosticism. His Religion of Humanity was a 'scientific' surrogate for those torn by honest doubt from the old moorings of faith. But it must be borne in mind that Comte's religion was coterminous with his whole social ideology. The priests of the Religion of Humanity were the intellectuals of the positivist society, for the spiritual realm, according to Comte, embraced all the realms of thought including science itself. Thus the Religion of Humanity was man-centred, like its science. Its object of worship was all those members of society who have contributed to it either by thought, action, or example, those worthy human beings who have gained 'subjective immortality' – that is, whose memory and achievement live on in the collective life of mankind. The greatest of these won the ultimate accolade of having a month named after them in the Positivist Calendar. Comte's religion, traditionally the butt of much ridicule, was in many respects quite sensible, though he gave unnecessary hostages to his detractors by prescribing in absurd detail the externals (borrowed mainly from Catholicism) of his church. Excessive detail is one of the traps of social prophecy into which Comte, unlike Marx, frequently fell.

Frederic Harrison in 1860 ignited the famous *Essays and Reviews* controversy with a passionate attack on that manifesto of the Broad Church *avant garde* who were attempting to propel the Church of England into the mid-nineteenth century and to place it on foundations which would be impervious to the disturbing findings of natural science and biblical scholarship. He was indignant that members of the established church should attempt to come to terms with the age by limiting the claims of religion – by 'subliming religion into an emotion and making an armistice with science.' Darkly characterizing the age in which he lived as one of doubt, hypocrisy, and indifference, he declared that such a severance of reason from emotion was 'the ultimate source of nearly all social confusion.' Although not fully committed himself to Comtism at this time, Harrison was arguing from an essentially Comtist standpoint. The great aim of the Religion of Humanity was to restore the balance between mind and heart, reason and emotion, and it therefore stood to benefit from this break-up of the old faith which he described with ill-disguised relish. But the 'wrigglings and prevarications' of the seven clergymen who obstinately refused to acknowledge the imminent demise of their creed presented an obstacle to the new dispensation.[12]

The Victorian Broad Church competed with Comtism in its wide and diffuse appeal for the allegiance of those who sought religious and social unity in a world of embattled sects. Comte's ideas aroused considerable interest among leading broad churchmen. B.F. Westcott detected a basic harmony between the opinions of Coleridge and Maurice and those of Comte; while J.M. Ludlow saw a parallel between Comte's three stages and the Trinity. Since it was Harrison's favourite debating tactic to show that his opponents were unwitting positivists, he was particularly annoyed to find men like Frederick Temple with his 'sham positivism' attempting to co-opt Comte into their own church. He felt also that the equivocations of the Broad Church leaders were responsible for the growing number of clergymen who were losing their faith. The saintly character and benevolently hazy doctrines of F.D. Maurice in particular attracted a number of well-intentioned but uncertain young men such as Leslie Stephen and Edward Carpenter into Holy Orders, where they became disillusioned and slid into agnosticism. The Victorian tragedy of the intellectual choked by the clerical collar was a real one – Pattison, Jowett, and Froude were examples well known to Harrison – and it was one of his hopes that Comtism would check this problem by providing a place for men with the sacerdotal vocation without confining their speculative capacities. He remarked in a letter to Beesly in 1859: 'Just look at Bridges. There must be something fearfully wrong when the men one fancies are worth most are perplexed and uncertain. There is one thing; such men don't carry their hopes and doubts into the all absorbing bosom of the establishment wherein so much half-formed good has been ossified.'[13]

Harrison's own initial reservations about Comte's church arose from his fear that it might prove itself to be an intellectually constricting institution. He had an interview with Comte in 1855 and was strongly attracted by his system, but the example of Congreve had an equivocal effect on him. The following year he expressed dismay at the 'fatal petrification of his fine mind' within the 'iron mould' of Comtism. Congreve rejoiced in the security of Comte's minutely detailed creed: 'As I get to live myself into the system I feel its logical coherence in all its parts, and points which were difficult become clear,' he declared in 1860. Harrison sought a coherent and comprehensive intellectual system, but unlike Congreve he wanted to expand within it rather than to narrow and channel himself. It was not until he had satisfied himself that Comte was no strict dogmatist, but rather 'full of broad practical tolerance,' that he was willing to commit himself. It was Comte the relativist and realist (for Comte had this side to him as well) that Harrison embraced. He also overcame his fear that Comtism was a mere sect, a set of crankish notions appealing only to the dissenting mentality and attracting only those motivated by the spirit of exclusion. Harrison was above all drawn to Comte's conception of the intellectual's place in the community, and he expressed his understanding of the creed and its founder's intentions in a way that clearly reflected the socially unifying aspirations of university radicals:

I cannot see that he ever contemplated forming a sect to which the human race were to be converted one by one. I conceive him to have drawn out a coherent *system of principles*, calling upon men to live by them, and to promulgate them. I believe his disciples and successors ought to seek mainly to make his principles actively felt in society, addressing first the most important and central sections of society. They ought to found a school, not a sect.[14]

Because ideas were the chief motive force in Comte's theory of historical change, he naturally gave a major historical role to men of ideas. It is important, therefore, to consider his theory of the development and functions of intellectuals. He claimed that the existence of an intellectual or speculative class was the 'indispensable preparation for the formation of all other classes.' It had come into being as the organ of primitive religion and ruled first as a theocracy – in Egypt, for example – through fear and superstition, its power being founded on the possession of the earliest scientific knowledge. Through the successive civilizations of the theological stage of history, Greece and Rome, its authority and prestige were somewhat diminished because the intellectual class was slow to renounce its pretensions to political power and to recognize that its true function was 'not to engross the conduct of life, but to modify, by its consultative or preparatory influence, the rule of material or practical power.' This was simply to recognize the contradictory demands of the active and the contemplative life which Comte, like many poets and philosophers before him, considered to occupy mutually incompatible spheres. It was an inescapable psychological fact to him that the spheres of thought and action demanded wholly different attitudes and abilities. Only at the end of theological stage in the mediaeval Catholic church was this truth finally institutionalized in the doctrine of separation of church and state, of the spiritual and temporal power. Monasticism above all provided for the special needs and functions of the intellectual class; communal life and celibacy ended the hereditary principle hitherto traditional to the recruitment of that class and at last enabled it to become a truly disinterested élite – a spiritual power.[15]

But this institutional perfection was shattered during the metaphysical stage which occupied the fourteenth to the nineteenth centuries, essentially a period of critical and negative reaction to the theological stage, and culminated in the concerted, systematic negations of the eighteenth-century Enlightenment. False pretensions returned to the intellectual class, particularly with the development of the universities and the parliaments. These produced the two great instruments of metaphysical reaction, the professors and the lawyers, who by the nineteenth century had become the chief forces of retrogression, the major obstacles to the realization of the positive era. The professors formulated the metaphysical mode of explanation which replaced supernatural powers with abstract principles, while the lawyers developed political abstractions such as natural right and popular sovereignty to replace theological notions like divine right. The Reformation with its emphasis on intellectual individualism consolidated the power of these new secular intellectuals in northern Europe and particularly in the universities, which now turned out increasing numbers of students unprepared for any specific career by their unscientific, largely literary education but intent upon some sort of intellectual vocation. These became 'members of that highly equivocal class of modern society having no express mental functions' – freelance intellectuals. According to Comte, however, such intellectuals, men of letters and lawyers, were a class whose negative function was now exhausted and whose very existence was purely provisional.*[16]

As academic radicals like Congreve, Harrison, Beesly, and others read Comte's historical analysis of intellectuals, they could hardly fail to recognize that he was talking about them. They were in fact twice damned: as members of the middle class and as university intellectuals. Their eventual extinction was clearly spelled

---

* In using the term 'intellectual' in the context of Victorian England, it is well to remember that as a noun at least it was rarely used, though unlike 'élitism' it was not entirely unknown. Thus Mark Pattison, appropriately, used it in a modern sense: 'It is the business of the intellectual to make statements about the things that concern him' (*Essays*, II, 415). Generally the Victorians made do with a variety of neutral terms such as 'man of letters,' 'scholar,' or 'thinker' which had a more specific connotation, as well as more value-laden terms such as 'ideologue' and 'doctrinaire' (usually applied unfavourably to intellectuals in politics), or the honorific 'sage' (for a Carlyle or Ruskin). Comte used a variety of terms, many having pejorative connotations such as 'litterateur' or 'pedant,' though his usual neutral term was 'man of letters.' These terms applied, however, to the unincorporated intellectuals of the metaphysical era whose existence he deplored. In the positive social organization, as in Coleridge's clerisy, the intellectual was a priest, and, collectively, the spiritual power.

out. But salvation was at hand, for they could enlist on the side of the future by joining the spiritual power, receiving dispensation since, for its initial generation, Comtism had no choice but to draw upon the old order. As Comte had come to realize after completing the above analysis, the retrograde general literary education provided by Oxford, at least, could be quite conducive to appreciation of his system, and the *tabula rasa* of scientific knowledge was all the more receptive to his bold dogmas. But having enlisted under the device of 'order and progress,' having joined the intellectual élite, what was the Comtist to do next? When the positive order was fully realized, his place would be clear. His teaching and guidance would be accepted without question by the people and he would be supported by his official salary (the amount of which Comte characteristically specified). But what to do in the here-and-now was less certain. Much of Comte's correspondence consisted of advice to perplexed disciples on what to do in this transitional phase. They had to support themselves in the least 'retrograde' way possible; they had to set an example of Comtist morality by their lives and they had to proselytize by teaching or by otherwise influencing public opinion. It is understandable that the transition to Utopia could not be legislated for as comprehensively as could the Utopia itself. The dilemma of the Comtist intellectual, trying to accommodate himself to the imperfect realities of the interim period while living up to the ideal standards of the positive social order, must be appreciated if one is to understand those who adopted the creed.

Frederic Harrison remained at Wadham as a fellow and tutor for two years after taking his degree and actively participated in university politics, but though he enjoyed it, for him as for many others, academic life did not really seem to offer a career or profession. Full of the academic radical's sense of public mission, he felt slightly ashamed of his cloistered ease – its 'sneaking annotation of the book of life' – and soon left it for a real profession. Again like many others, lacking any particular inclination but compelled to choose from amongst the limited number of gentlemen's professions, he chose the bar, the least demanding of the professions in its formal training and the most open-ended in its opportunities. Unfortunately, Comte considered lawyers a most retrograde group, scavengers living off the social and intellectual disorders of the declining metaphysical stage. It was in their professional interest to preserve the status quo, but even worse, their central principle of accepting briefs and advocating them without reference to private judgment made the practise of law extremely harmful to intellectual integrity and personal morality. (Thomas Arnold shared this view.) Yet a disproportionately large number of English Comtists were barristers and Comte eased their consciences by allowing that legal practice did at least provide empirical knowledge of the bad side of human nature. Harrison's guilt about his profession shows in his remark to George Eliot when she sought his help on the niceties of the law of entail in connection with the plot of *Felix Holt:* 'Points of law are so little connected with the happiness of mankind that I fall with a will upon one which I hope will be.' His interest in the law was that of a scholar and reformer, however, and he had the good fortune to study under Henry Maine, the jurist and pioneering legal anthropologist. The young student who found it 'a delight to come upon a huge, overgrown historic system with all its proportions untouched, upon which one is at liberty to thrust and pound in every direction without a change of a useless blow' was well fitted for the post of secretary to a government commission on the digest of the law to which he was appointed in the late 1860s. Yet Harrison retained at the same time a deep respect for the force of the law in shaping the history and institutions of human society, a respect which was integral to such conservative aspects of his character as his profound instinct for order. Comtism offered to satisfy this conservatism as fully as it did his desire for progress.[17]

Once established as a student at Lincoln's Inn, Harrison pressed his Wadham companions to leave the cloisters and join him in London to concert their efforts along the lines to which they had dedicated themselves as members of the Essay Society and the Wadham Confederacy. Bridges was working in hopes of a fellowship, while Beesly was teaching at Marlborough College. Bridges came to London after winning an Oriel fellowship, which now supported him in his scientific studies ('caterpillars in fact – ugh!' Harrison characteristically remarked of his work). In accordance with Comte's prescription for the intending Comtist priest, Bridges became a physician and was soon serving honourably as a public health inspector. Congreve also studied medicine but none of the other Oxford Comtists did so. Beesly came to London in 1859 as principal of University College Hall but Harrison had difficulty in co-ordinating their activities. Both were eager to speak out as heralds of the new order, but Beesly was more radical in his political responses, readier to take a strong line, while Harrison was anxious to seek a wider consensus which included his other university friends. Many of the latter were with him at the Inns of Court, young barristers enjoying considerable leisure in the long intervals between their first briefs, unmarried and financially comfortable thanks to their fellowships and their fathers. They were eager to take up the larger issues which their university education had prepared them to encompass confidently within the limits of an honours exam paper. Not surprisingly, the thoughts of such men turned readily to journalism.[18]

As we have seen, journalism was one of the means by which the university radicals hoped to bring Oxford into contact with the nation. Fortuitously for these ambitions, journalism was just attaining in the 1850s sufficient social acceptability to allow gentlemen to engage in it without serious fears of losing caste. Periodicals like the gentlemanly *Saturday Review* paid quite well, which made them, like the fellowship, a useful financial prop to clever young barristers getting established; the prevailing policy of anonymity protected them from, amongst other things, the envy of solicitors who might draw unflattering conclusions about their professional capacities from such evidence of leisure.[19]

Unfortunately, however, Comte viewed the practice of journalism, like the practice of law, with grave disapproval. He considered journalism an 'anarchical institution' spoiled of any power to do good by the grip of ambitious editors (a prejudice based on unfortunate personal experience). His virtual prohibition restricted his English disciples in utilizing this natural means of making known their opinions. According to Comte's own teaching, public opinion was the great moral force in society, the primary means by which the regeneration of human society was to be effected and enforced. And it was virtually an article of faith in the mid-nineteenth century that journalism was the great means by which public opinion, that vaguely defined but powerful entity, could be inspired and controlled. Journalists were thus the hierophants of public opinion, translating its undisciplined, incoherent force into a useable current which they directed into such channels as they divined to correspond with its intentions. But Comte declared that privately printed broadsheets and pamphlets appearing at irregular intervals were the only means of public communication which avoided the corrupting influence of journalism. Only such a purist as Congreve could acquiesce fully in Comte's injunction; Harrison and Beesly rather guiltily flouted it, Harrison most of all since he had a brilliant talent for higher journalism and could not resist exercising it. He assuaged his guilt, however, by speaking out against the practice of anonymity which deprived the individual journalist of responsibility for his opinions while giving editors such as John Delane of *The Times* enormous influence. Opposition among higher journalists to the principle of anonymity was in fact swelling at this time, and began to make headway in the 1860s as new journals such as the *Fortnightly Review* increasingly adopted the policy of signed contributions. Coleridge and Thomas Arnold had been early critics of the irresponsibility, the skulking unmanliness of anonymity. Thomas Hughes compared it to the secret ballot which, by concealing and depersonalizing the judgments of the élite, diminished their rightful authority. Voting in secret and writing in secret ran counter to one of the chief commandments of Comtism – 'Live openly.' Here, as at other significant points, Comtist teaching coincided with the ideal of the clerisy.[20]

5

The Search for the Proletariat

The happy ambiguity, particularly in French, of the word 'people' is a constant reminder that the proletarians in no way form a true class, but rather constitute the social mass from which emerge, like so many necessary organs, the diverse and special classes.

Auguste Comte, *Discours sur l'ensemble du positivisme*

The unfortunate confidence which [the proletariat] still bestow on literary men and lawyers shows that the prestige of pedantry lingers on among them longer than the prestige of theology or monarchy.

Ibid

Though certain awkward vocational problems hindered the English Comtists in their attempts to realize the 'spiritual power,' their duties at least seemed fairly clear. Frederic Harrison believed that Comte's disciples 'ought to seek mainly to make his principles actively felt in society, addressing first the most important and central sections of society.' Unquestionably the most important section of society in the Comtist scheme is the proletariat. 'The working class is the only class which (to use a paradox) is not a class. It is the nation'; so Harrison paraphrased Comte's dictum. The working class is the true body politic (the organic metaphor is appropriate to Comte); the other classes are but special organs fulfilling specific purposes. But against this ideal classless, functional society stood the reality of Victorian England where the middle class was the most important section of society. What part of society should the Comtist missionary chiefly concern himself with addressing, the working-class majority to whom the future belonged, or their middle-class masters, who held most of the levers of national life under the present dispensation but had virtually no place in the positive polity? Congreve, who hewed closest to the letter of Comte, stated in 1857 that his followers should provide examples in themselves of the 'adaptation of positivism to middle class life.' This was quite successfully done, for the Comtist movement in England was very middle class indeed. Barristers, academics, higher civil servants, and men of leisure predominated; proletarians were even rarer than businessmen (the group most in need of Comtist moralization). Comtism appealed to those whom its new order threatened: joining the élite offered security. In contrast the proletarian, whose future importance was assured, had no need to scramble for a place in the new dispensation.[1]

Yet Comtism had to establish some sort of relationship with the proletariat, who were after all the ultimate object of attention. Comte idealized them to a degree far beyond anything the young university radicals achieved in their unsystematic way. Comte has been aptly called the theoretician of the 'noble proletarian,' and, compared to Rousseau, the theoretician of the 'noble savage.' Both thinkers presented social abstractions, archetypes founded on intuition rather than empiricism. In both cases we recognize a prelapsarian man of nature who, despite his material deprivations, has been providentially spared from civilization's greatest misery – specialization. Comte attributed this good fortune to the proletariat's lack of education. Uncorrupted by the characteristic education of the metaphysical stage, they were empty vessels ready for the positive doctrines of the ultimate stage. Their moral superiority was another happy consequence of neglect: their social institutions, their family life, even their habits of improvidence which argued spontaneity, generosity, and social fraternalism were all providential indications that the proletariat were the chosen people of the positive stage.[2]

The peculiar aptitude of the proletariat for the positive stage, according to Comte, made them natural allies of the spiritual power. The 'decisive coalition' of workers and intellectuals would be facilitated by their intellectual and moral affinities. With characteristic antithesis, he noted that 'each proletarian is in many respects a spontaneous philosopher, just as every philosopher is in many respects a systematic proletarian.' Both were to avoid in their educations that specialization which, however indispensable for the administrative class – the practical directors of society and industry – was antithetical to the generalizing, synthesizing spirit essential to those classes embodying the morality and intelligence of society. Again, the habits of economy necessary for the accumulation and administration of capital, and therefore essential to the practical élite, were to be discouraged in both the proletariat and the intellectual élite as injurious to the character because they impaired the exercise of generous social feelings. Comte suggested that both the intellectual and the practical élites would come to envy the virtuous, carefree situation of the proletariat and 'with all their personal advantages often regret that they were not born or did not remain in the condition of workmen.' In the positive order the proletariat, contented and unambitious for temporal power or gain but exercising by sheer weight of virtue a moral authority over the other parts of society, would occupy according to Comte's scale of values the highest place in the social hierarchy. Ever mindful that social discontent was the great enemy of stability, Comte wanted to ensure that the proletariat, secure in its sense of superiority, would feel no envy towards the governing élites. Meanwhile the feeling of alienation from the community, traditionally so unsettling to the intellectuals, the smallest and most self-conscious social group, would be assuaged by a sense of identity with the largest and least self-conscious group.[3]

Harrison's undergraduate letters illustrate vividly the social and political attitudes which made him particularly susceptible to Comtism. He welcomed the aristocratic Aberdeen coalition government of 1852, hoping that it would polarize and unite in opposition the 'vigorous practical radicals ... plebeians to the backbone, sprung from the earth.' He looked forward hopefully to the foundation of 'a real people's party' which would 'wage war on the accurst barrier between the gentleman and the cad, the unholy assumptions of property, the arrogance of respectability.' Such sentiments are redolent of Kingsley and Carlyle and the confused situation of middle-class radicalism in the mid-century years. By 1856, in the disappointing aftermath of the Crimean War, Harrison was wishing for one hour on the floor of the House of Commons to curse all its hypocrites and liars, and to tell them that 'the only reform needed was one that would disenfranchise the middle class as unworthy and incapable of political power, and ostracize the upper classes as enemies of the commonwealth.' 'The horny handed millions' alone seemed worthy, with their leaders, the plucky Northern manufacturers. 'I am sick of those among whom we live,' he continued, 'Their stale sneers, their ignorant commonplaces, their mean fears disgust me. They stifle me. I will go and make friends with the hard hands and rough tongues in whom content has not overgrown human nature, nor success made selfish, nor convention hypocrites – who can trust and love and hope.'[4]

After leaving Oxford, like many radical young gentlemen of education and conscience Harrison was drawn towards the Working Men's College, founded in 1854 by Maurice and his disciples to enable them to learn from the working man by teaching him. Harrison noted of Maurice that he was 'a good man, but not at all dangerous' ('dangerous' was a laudatory epithet in the private conspiratorial vocabulary of Harrison's correspondence with Beesly). 'Christian Socialism,' he continued, 'means nothing at all, only that men and teachers are working very well and pleasantly together, and sometimes make remarks about Mammon worship.' The students were 'mostly working men of the first class (£2. a week) ... a gentlemanly, intelligent, improving breed.' During one of his lectures on the French Revolution Harrison was fiercely attacked by a 'rising carpenter,' who called him 'a republican, and an enemy of the British Constitution.' 'So low the aristocracy penetrates,' he growled in reporting the incident to Beesly. It was an additional complication in the dilemma of the middle-class Comtist, already vexed by his own precarious status, that in seeking contact with the working class he had to distinguish between its 'pure' and 'impure' members with regard to their attitudes towards society: 'I come home for the 20th time convinced that it is a mere waste of time to be improving the style of semi-literate youths aspiring to be correct. On the other hand, the strong horny hands who have something to live for are not given to literature and have no taste for study at all.'[5]

Maurice in fact emphasized the humanities and tried to exclude strictly vocational subjects, to avoid providing convenient educational facilities for men merely ambitious to improve their skills and advance in their trades. This was in keeping with his aim of dissolving class barriers through the sharing of cultural experiences between gentlemen and working men. But it opened the way to the even greater danger, for the Comtist at least, that workers might be encouraged by such contacts to try to leave their class altogether. Thus there was considerable demand among the students for a Latin class, despite Godfrey Lushington's attempt in the college magazine to show that Latin was not really an appropriate study for working men. But with Latin tags so freely used in parliamentary debates, in speeches and leading articles, it is hardly surprising that the uninitiated should attach almost magical significance to the language – as a key to wisdom and power held only by the upper classes. *Vox populi, vox Dei* – the Latin class was formed, and proved even more popular than history.[6]

Harrison enjoyed teaching at the college, but his attempts to systematize the courses in history in accordance with Comte's scheme met stern opposition from Maurice, who did not want any Comtist eggs hatched in his nest; so he decided to give a series of history lectures on his own in 1862. He was encouraged by the success of T.H. Huxley's special lectures for working men where he saw a large audience held spellbound by the similarities between man and the higher apes. So delighted was he by this *provocatio ad populum* (so he called it) that he wrote to Beesly to announce that 'the intimate alliance foretold by Comte between philosophers and the proletariat' had begun. Harrison found a secularist hall where he was free to dispense the pure milk of Comtism to working men and others on Saturday nights, and though most of his listeners seemed weary and inattentive, a few 'very desirable and intelligent' men asked to join his class for further instruction. His lectures, subsequently republished as a pamphlet *The Meaning of History*, were certainly no provocation, being richly Arnoldian in tone. History,

Harrison declared, revealed the power of public opinion and demonstrated how 'a man, provided he lives like an honest, thoughtful, truth-speaking gentleman, is a power in the state.' Unfortunately, the platform afforded no opportunity to gain an intimate knowledge of the working classes – 'to know the best of them personally as friends, to feel the quality of their minds and hearts, to enter into their spontaneous institutions and practices, and witness by personal inquiry the sufferings and necessities which weigh upon them.' All this he had resolved to do.[7]

Harrison's first active involvement with the 'spontaneous institutions and practices' of the working classes came in 1861 when the London builders' strike introduced him to trade unionism. In 1859 Congreve had made contact with George Potter, the leader of the more militant unionists, and put the Comtist seal of approval on his general aims and activities, since Comtism was sympathetic to trade unionism within limits and Congreve was anxious to establish his own relationship with the English proletariat. Harrison, Beesly, and Godfrey Lushington joined the Christian Socialists in preparing a statement of the builders' dispute for publication to counter the misrepresentations of the middle-class press, led by *The Times*. But George Potter, although Harrison admired his talents, lacked the character befitting an ideal proletarian; from the start Harrison suspected him of being unscrupulous. Indeed, London working men generally seemed to suffer from 'luxurious tastes' and general dissipation. An early student of urban problems, Harrison suspected that the 'great wen' was itself to blame. Comte had condemned the 'confused and monstrous' city of London and believed that Manchester, the embodiment of industrialism, was a much fitter centre of social regeneration. In October 1860 Harrison made his first investigatory trip to the North, that focus of the university radicals' mythology. He wrote in awe to a friend:

The first sight of the manufacturing world, brief as it was, has filled me with material for reflection and inquiry ... Nothing but ocular demonstration can make one feel that enormous weight, mass and power of the manufacturing districts. It is only by seeing that vast palpitating city 100 miles long that one can understand what it means. That which I think most strongly impressed and astonished me was to see the obvious comfort, power and intelligence of the best workmen. Everything in human life is within the reach of the more highly skilled mechanic.

But morally he found it a chaos. The whole experience confirmed his growing confidence that Comte had correctly analyzed the socially harmful consequences of the individualistic, competitive values of unmoralized industrialism and had prescribed valid remedies. The squalor and suffering that existed side by side with comfort and opulence were remediable, but 'the blood,' in Harrison's words, 'was on the hands of the employer. Of all men, he is his brother's keeper.' The captains of industry did not seem to be accepting the responsibilities that accompanied their power over men's lives.[8]

Harrison met some more promising specimens of the industrialist class the following year, when he made another tour of the northern cities, this time with J.H. Bridges, who had just commenced practicing medicine in Bradford. This city was a stronghold of the 'new model employers' who were becoming more numerous as the mid-century breathing space of capitalism gave their benevolent impulses a chance to emerge and expand. Harrison met W.E. Forster, the woolens manufacturer and future minister of education who had married the eldest daughter of Thomas Arnold. Forster had been, like Congreve, a backer of the *Leader*, a radical journal sympathetic to Comte, and contributed a series of strongly anti-*laissez-faire* articles on the 'Right to Work'; he seemed a promising prototype of Comte's moralized capitalist. Harrison also had 'immense fun ... hunting up Socialists, animists and secularists wherever he went,' but complained that the real working men were 'difficult to get at.' In 1863 he made a third tour, this time with Godfrey Lushington, at the height of the Lancashire cotton famine. The two men conducted a private inquiry into the effects of unemployment and the operation of the relief system, publishing their findings in two long letters to *The Times*. Harrison and his friends were rather disappointed by the apparent failure of the millowners to fulfil their moral obligations as capitalists towards the unemployed proletariat during the crisis. Bridges was particularly critical of the humiliating treatment of those claiming relief. Harrison's investigations were slightly more favourable: after observing a distribution of relief he noted in his diary that the examinations of applicants were 'not a model of delicacy of manner, but certainly free from rudeness and brutality.' However, they all agreed that the crisis dramatically exposed the utter inadequacies of *laissez-faire* voluntarism and demonstrated the need for large-scale state intervention through public works projects which would relieve the unemployed without degrading them, while producing lasting social benefits.[9]

Harrison was no nineteenth-century Orwell, eager to go slumming in search of the common man; thus he had to rely heavily for his information on the 'uncommon man' – the educated, articulate, often socially ambitious workers who by Comtist standards were the least desirable members of their class. (One of Harrison's sources of working-class contacts was G.J. Holyoake, the Owenite and Secularist agitator who took an interest in Comtism and had visited Comte himself in 1855.) Harrison described one such contact to a friend: 'At Leeds we saw a man who much struck me. An old Owenite who is a sort of general adviser and manager of the Mechanics Institutes; penny saving banks, and co-operative unions, etc., all 'round the country. He seems quite a practical genius, and everything succeeds. But besides this he has written a volume not unremarkable on Social Science, and he knows F. Newman and keeps alive with everything going on – religious, political, social and intellectual. He was in a ragged school and is now a managing clerk in a warehouse.' This Smilesean hero was hardly the archetypal proletarian. But such men often confirmed the Comtist doctrine; thus in Lancashire he encountered 'an excellent specimen' of the artisan class who had invested all his savings in a co-operative cotton mill, even though he admitted that such mills were usually harder employers than the large capitalist-run mills. Amongst the Rochdale co-operators Harrison found a clear demonstration of the consequences of labourers rising out of their class by successful investment in a co-operative cotton mill which had initially been founded on principles of worker ownership and profit sharing but had evolved within eight years into a straight capitalist venture for the more astute working-class investors. Social advancement bought in this way entailed a betrayal of true proletarian morality, as he emphasized by quoting from the 'Co-operator's Catechism' in which 'cash payments, small profits and quick returns' were exalted as articles of faith. [10]

A letter to *The Times*, that instinctive upper middle-class response to perceived social problems, was no means of communicating with the working class. Nor did Harrison and his friends have access to mass-circulation papers like *Reynolds'* and *Lloyd's*. In 1861, however, George Potter founded the *Bee-Hive* as an advanced working-class weekly newspaper giving special attention to the organized labour movement, and from 1863 Harrison and Beesly were regular contributors, on terms which suited them very well: 'One puts one's name, one says just what one likes, one has no need to regard editor, printer or subscriber. It is really a free platform one can mount without giving any pledge.' Unfortunately the progress of the *Bee-Hive* was marred by unedifying internal disputes over management and editorial policy which lent colour to Comte's warnings about the moral evils of journalism. When Potter's opponents in London trade union circles took over control of the *Miner and Workman's Advocate* (later renamed the *Commonwealth*) and ran it as a rival organ of labour, Harrison and Beesly wrote for it too. Writing for such *bona fide* proletarian journals, Harrison could hope that he was at last getting across to the working men, though how many, where they were, and what weight his words had with them was hard to tell (both papers had circulations of well under 10,000). [11]

Harrison did not preach Comtism directly to his readers though it was usually implicit in the treatment of his subject matter. Only when directly accused of using the paper as a Comtist pulpit did he indulge in an overt exposition of his creed, and then only to rebut the charge by emphasizing its very lack of demagogic appeal. The Comtists gloried in their purity, and Harrison even refused the offer of the editorship of the *Commonwealth* in spite of (and partly because of) 'the great opportunity and terrible power' which such a position might afford him. It was better that a working-class newspaper should be edited by a member of that class, and that they should simply provide articles 'presenting positivist theories under the garb of mere good common sense,' an art in which Harrison excelled. This was not mere irresponsibility, for Harrison honestly felt that his method of insinuating his doctrines was tactically realistic under the circumstances. As an editor he would have been compelled either to turn his journal into a sectarian organ, and find himself preaching to the converted who were few indeed, or else to compromise. It was better to compromise others. Then, too, the whole business aspect of journalism – deadlines, money, subscribers – was repugnant to his gentlemanly instincts.[12]

Though Harrison did not condescend in his proletarian journalism, he had a keen sense of his audience. In his letters to Beesly concerning their *Bee-Hive* and *Commonwealth* articles he frequently indulged in the sort of conspiratorial language, half-bantering, half-serious, which serves to illuminate the self-consciousness of the Comtists about their relationship with their proletarian clientele. Once again it was the tension between the mid-Victorian reality and the Comtist ideal, between the somewhat subversive appearance they created as middle-class gentlemen aiding and abetting the mysterious lower classes and the basically conservative ideal towards which their activities were ultimately directed. Harrison described one of his *Commonwealth* articles as 'violent beyond measure,' and called on Beesly to help him to prevent the paper from becoming 'too respectable,' adding, 'I put in some foul-mouthedness on purpose.' He was certainly forthright and trenchant in his style, but it was Beesly who excelled at summoning up the distant thunder of proletarian discontent and dropping veiled hints of social upheaval. When a more conventional friend took Harrison to task for being a bit too 'strong' in one of his articles, he protested: 'I would never say anything that could have an incendiary effect. It's impossible to produce any strong feeling, let alone action.' Significantly these words were written in 1866, on the very eve of the reform agitation. The apparent contradiction between Harrison's remarks is largely resolved by the distinction which he made between the standards of his own class, whose members might indeed find his articles in the working-class press 'violent beyond measure,' and the standards of the working class itself. He recognized that his own class was inordinately ready to feel threatened by the language of change, while the working class had a much higher threshold of sensitivity to such language. He felt that fairly strong words were necessary to prod the latter into an awareness of the need for political reform in the mid-1860s, and though a member of the middle class, he had to stimulate the proletarian consciousness to overcome the 'respectable' inclinations of their own leaders.

But Harrison and Beesly also knew that members of the middle class looked at the *Bee-Hive* and *Commonwealth*; after all, the *Saturday Review* had stated that they were influential organs of the working class. So if any stray bourgeois happened to look in, wondering 'what the people were thinking,' he would receive a salutary shock to his complacency.[13]

Harrison said little about Comtist economics – its moralized capitalism – in the working-class press, confining himself mainly to political subjects, foreign and domestic. On foreign policy his Comtist line would not have appeared unfamiliar to his readers. Anti-Palmerstonianism, anti-colonialism, internationalism – on these issues he appealed like other university radicals to 'the generous instincts of the working class.' On domestic politics Harrison was a bit further from the beaten path, though the thinking artisan who had been exposed to Carlyle or Kingsley's 'Parson Lot' would find the tone and language, the pervasive quietism couched in impassioned rhetoric, already familiar. As a Comtist giving practical political advice to the working classes in the mid-1860s, Harrison was in a somewhat ambivalent position. Like all the university radicals and like his Comtist companions, he was an advocate of reform as a matter of fairness and of faith. Reform meant enfranchisement, widening the sphere of political participation to bring the lower classes (or some of them, at least) into the nation. But the Comtist social system entirely excluded the proletariat from active participation in politics. They were to exercise moral influence over their governors by the force of their virtuous collective opinion, but were to be kept from the potentially corrupting influence of actual political power. The Comtist polity would have no elections, being governed – or rather, administered – by the ablest men, who were to be chosen solely by their superiors.

Hence Harrison's uncertainty as to his task *vis-à-vis* his proletarian readership – whether it was to preach Comtism, encourage reform, criticize the existing political system, increase proletarian political awareness, or educate them in the realities of politics. That he tried to do all of these things accounts for much of his confusion. This emerges in his *Commonwealth* article, 'A Scheme of Reform' (March 1866), in which he stated his views on the major issue of the day. 'Reform,' he declared at the outset, meant 'the placing of ultimate control of the State in the hands of the mass of the people.' But from this apparently unequivocal statement he almost immediately retreated into qualification and restatement from the Comtist point of view. First, he admitted that the governing classes would not allow such control until 'forced in a severe struggle.' And, 'this struggle, to be candid, we are not yet prepared to make.' Manhood suffrage, after all, had chiefly symbolic value as a sign of political purification. The substance of power would be in the people's possession through the indirect action of public opinion well before the legal formality of power. Harrison therefore urged the people to prepare themselves for the real power which they must eventually possess and exert. But, he warned, 'it would be a disaster to them, to this nation and to freedom if they came by this power before they are quite fit to use it. And for my part I say frankly that I do not believe they are yet fit.' These were not the sneers of an arrogant intellectual, Harrison assured his readers. The masses were better fitted for the franchise than the present electorate, for they had the sound instincts based on 'social and generous emotions, habits of sympathy called out by joint suffering and difficulties.' But because so much more was to be expected of them, they must perfect these virtues before coming to power. Harrison was concerned lest they compromise their virtue by compromising with the existing political system, being integrated into it so as to help prop it up: 'In some points of view it is not undesirable that the jealousy of the actual holders of power keep the bulk of working men outside these constitutional rights. They have full time to ponder and prepare the real questions of political importance, without having thrown off the true line by the puerilities of Parliamentary shuffling.'

The people were to come into power in a completely new atmosphere to develop a new political order bearing only the remotest likeness to the existing system. Harrison's whole message is richly Comtist in aspiration, though very inexplicit. He outlined briefly six large areas of reform, urging the workers to develop schemes which 'in good time they will be prepared with united action to enforce.' The magnitude of these reforms would be great, he hinted, but the details are vague. At the close of the article Harrison left his reader contemplating bright but misty horizons, while the note of caution echoes in his ear, warning him against the demagogue and urging patient discussion. In the realm of immediate action, it was the counsel of quietism.[14]

Harrison was quite aware of the awkwardness of his position as a proclaimed radical and sincere advocate of the political nationalization of the lower classes, yet throwing lukewarm water over their legitimate aspirations for political participation. In the Comtist view manhood suffrage was itself a *pis aller* since elections were a very crude means of expressing public opinion. The Comtists therefore accepted manhood suffrage, which to many of the working classes was the political panacea, without enthusiasm, viewing it as an interim compromise forced upon them by political realities. However, the Comtist ideal of proletarian non-participation represented the logical conclusion of intellectual populism – the purest version of élitism and of the alliance of brains and numbers. On the other hand, the ban on political activity which Comte imposed upon the spiritual élite in accordance with this theory of the separation of powers was less in harmony with the gentlemanly ideal. The university radicals were not politically alienated intellectuals. As members of their class they participated in politics both as a historical right and a social duty. Some might not choose the political life, but a creed which expressly barred them from it on principle would seem very ill-suited to gentlemen so intensely conscious of politics as were the English Comtists, Beesly and Harrison especially. There was a certain compelling logic to Comte's ban within the context of the Comtist polity, but in the context of mid-Victorian England it was once again a case of ideal versus reality. Harrison and Beesly accepted Comte's edict but characteristically did not observe it to the letter, though in Harrison's case at least there is evidence of a temperamental inclination which facilitated acquiescence – a fastidious distaste for the heat and dust of the political arena.

In the spring of 1864 Garibaldi visited England and was greeted with remarkably well-organized enthusiasm by the English working men – further evidence of their instinctive democratic internationalism. When Garibaldi's visit was unexpectedly cut short (many of the radicals suspected it was because of the government's concern about the democratic enthusiasm he evoked), a public open-air meeting was held in protest, and when this was broken up by the police a meeting was called to uphold the right to hold such public meetings in the parks. Harrison and Beesly were members of the working men's Garibaldi Committee, but when it got involved in these protests they became rather unhappy about the growing agitation and were anxious to extricate themselves from the movement. Harrison wrote disapprovingly of its 'revolutionary' implications but he did not wish to appear a deserter to the working men. He hesitated about the meeting but finally went, arriving only just in time for 'the Queen' (not entirely by accident perhaps) and made his excuses to members of the committee, one of whom remarked pointedly on his defection. 'It is rather a bore,' he wrote to Beesly describing the incident, 'after having come to the scratch to be told that one shirked. We are out of the thing now ... let us return to our diggings. These platforms and committees are beastly.' Not all platforms and committees perhaps, but certainly those which might lead to something unintended and which leaned too heavily on popular support were to be avoided. The Garibaldi parks protest in fact led directly to the formation of the Reform League, in which the involvement of the Comtists was relatively small.[15]

Prior to the 1868 elections Harrison described his Lincoln's Inn chambers as 'a sort of proletarian caucus,' frequented by 'electioneering vipers' seeking tips and support because of his reputation as a friend of the working man. He could probably have found a nomination in 1868 and might well have won a seat, but Comtist scruples reinforced his temperamental disinclination. In 1870 he did agree to stand as a candidate in Westminster for the first school board election, though this lapse was extenuated by the fact that he did not seek the nomination and emulated Mill by demanding complete freedom of opinion and by neither canvassing nor spending anything on the campaign. He was not elected.[16]

A much more acceptable avenue of involvement and influence with the working class was provided by the trade union movement. Here at least it was possible to follow the Comtist line fairly closely. According to Comte unions were not permanent organizations, certainly not instruments for effecting significant economic or political change. Their chief virtue resided in their educational function, which was to accustom the labourer to group discipline (a microcosm of that public opinion which would be the mediatory force in the positive society) and to collectivist ideals. They were also of some immediate practical use to the working class in that they palliated exploitation and tended to elevate the status of the worker. Harrison admitted the defects of the unions – particularly the spirit of exclusiveness and selfishness which they tended to promote, sacrificing the wider solidarity of the proletariat to the more restricted solidarity of the trade. These defects were excusable, however, in view of their provisional character. Unions were only a temporary expedient which would ultimately cease to be necessary. In the meantime, however, it was to their credit that they were 'at bottom, truly conservative, mainly protective, and essentially legal.' It was an essential requirement of provisional institutions that they should harbour no radical impulses which might lead them off in a direction different from the path of positivism. Society had to arrive more or less spontaneously at the point of receptivity to positive ideas. The status quo (or provisional order, in Comtist terminology) was in fact nearer to positivism than some reformed state of society – however much better than the status quo – which happened to be based on principles different from those of positivism (such as communism, for example). It was better for society to linger at the fork of the road than to veer in the wrong direction. Such reasoning makes clearer the desirability to the Comtist of conservation in the institutions of the provisional order.[17]

But such conservatism must not imply any distinctly retrograde tendency: this was the trouble with the co-operative movement. Harrison accepted without enthusiasm the idea of consumer or distributive co-operation – again as an immediate, temporary palliative. The fact that working-class co-operators were induced to save small sums was acceptable, though ideally the proletariat should not be encouraged to save since it tended to check their spontaneous instincts of generosity. Consumer co-operation was relatively unimportant as it did not directly affect the basis of the labour question, which centred on production. When applied to the production of goods, however, it was harmful, as Harrison saw in the results of the Rochdale co-operative cotton mill with its unhealthy stimulus to middle-class ambitions amongst the proletariat.[18]

The trade unions were legitimate proletarian social organizations and from 1861 onwards the Comtists were their most tireless and effective defenders. It was for this service that the working classes were most appreciative of the Comtists, while their political quirks were probably dismissed by many trade unionists simply as more of those eccentricities which were the traditional prerogative of their upper-class friends. It was exciting and flattering for the Comtists to have the support and approval of the working class, but it was a source of constant concern to know the basis of this approval. In 1862 a group of Northern trade unionists, greatly pleased by one of Harrison's *Bee-Hive* letters, asked him to come to Preston (expenses paid) to receive a framed address. Harrison refused graciously, protesting that he had done them no special favour, but remarked to Beesly that their singular gratitude made him suspect there 'must be something wrong to make them so eager for a good word.' He added: 'I hope they won't think I am ashamed of them.' Harrison was also aware that the world at large, particularly those of his own class, interpreted his involvement with the unions as signifying complete approval of their activities. Thus in 1864 he wrote to Beesly, a fellow member of the Miners' Council, about a violent strike in South Staffordshire 'of which we know nothing and can do nothing ... We are in a false position having our names paraded as friends and advisers of the colliers whilst absolutely ignorant of a great crisis. We ought to act or resign.'[19]

In the decade following the builders' strike Harrison and Beesly became semi-official advisers to the trade union movement, particularly the London Trades Council which grew out of the strike and attempted to provide co-ordinated national leadership to the movement. The leading figures in this body, the 'Junta,' were responsible and respectable trade unionists who wished to impart their own values to the movement as a whole. It is often suggested that the emphasis on respectability in the New Model unions which the Junta represented helped to push the movement towards an acceptance of middle-class values and attitudes, thus deflecting it from its true task. It is perhaps significant that a number of members of the Junta expressed an interest in Comte which was probably more than mere politeness. Robert Applegarth and George Odger were particularly close to the Comtists, and the testimony of Beesly and Harrison, who had keen noses for the taint of middle-class ambition, portrays both men as exemplars of the proletarian virtues – unaffected, generous, free of envy, and above all devoted to the interests of their own class. (An exception was George Howell, who despite his expressions of interest in Comte, proved ultimately vulnerable to the middle-class embrace.)[20]

The Comtists were committed to the large London-based New Model unions, the 'Amalgamateds,' because they embodied the virtues of concentration and conservatism. In the mid-1860s the trade union movement received two very serious blows – the revelation in 1866 of terrorist tactics being used by the Sheffield saw-grinders union against non-unionists and the *Hornby* v *Close* decision of 1867, which called into question the legality of all trade unions. The Sheffield union was precisely that sort of small, local, independent, and irresponsible union which the New Model repudiated, but the public did not discriminate in condemning the whole movement by association. Beesly boldly counter-attacked in a speech which earned him considerable notoriety by suggesting that the perpetrator of the Sheffield terrorism (one Broadhead), whose acts he of course did not condone, was no worse than Governor Eyre, the current hero of respectable society. Harrison, who was somewhat taken aback by the violence of Beesly's speech, shortly found himself appointed by the Conservative government as labour's representative to a Royal Commission on trade unions which was inspired by the Sheffield outrages. Membership in a Royal Commission was perhaps as close as Victorian reality came to realizing Comte's spiritual power; certainly Harrison could hardly have done more for the union movement than he did in this capacity. He worked tirelessly and against considerable odds (Thomas Hughes was also on the commission, but less actively) to turn its proceedings into a showcase for the respectable and responsible New Model unions, calling attention to their organizational and financial stability and their emphasis on security and benefits over industrial action, while diverting attention away from the activities of the noisy, unstable, local unions. So successful was he that with the help of some allies on the commission and the assistance of his Junta friends, who privately fed him information while he skilfully fed them leading questions in testimony, that the initially hostile intent of the commission was reversed and its ultimate effect was to encourage legislation giving further recognition and protection to the unions. The conservative, non-revolutionary proclivities of trade unionism which made them acceptable interim institutions to Comtists appealed equally to middle class opinion. No one could have argued this brief more sincerely or effectively than Frederic Harrison. [21]

In their search for common ground with the working class another institution which attracted its middle-class apologists was the club. Clubs played a major role in Comte's social system as proletarian salons where public opinion would be formed and social sympathies developed. Harrison became an ardent supporter of working-men's clubs, gratified that in the present, and not just in the ideal future, gentlemen of his class should share one of their quintessential institutions (the idea of course, not the same club) with the working class. The idea of using the club as an institution of social improvement was very much in the air in Victorian England. The clubs of Pall Mall were examples of the communitarian principle, enabling the gentlemen with £200 PA to partake of luxuries which he would need twenty times his income to provide for himself alone. The same principle was urged by some as a solution to the problems of the lower classes. Harrison participated in the work of the Working Men's Club and Institute Union and tried to recruit trade union support for the club movement, hoping that the unions would recognize that raising the tone of their class was more important than raising wages. He was able to work with men like the Rev. Henry Solly, secretary of the Union, even though Solly viewed the clubs as a means of dissolving class conflict by introducing the working class to the delights of the middle-class life-style. For Harrison such an intention was of course abhorrent; he saw the clubs as a means of crystallizing the innate proletarian virtues of solidarity and mutuality. Like the trade unions, the clubs happily combined agreement with Comtist teachings, which put them on the side of progress for the future, and a strong and immediate tendency towards conservatism and respectability, which put them on the side of order for the present. [22]

6

Rhetoric and Respectability

British surroundings, or perhaps Protestant inconsistency, dispose the English towards sympathy for revolutionaries whose triumph, if it ever became for a moment possible, they would be the first to deplore.

Auguste Comte, *Lettres*

'The Revolution' as a name for any sort of principles or opinions is not English. ... I cannot think it is good to adopt this mode of speech from the French. It proceeds from an infirmity of mind which has been one of the main causes of the miscarriage of the French nation in its pursuit of liberty and progress; that of being led away by phrases and treating abstractions as if they were realities ...

John Stuart Mill, *Letters*

In describing the transition to the positive polity, Comte spoke of a temporary dictatorship of the proletariat, or at least of a few 'eminent proletarians,' as a transitional arrangement preceding the final organization of society. Unlike Marx, however, Comte did not consider this a necessary development. It was the unfitness of the upper class which obliged him somewhat reluctantly to appeal to the lower, for Comte's authoritarian nature was predisposed to the idea of revolution from above as a more orderly and effective means of social transformation than revolution from below. He even considered Czar Nicholas of Russia and the Grand Vizier of the Ottoman empire as possible leaders of the great transformation, hoping that such theocracies might proceed directly to the positive society, skipping over the disagreeable metaphysical stage. Comte also considered the possibility of granting England exemptions. According to his historical theory England was ill-placed for progress towards the positive state because of her unhealthy historical precocity; while apparently a more advanced society, she had unfortunately advanced in the wrong direction. One of the problems of England's development was that instead of following the normal development from feudalism, wherein the crown allied with the commons to restrain the nobility (typified, as usual, by the French case), the English aristocracy had combined with the commons to restrain the crown. Thus as the feudal system declined, political power, instead of being centralized and concentrated in the monarchy where it could easily be captured, was dispersed and ramified throughout the aristocracy, where it was much more resistant to the necessary and inevitable transformation. Britain was a latter-day Venice, enjoying short-term political success through her parliamentary institutions (a cunning modification of aristocratic feudalism) at the expense of long-term retardation. Yet Comte was sufficiently encouraged by the response of English gentlemen to his doctrines to hope that the English aristocracy (in which he apparently included his Oxford followers) – 'the ablest patriciate the world has seen since the Roman senate' – might demonstrate further its extraordinary capacity for adaptation by making itself fit to direct the national reorganization. In this way England might escape the 'temporary anomaly' of the dictatorship of the proletariat. In view of this notable exception the English Comtists were clearly justified in exposing the upper classes to Comte's ideas, in however dilute a mixture.[1]

Contact with these classes was an easier matter than with the proletariat. The obvious avenue, despite Comte's anathema, was journalism. In 1865 the *Fortnightly Review* first appeared – an open forum for intellectuals of all shades of opinion each writing under his own signature. This was a golden opportunity for the Comtists. Its editor, G.H. Lewes, was an early admirer of Comte though he did not entirely accept Comte's later social and religious doctrines. Beesly and Harrison soon became frequent contributors, and apparently Lewes even suggested affiliation of some sort, which they of course refused. Here was an excellent platform for addressing intellectuals of the more radical persuasion, among whom many had some prior knowledge of Comte. The *Fortnightly*'s readership was already an élite, non-sectarian though not exclusively establishment – an enlightened group predisposed towards large and systematic ideas who might easily be won to the élitist doctrines of Comte.[2]

In the *Fortnightly* Harrison developed the socioeconomic aspects of Comte's creed which he tended to avoid in his working-class journalism but which had much to recommend them to the propertied classes. He also anglicized them as much as he could. Comte believed that the increasing concentration of ownership in industry was a desirable and stabilizing feature of modern capitalism; the possession of power and of property being necessarily linked in society, he believed in the concentration of both. The distinction between public and private property did not greatly concern Comte, for the important point was the moralization of property and power; herein lay the key to social harmony. Property was a matter of stewardship rather than possession, and what mattered most was not its present ownership but the traditions of civilization and the exertions of human beings through the ages incorporated in it. Comte's ideal capitalist society was in fact a sort of industrial feudalism governed by a moral code similar to the romantic notion of chivalry which would create a genuine community of interest between proletarians and capitalists.[3]

From Carlyle's *Past and Present* (one of Congreve's favourite books) to the positive industrial order was but a short distance, and from the Gothic capitalism of Ruskin's *Unto this Last* (1860) it was shorter still. Harrison was a great friend and admirer of Ruskin with whom he had been a fellow teacher at the Working Men's College. They met and corresponded frequently and Harrison urged him to study Comte, realizing the closeness of their views on society and hoping for his possible conversion (Comte himself viewed Ruskin quite favourably). Ruskin certainly praised those of Harrison's *Fortnightly* articles which were most explicitly Comtist. Comte had bitterly reproached the economists of his day for their narrow terms of reference and for studying, instead of man the moral and social creature, a metaphysical abstraction - *homo oeconomicus* - whose conduct was amoral and anti-social. Harrison perceptively remarked on the tendency of the language and categories of orthodox political economy to stimulate class tensions and to promote the alienation of labour. To the hardheaded employer who regarded labour as if it were a commodity like pig iron, and talked of buying 'fifty shillings worth of puddling,' he urged that just as one did not go to Tattersall's for '£1000 worth of wife,' or haggle over the fee with a doctor, lawyer, or priest, so in industry the man was inseparable from his work and had to be treated accordingly; to ignore this was not only immoral but unrealistic. This was of course a central Ruskinian theme as well - the need to reintroduce the moral element into all the economic transactions of mankind, down to the smallest. But Harrison's coherent and judicious exposition avoided Ruskin's impressionistic generalizations, eccentric examples, and frequently ranting tone. Harrison also left many points of Comte's doctrines untouched, preferring to emphasize those which could most effectively be tied to the immediate concerns of the English reader while taking advantage of their familiar Carlylean and Ruskinian resonance to win sympathy for Comte.[4]

Harrison described the true role of the capitalist, the captain of industry, in the military metaphors beloved of Carlyle and Ruskin, industrialist and workman becoming 'fellow soldiers in the battle of labour.' He portrayed an heroic future when capital would no longer receive 'the mere inglorious toleration ... which it now scarce openly dares to ask' but would instead command 'chivalrous loyalty in return for knightly services.' He dismissed as 'bastard communism' producer co-operation, which weakened capitalism's power for good far more than its power for evil. He became positively lyrical in describing the speed and concentration of response, the flexibility of action, and benevolence of attitude which could spring only from the accumulation of capital and the corresponding convergence of responsibility and command in the person of the individual capitalist. This was indeed the apotheosis of the entrepreneurial ideal of nineteenth-century capitalism. But such effusions gave him certain pangs: 'the working men will never trust me after this,' he remarked to Beesly of one of his *Fortnightly* articles. Of course few if any working men read the journal.[5]

Another aspect of Comtism for which Harrison could take advantage of the existing prejudices and inclinations of his audience was international policy. Comte's idea of an international 'republic of the West,' his moral hierarchy of European nations, his advocacy of international congresses and national altruism – all these were remarkably congruent with the persistent English tradition of belief in international co-operation whose greatest nineteenth-century advocate was Richard Cobden (Comte acknowledged the similarity between Cobden's views and his own). It also coincided with the widespread opposition to colonialism of the 1850s and 1860s. Comte urged that England, as the chief imperial power, should lead the way in renouncing imperialism by abandoning her colonies, particularly Gibraltar and India. Congreve, who enjoyed flaunting his allegiance to the point of antagonizing his audience, published pamphlets in the 1850s urging this course of action. Harrison remarked disapprovingly of Congreve's head-on tactics: 'It is as though a man were to get on a post and say "Gentlemen! I am an atheist and strongly advise you to cut your throats." '* Harrison preferred implicit to explicit Comtism, and constantly tried to show how closely it accorded with what any reasonable, intelligent English gentleman must think. When he wrote on the Italian Risorgimento, the American Civil War, the troubles in India, the bombardment of a Japanese town by the English fleet, the martyrdom of Poland, or the massacres of Jamaica – issues in which he felt England played an immoral role, either by bullying intervention or more frequently by conspicuous and cowardly abstention – he was able to preach an aspect of Comtism which was quite palatable to many English tastes. In 1866, when a collection of remarkably intelligent essays by English Comtists was published under the title *International Policy*, even the *Saturday Review*, not usually friendly to Comtism, remarked of Harrison's contribution: 'Except that the language is much clearer, and the thoughts appear

---

* *The Times* attacked one of these pamphlets so savagely that Congreve nearly lost his livelihood. He gave private tuition preparing pupils for Oxford, most of whom were withdrawn by their parents who assumed on the basis of *The Times'* review that he was a madman.

to be those of a man who can think two days running the same way, we might be reading a leader in the *Times*.' It is unlikely that Harrison was offended by the comparison.[6]

Radical causes tended to cluster in the 1850s and 1860s, involvement in one often leading to involvement in another. The Comtists, like the other university radicals, moved in various radical circles and thus came into contact with the many enthusiasms and sectarian causes which marched, often out of step, beneath the common banner of liberal individualism. To many onlookers the Comtists appeared to be just another group of crotcheteers; yet they differed from the rest in their rejection of sectarianism. Harrison particularly strove to avoid the minority mentality which characterized the traditional radicals whose very hobbies were so often purely negative – campaigning for the abolition of some law or obstructing progress towards another in the name of individual liberty. In contrast, Comtism was marked by a collectivist strain and lacked that instinctive distrust of the state which so frequently coloured the radical viewpoint. The Comtists rejected the self-image of the outsider, of the irregular band besieging the citadel of customary abuses and established institutions. Men like Harrison and even Beesly preferred to regard themselves as insiders, effecting changes and influencing people from within, not as soldiers, but as agents. The Comtists had no real desire to lose their respectability, though they derived a certain pleasure from making their bold sallies in print or in deed against the bounds of acceptable behaviour. Congreve and Beesly went farthest; both of them were fascinated by social martyrdom, though neither really achieved it. After all, the Comtists were gentlemen and as such were permitted the traditional latitude for eccentricity. Yet they were serious in their beliefs and, while taking advantage of the permitted margins of unconventionality, they were aware of the risk of simply being dismissed by an indulgent and complacent society as eccentrics.

Most of the Comtists were devoted clubmen. Since the eighteenth century the club has mediated the political and intellectual life of the English upper classes, enforcing a certain sense of solidarity and spirit of tolerance amongst members. Harrison's correspondence documents his efforts to gain election to the Reform Club in 1864. His father, concerned that he should get on in the world, was anxious that he should be elected: it was, he stated, 'a very solemn act.' Though he self-consciously made fun of these gentlemanly rites of initiation, Harrison took them seriously enough to mobilize his impressive battery of aristocratic, academic, and legal connections, thus ensuring election despite fears of black-balling from the '*Times* clique.' Now that he was well and truly within the citadel his conspiratorial and revolutionary fantasies took on added piquancy. The following year he could write to Beesly (on club stationery) about an iron masters' lockout: 'The only thing is for society to see the entire proletarian force concen-

trated and agitated. I want to talk to you about these things. Are you to be dining at the Club on Thursday?' There were other clubs as well – one for every facet
of Harrison's personality: the intellectual Century Club, the Alpine Club (like so
many Victorian intellectuals Harrison was a keen mountaineer), the prestigious
Athenaeum (where he was elected under Rule II as an intellectual of 'distinguished
eminence' in 1878), the convivial Cosmopolitan Club, the sober Cobden Club,
and (briefly) the pragmatic Radical Club. Inevitably Harrison was also a member
of the Metaphysical Society where, with such notables as T.H. Huxley, W.E. Gladstone, and Cardinal Manning, he earnestly attempted to resolve the spiritual uncertainties of the age (and also to gain a few converts: Manning apparently had
the same idea and they seem to have ended up trying to convert each other).[7]
Even the profession to which so many of the Comtists belonged was organized
like a club: one became a barrister, after all, by eating dinners at one of the Inns
of Court. In extenuation of Comte's anathema, most of the Comtist lawyers
worked in specialized and highly influential areas of the law – such as legal
draughtsmanship, pleading at the parliamentary bar, judicial work and legal education which were most congenial to the aspirations of an intellectual élite. Here
they were working at the very centre of English institutions. Both the Lushing-
tons employed their legal talents as higher civil servants – Godfrey was the Home
Office official responsible for draughting the Trade Union Act of 1871. Henry
Crompton, another Comtist, was for forty years a Clerk of Assizes and became
an authority on criminal law; he was also a legal adviser to trade unions and a
leading exponent of industrial arbitration and conciliation procedure (one of
Comte's more practical social panaceas). Charles A. Cookson became a judge in
the British Consular Service, helping to bring morality into the sphere of international trade, and Harrison himself became a professor of law.[8]
Most of the English Comtists were comfortably circumstanced; a number of
them had private means which gave them some uneasiness of mind. The richest
and uneasiest was James B. Winstanley, a young landowner, briefly high sheriff
of Leicestershire, whose mysterious death hints at a minor Comtist tragedy. One
of Congreve's Rugby pupils and Oxford intimates, Winstanley suffered from ill-
health and excessive sensitivity. His morbid lack of self-confidence made him extremely susceptible to a creed that offered spiritual and intellectual certainties,
and he turned to Comtism after a flirtation with Catholicism. On inheriting his
large estates he fled to Paris and placed himself under the personal guidance of
Comte, whom he called 'Père' and who taught him the duties of a member of the
Agricultural Patriciate, which included getting rid of the middlemen on his estate
and exercising concentrated and direct benevolent authority over his tenants. He
built them a church and spent heavily on model cottages for them. He also contributed a large sum to institute a similar Comtist agricultural scheme in France,

as well as becoming the main financial supporter of the other Comtist activities. He inexplicably disappeared in 1862, apparently a suicide. The affair was hushed up and some blamed Congreve for Winstanley's aberration, though he appears to have collapsed in spite of, rather than because of, the influence of Comtism.[9]

Other Comtists did not find their means quite so great a burden but did however express guilty sentiments. When Beesly came under heavy attack in society and was threatened with the loss of his University College Chair in history on account of his pro-trade union 'Broadhead' speech of 1867, he still had £500 a year of private income to fall back upon. He remarked to Henry Crompton: 'I almost feel ashamed sometimes that I cannot thoroughly test my mettle, just as one always feels that his invulnerability made Achilles a very questionable sort of hero.' Frederic Harrison also expressed doubts about his own dilettante existence. He complained in 1863 to his confidante Mrs Hadwen about 'irregularly wasting my time fussing over public questions which I have no vocation to deal with and no capacity to take up in a worthy manner. One will soon be as bad as those half crazy "ne'er-do-wells" who muddle about at the Social Science Congresses.' Had he wished he might have done very well at the bar; he had the talents, the energy, and the connections; his brother was a very wealthy solicitor and his father was a close friend of Westbury, the Lord Chancellor (whose friendly interest in Harrison's legal career was alone sufficient to ensure his fortune). But he resisted success in his profession and lived contentedly with his family, supervising the education of his intended wife (a pretty cousin, twenty years younger than himself). Until his marriage he also kept his Wadham fellowship, in spite of occasional fears that he might be ejected from it for religious reasons. 'I know few persons who have less to contend with. Social difficulties have I none,' he remarked almost peevishly.[10]

In 1864 one of Beesly's friends who was sympathetic towards Comtism, the proprietor of a large auctioneering firm, offered to take Beesly into the firm at a salary well above the £300 PA which he received for his not very onerous duties at University College. Beesly was tempted and wrote to Harrison for advice. Harrison's reply illuminates some of the tensions inherent in the dual roles of Comtist and gentleman. Auctioneering was not a very gentlemanly occupation, Harrison admitted, but this was a matter of breeding. To be born an auctioneer was no doubt a social stigma, but for a gentleman of education, good family, and reputation such as Beesly, to become one would be a 'piquant curiosity' which would 'strike flunkeyism dumb.' Such acquaintances as would cut him for this were not worth having. It might harm his matrimonial prospects a bit, but this was not a major consideration either. Unfortunately an auctioneer was hardly a 'captain of industry'; in Comtist terms the job did not entail managing men and would give Beesly only 'a very modified and minor place among the directors of industry.'

Therefore Beesly would still remain primarily attached to his 'intellectual functions (positivist sense)'; but in performing these functions such a job might prove
a hindrance. It was best not to be tied down, best to travel light. Harrison then
launched into one of his intriguing half-fantasies about their position in society.
He was himself 'sitting very loose' in the anticipation of possible developments:
'I now go a great deal into general society and amuse myself with all sorts of mere
butterfly acquaintances because I feel certain of being forcibly expelled from it
before long. I find a little fun in it before it is closed to me which it might be at
any day.' 'This must apply to you,' Harrison added. It was the price of being in
the vanguard. At any time the call might come; within the next fifteen years anything was possible in the industrial, political, or religious situation. 'We are like
members and agents of the national party at Warsaw – perfectly quiet ordinary
citizens, but at any moment the reign of terror might set in, and we whirl into
action.'[11]

The expulsion from society never came. Beesly perhaps came closest with his
'Broadhead' speech but he rode out this brief squall, aided by his friends and his
own dignity: 'I have dined at the club most days and kept my head up,' he wrote.
Harrison continued to move in 'the most sacred circles ... elbowing cabinet ministers and making the acquaintance of the Russell family' (the Amberleys particularly liked 'a little playful radicalism,' Harrison noted unselfconsciously). 1867
was the *annus mirabilis* of Comtism: besides Beesly's speech the Comtists further
offended respectability with a controversial petition, signed by thirteen of them
and presented in the House of Commons by Bright, requesting leniency for imprisoned Fenians and redress for the legitimate grievances of Ireland. Harrison
was busy with his private practice but found time for the Royal Commission on
Trade Unions, two articles in the *Fortnightly*, a handful for the *Bee-Hive*, and his
contribution to *Questions for a Reformed Parliament*. He was also busy trying to
manage the election of a promising young student of Comte to a Wadham fellowship. For relaxation he managed a trip to the continent in the summer, met Garibaldi, and attended both the Lausanne Congress of the International Working
Men's Association and the Geneva meeting of the International Peace Congress.
It was a time of great optimism for the Comtists. 'Upon the whole we are not an
inactive body when it is considered that we are pounding away at the lower strata
of society as well as the higher,' Beesly cheerfully observed. The journalist Justin
McCarthy wrote: 'A small drawing room would assuredly hold all the London
Positivists who make themselves effective in English politics. Yet I do not hesitate to say that they have become a power which no-one, calculating on the
chances of any coming struggle, can afford to leave out of his consideration.'[12]

In 1867 also the London Positivist Society was founded. This seemed to be a
good way of taking advantage of public interest and consolidating the influence

of English Comtism. But it also brought into the open a number of difficulties which hitherto had largely been evaded within the movement, difficulties centring upon the role and influence of Congreve, its officially sanctioned English apostolic head. One problem endemic in religious and ideological movements is that of balancing the twin necessities of attracting support and preserving doctrinal purity. Comte's earlier writings, especially his *Philosophie positive*, attracted a large number of followers, many of whom were unenthusiastic about the later *Politique*. As we have seen, Comte anathematized those who did not stay for the second half of his programme. He considered purity and strictness of adherence far more important than mere numbers: spiritual commitment to the Church of Humanity meant more than intellectual attraction to the law of the three stages. While Pierre Laffitte, Comte's heir and successor as 'director' of the movement, leaned increasingly towards the broadcast dissemination of Comte's ideas even at the expense of the actual cult, Congreve followed Comte in believing that the mere intellectual spread of positivism was not enough – and possibly even detrimental to true moral progress. [13]

Congreve took a very proprietorial attitude towards English Comtism and possibly feared that the movement would get out of hand – or out of his hands, at least – if it grew too rapidly. He wanted disciples, but only faithful and obedient ones. Like the other Comtists he was anxious to establish ties with the working class: 'It is a great pleasure to receive such communications and to feel that one is in some contact with the working man,' he wrote gratefully to one proletarian correspondent who had expressed a promising distrust of the delusive panacea of franchise reform. He commenced giving lectures to the proletariat in 1860; the audience was chiefly old Owenites with whom he took no chances of jeopardizing his authority: 'I refused any discussion for which the men, some of them at least, had a hankering.' Beesly (who also gave occasional Comtist lectures) steered a few workmen Congreve's way, but on the whole the audiences were decidedly upper middle and upper class. By 1867 Congreve's lectures were quite in vogue, according to George Eliot: 'at the first lecture on the 5th of May there was a considerable audience – about 75, chiefly men of various ranks from lords and M.P.'s downwards, or upwards, for what is called social distinction seems to be in a shifting social condition just now ... Curiosity brings some, interest in the subject others, and the rest go with the wish to express adhesion more or less thorough.' Inevitably, the arch-eclectic Lord Houghton was present, 'sleeping exactly as if he had been in Church.' Despite her sympathy, George Eliot found Congreve a rather dull lecturer, and few stuck out the full course of lectures. [14]

Converts were few in spite of the stir which the Comtists made. But even among the converted all was not harmonious. Congreve was directly or indirectly responsible for nearly all the leading adherents to English Comtism, but his former students showed a disturbing spirit of intellectual independence. In 1868 Bridges, whose first wife had died some seven years previously, decided to remarry in contravention of Comte's doctrine of 'perpetual widowhood' (Comte had erected his personal grief at the death of his beloved Clotilde de Vaux into a universal principle of which Queen Victoria herself might have approved.) Congreve protested with Bridges, whom he considered one of the few 'within the pale.' But Bridges replied: 'What *is* the pale? What is the degree of adherence necessary to constitute a positivist?' For Congreve it was rigid adherence to every detail of a creed which sagged beneath the weight of detail. But the submission in which he rejoiced was for the others a chief obstacle to the propagation of positivism. Congreve became increasingly suspicious of the activities of his former students, especially Harrison who wrote too much 'for his sake and for ours – too rashly and often very compromisingly.' Congreve understandably resented the prestige and publicity which men like Harrison and Beesly acquired because it eclipsed his own authority. But Harrison, Beesly, and the other Comtists regarded positivism as not so much a church requiring strict discipleship but a school preparing the ground for the future transformation of the whole society. [15]

With the formation of the London Positivist Society Congreve was anxious to proceed to the foundation of a Church of Humanity, for he was above all a priest. Harrison feared that he was moved by the sectarian impulse and argued that the real obstacle to the spread of positivism was precisely this obsession with institutionalization; this had only led to the formation of formal societies, pitifully few in membership and scattered over various countries, in which worthwhile activity was sacrificed to maintain the pretence of realizing an ideal. The important thing was to disseminate conviction and example, and let the actual church arise spontaneously when the time was ripe: 'To form a Church without such an existing body of members is to form a sect from which public opinion, the life of Positivism, is excluded.' Otherwise the church would be condemned to an artificial existence outside 'practical society,' in which, after all, they had to live. But Congreve had defiantly stated in his inaugural sermon: 'We need, I hesitate not to say, to live as little as we can in the present, as much as we can in the past and future.' To live as if the positivist dispensation had already arrived was the sort of sectarian flight from reality which was abhorrent to those who, like Harrison and Beesly, considered themselves members, even if slightly subversive ones, of the establishment. [16]

How did other members of the establishment view the activities of the Comtists within their midst? Of those who were moved to comment Matthew Arnold is the best known. Many today recognize Frederic Harrison's name only as one of several (along with the Rev. W. Cattle, Mr Murphy, and others) in the Arnoldian litany of opponents of culture. He incurred Arnold's displeasure by scornfully dismissing his ideal of culture. 'The man of culture is in politics one of the poorest mortals alive,' Harrison wrote in 1867; 'a turn for small fault-finding, love of selfish ease and indecision in action' were his distinguishing political characteristics. Harrison saw in Arnold's 'man of culture' one of Comte's despised class of pedants and *littérateurs* – that retrograde body of destructive critics who impede society's progress into the positive stage. Ironically (in the light of his own views), he accused Arnold of promoting political quietism among the intellectual class by over-intellectualizing the process of social change and disparaging programmes of definite political action. Arnold replied in an essay, which subsequently became the opening section of *Culture and Anarchy*, accusing Harrison of anti-intellectualism. Both accusations had some foundation but both were based on misunderstanding. (The very real anti-intellectual strain in Harrison and Comte is discussed in a later chapter.) 'Mr. Frederic Harrison is very hostile to culture, and from a natural enough motive; for culture is the eternal opponent of the two things which are signal marks of Jacobinism, – its fierceness and its addiction to an abstract system.' Thus Arnold placed Harrison and the other disciples of Comte among the apostles of anarchy and Jacobinism, of 'violent indignation with the past.' Arnold sketches for the unwary reader a figure bearing little resemblance to the real Harrison, whom his close friend, Sir Frederick Pollock, described as 'by nature English, conservative and historical rather than philosophical.' Nor is he altogether fair to Comte, who scrupulously acknowledged his debt to past thinkers and reverentially created a calendar of great men to replace the calendar of saints.[17]

The misunderstanding was at least partly wilful, for both men were brilliant debaters. Arnold caricatured his victim's views quite ruthlessly by pillorying a chosen phrase or sentence and never deigning to argue. Harrison, equally urbane, neatly parodied Arnold's style and resorted to his own favourite controversial tactic which was blandly to insist that his opponent misunderstood Comte, and was in fact a Comtist without knowing it: Sir Henry Maine, Goldwin Smith, and Fitzjames Stephen were among his other distinguished, unwitting conscripts. This tactic also avoided argument (which degraded the authority of the spiritual power) while impressing readers with the irresistibility of the doctrine. Harrison was not insincere for Comtism could be extremely accommodating in his hands: he was the Jesuit of Comtism. Not surprisingly in his witty rejoinder to Arnold, 'Culture: a Dialogue,' he suggested that Arnold was unconsciously affected by Comte. (Once Arnold was safely dead and buried Harrison revealed that he had 'constantly talked Comte without knowing it.') Both men were reluctant to recognize the full extent of their agreement; but Walter Bagehot, a judicious outsider, saw a striking resemblance in the shared Francophilia and cultural authoritarianism of Arnold and the Comtists. Harrison concentrated his attack on the Arnoldian ideal of culture, ridiculing its vagueness and calling attention to the impossibility of translating its inflated aspirations into a programme for social or political action. This was indeed Arnold's weak point and Harrison identified it all the more clearly for his unconscious knowledge that Comtism was weakest at precisely the same point. Both doctrines showed a marked distrust of political activity; neither was altogether successful in formulating an effective alternative to politics as a means of translating ideas into realities. It was as if the two men had more in common than could be tolerated; certainly a common deficiency in their doctrines was the very last bond they would have been willing to admit.[18]

Arnold pilloried Harrison's claim, in a *Fortnightly* article, that the best part of the working class was fittest for political influence, having the 'brightest powers of sympathy and the readiest powers of action.' Arnold repeats this assertion time and again, presenting Harrison not merely as an example of philistinism but of class apostasy: 'There is a sort of motion of Mr. Frederic Harrison's tongue towards his cheek when he tells the working class that "theirs are the brightest powers of sympathy and the readiest powers of action." ' Arnold was accusing him of pandering to the masses; flattering the proletariat was a very serious sin for a Comtist as Arnold knew. Arnold, whose own apostate inclinations tended towards the aristocracy rather than the proletariat, had a sharp eye for the ironies of social dislocation and he directed a telling shaft at Harrison in a letter to the *Pall Mall Gazette* which told how from his 'elevated window in Grub Street' overlooking Harrison's spacious and secluded backyard he could see him 'in full evening costume furbishing a guillotine.' This vignette neatly impaled Harrison's rather fastidious radicalism.*[19]

Congreve wrote in November 1870 to a disciple in India:

I cannot think we are open to the charge of flattering the proletariat. Beesly is especially free. It is the soundest part taken *en masse* of our social system, with due allowance for its great deficiencies and faults, and so far as I know we always keep the whole in view. Most troublous times be before us and the real hope is in our conciliating the proletariat in its best position and making ourselves listened to by the capitalist who is otherwise inclined to dismiss us as dreamers but will quickly change his mind if he finds that we have extensive working class sympathies.

* The sartorial detail was also rather apt; both Beesly and Harrison were notorious for their elegant attire. Henry James unkindly remarked on the singular contrast between Harrison's unorthodox opinions and his conventional appearance – that of a 'provincial second-rate dandy.' Leon Edel, *Henry James: The Conquest of London* (London 1962), 333

'Troublous time' perhaps, but times of hope for Comtists. The Franco-Prussian war had swept away Napoleon III, by now a fallen idol even for them, but the melancholy triumph of Bismarck was suddenly relieved by the heroic siege of Paris and the subsequent appearance of the Paris Commune, an event which called the Comtists once more to the journalistic barricades. They were always particularly sensitive to the fortunes of France (Austin Harrison tells of his father once hitting him on the jaw for making fun of the French army). When the proletariat of Paris showed signs of resuming its historic mission of leading Europe towards the new social dispensation by spontaneous political action, the Comtists could not sit still: 'There the great social struggle between capital and labour, that prolonged struggle on which England is entering and to which Germany is approaching, is already far advanced,' Harrison announced. Issues of foreign politics placed fewer restraints on Comtist rhetoric than did domestic politics. They demanded English intervention as Prussia revealed her territorial demands. They defended the Commune against the misrepresentations of the hostile London press, Beesly interpreting events to the *Bee-Hive*'s readers, Harrison to the *Fortnightly*'s. The crisis in France seemed an excellent opportunity for the Comtists to extend their connections and influence with the proletariat and they succeeded in promoting a considerable pro-French agitation with extensive organized working-class support in London during the latter part of 1870 and into mid-1871. Harrison exuberantly wrote to his friend John Morley, editor of the *Fortnightly Review*, of a meeting of the Workmen's Peace Committee which he and his bellicose friends succeeded in capturing: 'War cheered to the echo ... I unluckily got up an opposition by calling the peace people "psalmsinging fanatics." ' (Frederick Engels sourly remarked that they were dividing the working classes with unrealistic demands.) Harrison boasted of giving 'blood red' lectures to his positivist audiences: 'Don't be afraid,' he wrote to Morley, 'Don't turn pale at the sight of a little blood. It is good honest stuff. I won't serve up such a blood pudding to the weak stomachs of your cultured public in the *Fortnightly Review*.'[20]

Not surprisingly the apparent contrast between the heroic proletariat and the contemptible bourgeoisie of Paris during these stirring events gave Harrison strong twinges of guilt about his own social position. He had just married and chosen a house which happened to stand near a public house. His father decided that such an address was disreputable and offered to meet the cost of finding a more respectable one. Harrison yielded, all the while writhing at his own descent into the foul slough of respectability. When his father also paid for the redecoration he wrote to Morley: 'Here I am rampaging about the new Social and Industrial order and I have had a dozen men, anyone of them as good as myself, employed for six weeks in trying to hit the exact tint which I, or rather my art-crazed family, think indispensable to decent life on earth.' He felt the falseness of his position even more acutely when he became actively involved with the other Comtists in assisting the Communard refugees: 'I have got a house into which I am ashamed to bring one of those starving devils whom I call citizen and address with *fraternité* and whose shoes in the kingdom of heaven I am not worthy to black.'[21]

Harrison's articles were certainly trenchant but could only have been considered inflammatory to a Prussophile. No member of the proletariat, were he to pick up a copy of the *Fortnightly*, would have found incitement to revolution in them. Harrison was careful to dissociate himself from the reported violence (most of which he denied). As for the reported communism, he was as a Comtist utterly opposed to it. Unfortunately it was widely believed that Comtism and communism amounted to much the same thing, a misconception equally annoying to Comtists and communists. Beesly had in fact chaired the inaugural meeting of the International Working Men's Association in 1864 as part of his activities encouraging working-class involvement in foreign policy issues but was never a member of the International. He was also on quite friendly terms with Marx despite their ideological differences (Marx contemptuously dismissed Comte's social prescriptions as 'recipes for some greasy spoon restaurant of the future'), and in November 1870 had published a sympathetic article on the International in the *Fortnightly*. On the Commune it was Beesly, as usual, who was most outspoken in his *Bee Hive* articles, about which Harrison privately expressed certain reservations. The Comtists, or Harrison at least, shared Marx's view that the Commune was lost from the start. But it was a hopeful sign, however. Harrison wrote to Morley just before its collapse:

Comte's followers are very few in Paris but their influence has been felt wonderfully in this movement. As Lafitte [sic] says, haughtily standing aloof as he does – 'Le positivisme n'y est nullement étranger.' That is enough for the present. Positivism, as I have always said is not an effusion, an idea, a passion. It is no ecstasy like Christianity, no dogma like the Social Contract. It is intellectual, moral and practical all at once and all equally. Therefore it cannot move mountains like faith and convert 5,000 at once. We are certainly not preachers and had better keep sober thought of our limited range. We are much more practical people.

Harrison then revealed to Morley his conception of the Comtists' role in English society. They were potentially dangerous men – 'a knot of revolutionists' working from within:

We belong by education, habit and even sympathy, to the old thing; from our compromising creed we have patience to study it inside and out. We understand its strong and weak points just as well as those who work it; we are on the very edge of the official world and socially and politically perfectly behind the scenes. They admit we understand it and actually use our help in pulling the old machine along. And yet we would turn the old thing inside out as completely as Rousseau – though more constructively and cautiously.

'I do feel dangerous,' Harrison concluded; but he admitted that it was most improbable – 'in fact, impossible' – that his dangerous propensities would find any encouragement in events.[22]

To many of their social and intellectual peers the Comtists certainly seemed dangerous at this time. Lord Arthur Russell, a member of the Metaphysical Society, was quite alarmed by their letters in the *Bee-Hive*. Canvassing his acquaintances in the Pall Mall clubs he claimed to find general agreement that their writings were 'positively criminal' in their incitement of working-class passions. However, his cousin, Lord Amberley, defended the Comtists, calmly maintaining that even if their views were wrong they did good by penetrating the hard crust of unexamined prejudice which passed for wisdom in conventional society. This assessment was sound; all the Comtists wrote with at least one eye upon their own class. Thus Beesly's 'Letters to the Working Classes' published in the *Birmingham Daily Post* in 1870 were according to Harrison 'not so much plain advice to the workmen, although so in form, but rather invective and threats aimed at the Middle Class.' Yet the *Pall Mall Gazette* attacked the Comtists as reckless and cold-blooded 'revolutionaries.' A major source of such misapprehensions was their use of a rather alien vocabulary and phraseology: terms like 'bourgeoisie' and 'proletariat' had a sinister ring in English ears. More alarming still was their persistent use of the word 'revolution' itself. 'Revolution,' as Mill pointed out, meant in plain English 'a change of government effected by force.' But in the ideological vocabulary of Comtism, where it was a crucial term, it referred rather to the degree of change than to its manner or suddenness, and to cultural rather than mere political phenomena. Mill and Arnold talked of their age as a 'critical era' or 'age of expansion' – the idea of cultural history as a grand dialectical process was common intellectual coin at this time. Comte's 'revolutionary period' was in many respects an equivalent concept, but as a son of the French Revolution Comte naturally resorted to a terminology which had more dramatic connotations to the English. Yet the English Comtists were not unaware of these associations and were not above occasionally taking advantage of them *pour épater les bourgeois*. Thus Beesly: 'The European revolution is a vast regular drama proceeding before their eyes. The curtain was raised in '89 and many acts still remain to be played. The unity of place is not indispensable on the modern stage and it will be found, we venture to say, that the scene will not always be on the continent of Europe.'[23]

The university radicals, as we have seen, were fascinated by the French Revolution, and its subsequent eruptions of 1830, 1848, and 1870-1 gave credence to the notion of permanent, ongoing revolution. The English had always tended to regard revolution in terms of their own glorious 1688 as a one-time affair, a discontinuous phenomenon, and even after their second 'revolution,' that of 1832, they clung to the official doctrine of 'Finality.' But in the later 1830s and 1840s the feeling grew that even this modest revolution was open-ended, as 1867 indeed proved. The writings of Comte, for whom permanent revolution was a central historical concept, introduced many English intellectuals to it, and by depoliticizing the term helped to prepare the way for wider applications such as Toynbee's 'industrial revolution.' Comte urged Richard Congreve to write a history of the English Revolution, claiming it would have 'a powerful effect in Britain by correcting the complacent official view of it which is preponderant among your aristocracy and bourgeoisie. They consider England wholly protected in advance against the present crisis of the West by their dynastic revolution of 1688. No work can have greater importance today for the social inauguration of western positivism than that of re-establishing the true historic filiation between the two great republican revolutions of England and France.' Unfortunately Congreve never completed this task. According to his notes he intended to represent the English Revolution in its two aspects – the spiritual embodied in Milton, the man of thought, and the temporal embodied in Cromwell, the man of action. Interestingly Lord Acton later took up the Comtist view (though it is unclear whether directly from Comte) that there was no basic dividing line between the French, American, and English revolutions, and the idea has since proved increasingly attractive to historians unaware of Comte's pioneering insight. Against this background the apparently provocative effusions of the Comtists during the 1860s and early 1870s become an aspect of the university radicals' concern to establish the place of their own country and their own times within the broader historical context of progress. [24]

The events of 1870-1 in France proved the last major occasion for rhetorical provocation from the Comtists. Henceforth their outbursts were increasingly sporadic and less alarming. Respectability asserted itself over rhetoric, particularly in Frederic Harrison's case. Comtism had reached the zenith of its notoriety in England through the publicity attracted by its few but talented adherents. In 1870 they rented a small hall in Chapel Street which was called the Positivist School, and in which was installed (at Congreve's insistence, and over the protests of Harrison) a marble tablet inscribed 'The Religion of Humanity.' After a decade of lectures in various hired halls around London they finally had a permanent home, a centre for their activities where they could offer the continuing lecture courses that were necessary to convey systematically the coherence and comprehensiveness of Comte's doctrines. Physically establishing themselves in this modest way, and thus regularizing their activities, no doubt dispelled some of the fears that the Comtists had aroused in orthodox breasts during the 1860s, when their frequent and irregular forays in various directions created exaggerated impressions of their strength. Tucked into their little Chapel Street hall they could more easily be dismissed as just another curious piece in the mosaic of London heterodoxy.[25]

In the school the quest for 'true' proselytes continued under more suitable conditions. Almost immediately on its opening a group of Hindu students began to attend, attracted by the academic, professional, and social eminence of its lecturers and by the activities of a small number of Comtists employed in the India Civil Service. The English Comtists believed that there was an affinity between positivism and Hinduism in its religious and social aspects, and thought it possible that India might be able to avoid the metaphysical stage and pass directly to the positive. Unfortunately, the Hindu students regarded the Positivist School as an excellent free cram school and were more interested in discussing their competitive exams than Comte. The dialogue between East and West ended with the Comtists having to speak on behalf of the Hindu peoples, and not 'these ambitious natives hungering to get into the official class.' 'We must not be exploited by them,' Harrison warned Beesly. The Comtists had no intention of being exploited by ambitious *déclassés* of any colour. Many years later Harrison described the educational activities of Newton Hall, the secessionist offshoot of Chapel Street, proudly contrasting its intention, 'neither literary nor professional,' with that of the Mechanics Institutes, those notorious resorts of the upwardly mobile. The Comtist School avoided the desultory and miscellaneous information, 'the lantern slides and recitations from Pickwick,' while enabling many men of all sorts and conditions to acquire 'a general conception of history, science and literature such as many a B.A. has never heard of.'[26]

Even Beesly, who claimed that they could easily attract mass support if they so desired by dwelling exclusively on 'the popular side of Positivism,' scornfully rejected this course followed by 'so many a Socialist quackery which has lived and died in a generation.' They did not want ignorant or calculating adherents who would 'hamper us with their crotchets or discredit us by their backslidings.' Fear of exploitation and fear of numbers were characteristics of the English Comtists which became increasingly evident as they institutionalized their movement. This is partly to be accounted for by the exclusive character of the movement's leadership, with its early and continuing ties from undergraduate days onwards. The English Comtist movement in many respects resembled a rather exclusive club more than it did a religious or political society. Having no wish to exploit their adherents for political ends, its leaders had no great need for a mass following; moreover, they were temperamentally and ideologically hostile towards the machinery necessary for large-scale organization in the pre-positive dispensation. They contented themselves with the cultivation of that small leavening which might eventually initiate the social transformation in a properly organic manner. They remained an élite rather than a sect.[27]

Another important factor in the Comtist subsidence was marriage. The prolonged bachelorhood of the leading Comtists came to an end in 1869–70 with the marriages of Beesly, Bridges, Henry Crompton, and Harrison. Beesly married Crompton's sister, who was if not a Comtist, very sympathetic to her husband's activities. Crompton married the daughter of a Whig law lord; Bridges and Harrison both married young women whom they had known since girlhood and whose education they had actively supervised along the proper channels. These English Comtist wives were a remarkable group in their own right; they were notably attractive and clever, and the marriages were by all accounts highly successful. According to Comte's doctrines women had the same ideal moral superiority over men that the proletariat had over the functional élites in society. But ideal superiority meant practical subordination, and the activity and influence of women was confined to the family (which was, however, the central institution of the positive social order). With fervent sincerity Comte incorporated into his system most of the stereotypes of the role and temperament of women which underpinned the official bourgeois protocol of sexual relationships. Yet by the standards of the time the Comtist wives were quite liberated. They participated largely in Comtist activities in their official feminine capacities, and it appears that with them at least the mysterious feminine influence over men which Comte extolled was in fact real. But domesticity placed restraints upon activism, and respectability slipped in on domesticity's coat-tails. 'There goes another piece off the board,' Harrison had remarked to Beesly when Godfrey Lushington married in 1865. 'I shall be expecting you to marry next and sinking without a struggle into the great social ocean, and then farewell to Unions, causes, positivism, republicanism et al.' The consequences were not quite this extreme, yet Harrison's remark was prescient.[28]

The cautious institutionalizing of Comtism by its English adherents ended a decade of unsystematic but remarkably effective propagandizing in which they infiltrated the labour movement with considerable success (and benefit to labour) and made use of working-class press to propagate their version of society and to offer an alliance with that class. Their energy, sincerity, and ambiguous mode of expression – the effect of which was heightened by the fluid political situation – created high hopes of such an alliance, as it had among university radicals generally. But here again the end of the decade called these aspirations into doubt; or at least made it apparent that aspiration alone was insufficient and that analysis was required to determine the practical possibilities for leadership by an intellectual élite. This meant exploring the poorly charted terrain that lies between political thought and political action.

PART THREE

POLITICS AND THE INTELLECTUAL:
JOHN MORLEY AND FREDERIC HARRISON

7

The Vocation of the Intellectual

The real vocation of the Intellectuals is the exploitation of politics.

G. Sorel, *Matériaux d'une théorie*

The more closely literature approaches to being an organ of serious things, a truly spiritual power, the more danger there is likely to be in making it a path to temporal station or emolument.

John Morley, *Voltaire*

The intellectual may be defined broadly in two ways: as one who, conscious of certain mental attributes which set him apart, feels a private commitment to intellectual activity which he regards as ultimately beneficial to society; or as one who publicly practices one of the professions involving the formulation, interpretation, or transmission of ideas in society, such as the law, education, or journalism. These two types of intellectuals (the definitions are not mutually exclusive, of course) may conveniently be labelled the amateur and the professional. The latter are socially definable by their professions, which reinforce their self-identity as intellectuals by making them readily definable as such to the world at large. The university radicals were intellectuals in the first sense, but in mid-Victorian England there was, as we have noticed, no real academic profession, while the law did not necessarily demand a professional commitment either, being still a stronghold of amateurism. The social status of gentleman inherent in these occupations tended to counter-balance the status of intellectual, thus blurring it. This was the strategy of the dominant clerisy ideal, the aim of which was precisely to prevent the formation of a self-consciously separate body of intellectuals. As for journalism, it was a lively issue at this time whether this was a profession at all. Coleridge's advice to young writers, 'Never pursue literature as a trade,' reflected his fear that the professional man of letters was one of the potentially most dangerous elements in society. Certainly the trade of journalism was viewed by respectable society in his time with a mixture of social contempt and political suspicion. The founding of the great reviews, the *Edinburgh* and the *Quarterly*, had since dispelled a certain amount of prejudice by their intellectual eminence and gentlemanly tone, but above all they did so by strictly observing the practice of anonymity. The gentleman could write for them anonymously, thus retaining his public amateur status and protecting his name from the taint of journalism. The professional journalist also wrote anonymously, partly to take advantage of these gentlemanly implications. Thus English journalism was bound in a pact of shame-facedness sustained and enforced by anonymity, which hindered its development as a respectable public profession for the intellectual.[1]

This independent profession of journalism was still not fully established when John Morley came to London in 1860. His promising Oxford career had been cut short by a dispute with his father, apparently over his refusal to enter the clergy, which resulted in his leaving the university with only a pass degree, rather than the first class and the fellowship which his already recognized talents would probably have won him. He was forced to make his way in the world unaided, and so came to London and journalism. Success came quickly: he was soon a regular contributor to the remunerative *Saturday Review*, and his cleverness and a talent for friendship brought him rapid entry into leading literary and intellectual circles, particularly those of Mill and the Comtists. Unlike most of the other university radicals who were amateur journalists, Morley sustained himself wholly by journalism. He proudly called it his profession, adopting the lofty definition of Carlyle, who in *Sartor Resartus* hailed journalists as the 'true kings and clergy' of the modern world. A very different breed of professional journalist from the irresponsible bohemians of Grub Street, Morley was a highly educated and self-conscious member of a new and powerful élite. Not surprisingly he was opposed to anonymity on professional grounds because it subordinated the personality and personal responsibility of the journalist to the larger corporate personality of the journal. Morley was barred on account of his radicalism from writing political articles for the *Saturday* and confined to innocuous social comments which he wrote in the tart, wordly style that the *Saturday* imposed on its writers (Leslie Stephen, another Saturday Reviewer, subsequently had difficulty even identifying his own pieces). Such consequences of anonymity, Morley claimed, demeaned the journalist and encouraged irresponsibility. With the periodical press growing daily more powerful it was in the public interest as well as their own that journalists be allowed the privileges attendant on professionalism – public respect and recognition, as well as self-respect. One of the chief defences of anonymity, however, was that it not only enabled members of other professions, such as barristers, clergymen, civil servants, to practise journalism as a profitable sideline without undesirable publicity, but that it allowed them to express their opinions without fear of possible reprisals from superiors. Anonymity, in short, could be defended as a functional mechanism for preserving the amateur ideal of the clerisy. But Morley, as a professional journalist, did not want his profession kept in the shadows just so amateurs might poach on it.[2]

In 1866 (at the age of twenty-seven) Morley became editor of the *Fortnightly Review*, which stood in the vanguard of intellectual journalism and owed much of its initial influence to the policy of signed articles and openness to all shades of opinion. It embodied the Millite doctrine of competition among ideas in the intellectual marketplace as the surest way to truth and progress: appropriately, Morley was an ardent disciple of Mill. Morley argued strenuously against the vulgar liberal notion that progress was automatic, and maintained that only by human agents and human efforts was it assured. By investing progress with the character of inevitability men did it injury, for a deterministic attitude was hostile to the climate of sensitivity and receptivity which new ideas, the stuff of progress, required in order to flourish. But although free trade was necessary in the realm of ideas, the model of *laissez-faire* could not be extended to the point of leaving the success or failure of ideas merely to the marketplace decision of public opinion. There was an ignorant public opinion guided by prejudice and sentiment, as well as an educated public opinion guided by truth, and the former tended unfortunately to be more powerful than the latter. Public opinion was not necessarily the handmaid of progress, Morley warned: 'Every reform, it should be remembered, has been carried out in spite of hostile public opinion.'[3]

Morley's conception of the nature and formation of public opinion was at variance with the popular and demagogic view of it as a sort of self-activating and self-legitimising force, spontaneously arising out of the instinctive reactions of the common people. This naïve view of public opinion was encouraged by the increasing numbers of popular journals and newspapers which liked to regard themselves as the organs rather than the guides of their audiences. This sort of flattery hid a more complicated reality, as Morley and other intelligent journalists realised. One of the dangers of anonymous journalism was that it tended to conceal the very crude mechanism by which individual writers and their opinions became transformed into the transcendant editorial 'we,' and thence even into very 'public' itself, these inflated metamorphoses lending a specious authority to private and individual opinions. *The Times*, as Matthew Arnold commented, 'tells us day after day how the general public is the organ of all truth, and individual genius the organ of all error,' but university radicals knew very well how 'public opinion' was manufactured by men like themselves, clever leader writers writing at Printing House Square under the directions of its editor. Too often it was simply to pander to the prejudices of readers or, in the case of *The Times*, to be 'strong on the stronger side.' Yet Morley firmly believed in public opinion, responsibly led, as a powerful force for social improvement.[4]

Such leadership, Morley hoped, would come particularly from the intellectual élite who read and contributed to the *Fortnightly Review*, which became under his editorship the most articulate organ of intellectual radicalism. Morley was a vehement exponent of this creed, greeting the reform essays of 1867 with a manifesto of his own, 'Young England and the Political Future,' in which he hailed the advent of the alliance of 'brains and numbers.' In his capacity as publisher's reader for Macmillan's (publishers of the reform essays) he used his influence to persuade Alexander Macmillan to publish a book on the Irish question by his close college friend, James Cotter Morison, whom he characterized as a representative of 'the extreme left.' 'Depend upon it,' he urged, 'the tide is rising: the younger generation of thinking men must come to the top and their views triumph.' Like so many of his fellow university radicals, Morley travelled to America in the autumn of 1867 and 'catechized' many of the 'central men' of the country with the intention of writing a book on the 'dominant social ideas' of the United States. Unfortunately it was never completed – no doubt because of the pressure of all his other activities which included his first parliamentary candidature and, for a part of 1869, the editorship of the radical daily *Morning Star* (founded by Cobden and Bright).[5]

In the midst of all this activity, Morley was turning out a regular succession of fiery political articles for his review. With the passing of the Reform Act he announced the advent of the first stage in 'the New Revolution' – political power had at last been transferred 'from a class to the nation.' Morley wrote excitedly, of the 'national will,' of 'national aims,' and of the new 'national party' which would realize them. And in case existing politicians failed to appreciate these new circumstances, he uttered dark hints suggesting that in another wave of European revolution, like that of 1830 or 1848, England might not escape now that political power was in the hands of those 'most keenly stimulated by foreign agitations.' Morley shared the characteristic university radical's confidence in the working men. As they became more aware of their political power, learning to use 'their weapon' with increasing confidence as they reached 'perfection in their drill,' Morley looked forward confidently to seeing 'ever-increasing power given to politicians with a policy, and those objects accomplished for which parliamentary reform was only desired as a means.' The new voters would respond to guidance from 'courageous and instructed men who know what policy means.' Here was a challenge to the élite: 'The result will depend upon the number of men who can be found with will and faculty to help, in the press and on the platform, in the creation of a virtuous public opinion.' Morley's message was frankly manipulative. The drillmasters of the workers would be the intellectuals – journalists particularly.[6]

At the time he was writing these words, Morley was becoming increasingly involved with the Comtists whom he inherited from Lewes as frequent *Fortnightly* contributors. He was probably introduced into these circles by Cotter Morison, a rich (thanks to the 'Morison's Pills' beloved of Carlyle and Matthew Arnold), clever Comtist dilettante. Morley studied Comte with interest, attended their meetings, went to Paris to consult Pierre Laffitte, their director, and became particularly close to Frederic Harrison. Though he never became an overt adherent to Comtism he was far more deeply influenced by it than is generally recognized, especially by the Comtist conception of the intellectual's role in society. Morley's own social background was different from that of the other university radicals – not quite so gentlemanly, perhaps. He was actually born in the heart of the industrial North which they tended to idealize, and he saw it through somewhat different eyes for that reason. He grew up in Blackburn, Lancashire, during 'the hungry forties.' His family was rooted in the soil of puritanism and nonconformity. His father had certain social ambitions however: a prosperous surgeon who changed from chapel to church-going, he sent his son to Cheltenham College and wished him to enter the clergy. Morley too was a man of considerable ambition. He had the confidence of the self-made man, proud that he owed what he had to his wits and effort and confident that he deserved his success. He had none of the gentlemanly doubts about undeserved ease that afflicted Harrison, for example. 'I was a scrawler when I first came to town, and have scribbled many a day before now with a hungry paunch, but 'twas all honest and honourable, and since I've had the *FR* I played and lived cleanly,' he remarked with defiant satisfaction in 1873.[7]

Morley's fascination with ambition and social mobility emerges in his earliest essays. He dealt with these themes in the 'ventriloquial manner' which characterizes much of his writing, generalizing and projecting in an apparently impersonal manner his personal experiences and concerns. He mocked the rationalizations by which mediocre men excuse their failure to get on, noted the vulnerability of declassed gentlemen to dangerous political notions, and commented generally on the problem of maintaining social stability where many were discontented with their lot. Ambition was a disruptive force in society, and yet it was necessary to progress. Comtism offered answers to this problem. In 1876 at a prize-giving ceremony of the Midland Institute Morley told his audience, of which a large proportion was working class, that it was a questionable policy to encourage the cleverest members of that class to go to university, leaving their class instead of making their talents available within it and so helping to raise the whole class. The following year he addressed a group of miners and remarked that he came as 'a student and man of the pen' to talk to those who were 'doing the hard work and carrying on the great, indispensable work of the world'; but there was no self-deprecation in his comment that 'head work is sometimes as hard and exhausting as even the work of hands such as yours.' No one could say this with a clearer conscience than the diligent Morley. He then proclaimed to them his belief in trusting the worker, telling them that although they could and did make mistakes, when they went wrong it was usually because 'those who knew better were too superfine or too lazy to go down into the crowd honestly and courageously to tell them their minds.'[8]

Morley adopted the Comtist formulation, according to which the workers constituted not a class, but the nation, embroidering it with the more traditional rhetoric of English radicalism. Thus he wrote in the *Fortnightly* in 1870:

Some of us, it is to be hoped, may live to see a day when all this talk about classes shall be at an end and when every citizen shall be able to rise to the conception of a national life, and every politician to follow and grasp the idea of a united and national action. But two conditions are essential to this consummation. First the demolition of privileged orders and privileged creeds, and second, the recognition of the cardinal doctrine that in the multitude you have the only body whose real interests can never, like those of special classes and minor orders, become anti-social; while it is the essence of all other separate classes – capitalist, aristocratic, monarchic, and so on – to be in our modern stage more or less antisocial, until they have learned by disinterested and human meditation that the claims of the multitude are sovereign and paramount, exactly because it is the multitude.

He could speak of how, during the Franco-Prussian war, 'the London workmen, with that sure instinct which is an inexplicable mystery to any but the believer in democracy,' showed by their sympathy with France that her social ideals were their own. He charged the middle and upper classes, rather than the workers, with encouraging and sustaining the idea of class conflict through their own press and political leaders. He stigmatized the middle class for their contempt of ideas, their cultural philistinism, and noted with dismay their obsession with money and position, symbolized by the propensity of successful mill owners in his native Lancashire to set themselves up as country gentlemen and dream of a 'pedigree and a motto in old French.'[9]

Ironically, Morley was himself becoming increasingly attracted by ambitions which Comte warned against most explicitly – the temptations inherent in journalism which made him prohibit it as a vocation for the intellectual. Journalism in Victorian England was becoming increasingly an important political stepping stone: Roundell Palmer, Robert Lowe, and Leonard Courtney were three *Times* leader writers who rose to cabinet rank. It was in fact one of the chief disqualifications of journalism as an independent profession that it was so transitory, so easily entered and left, so often taken up by its ablest practitioners as an avenue to some different goal. Morley's own commitment to journalism as an independent profession declined as he became increasingly successful in it. The former critic of interloping barristers became a barrister himself (not so much with a view to practice but as a confirmation of gentlemanly status and a useful preparation for politics). Moreover, his activities as editor of the *Fortnightly* pointed up other aspects of journalism which distinguished it from the liberal professions. The perspective of journalism alters significantly when viewed from the editorial chair. The *Fortnightly* had been founded as an open forum, and Morley was an apostle of Mill, but there were certain disparities between the doctrine of freedom to contributors and the traditional prerogatives and functions of editorship. Morley was a more authoritarian editor than his predecessor and was quick to impose his personality on his journal, changing it from a cock-pit of eclecticism to an organ of radicalism. Inspired by Comtism, Morley began to regard the *Fortnightly* as a nineteenth-century counterpart to the *Encyclopaedia*, casting himself in the role of Diderot. (The identification shows clearly in his study *Diderot and the Encyclopaedists*.) Comte rated Diderot the greatest genius of his century and regarded the *Encyclopaedia* as an informal precursor of the spiritual power. Diderot had forged a coalition of metaphysical men of letters, turning them into a coherent and disciplined force, a battering-ram directed at the crumbling edifice of the metaphysical era. Morley spoke of his own editorial role as that of 'entrepreneur of the spiritual power,' concentrating the dispersed activities of men of letters in his own day by gathering them together to write under 'the general device of progress.' By firmly exercising editorial discipline he tried to make his review into a coherent organ, focussing it particularly on the political matters that most concerned him. [10]

By occupying the ill-defined border areas of political activity, journalism breaches the integrity of the two spheres, thought and action, central to Comte's doctrine of the separation of powers. Morley's politicization of his review suggests that he was using it both as a surrogate for politics and a spring board. The electoral defeats of the university radicals, including himself, had led him to remark bitterly on the 'unmistakeable proof that people do not recognize the necessity of giving supreme political power to supreme political intelligence.' Yet he remained confident that the nation's needs would eventually 'force the thoughts of men of vehemence into political channels.' Morley's own political interests became increasingly specific as his dissatisfaction with Gladstone's government grew steadily in the early 1870s. W.E. Forster's Education Act particularly offended him as a secular nationalist because he felt it was anti-national, perpetuating sectarian and clerical influence in primary education, the one institution which had the greatest potential for creating a sense of national unity. Morley wrote a series of blistering articles on 'National Education' in 1873 and became active in the work of the nonconformist National Education League organized to fight Forster's legislation. It was this organization which first brought him into contact with Joseph Chamberlain, who further sharpened his political enthusiasm. By 1873, with the Liberal government on the edge of defeat – disunited, drifting, apparently exhausted after five years of strenuous rule – Morley felt the moment had come for a radical initiative, an intervention from the spiritual power of the *Fortnightly*. Like many academic radicals he was opposed to formally organized political parties because they were anti-national, encouraging and indeed depending upon divisions within the nation, and because they were anti-intellectual, hindering the individual initiatives of men of ability which made for progress. But he saw the possibility of a higher, more virtuous party – 'the party of active humanity, of political initiative, of the republic in the true sense' – which might be realized through his journal.[11]

Such was Morley's enthusiasm that he succeeded in tempting Frederic Harrison dangerously near the frontier of political action. Harrison had become one of the *Fortnightly*'s most regular contributors, but always with an equivocal attitude towards literature – one of fascination mingled with contempt which shows again and again in his correspondence with Morley: 'Quite in earnest I regard the literary trade as a trade, as very degraded and producing an infinity of harm. The more valuable and sacred is the subject of commerce, the more is commerce demoralising, and in sober truth I take the publishing trade as a trade to be mere simony.' Thus Chapman, the *Westminster Review*'s editor, was a 'literary pimp'; Morley was a 'tyrant,' and literature 'like pitch' in Harrison's hyperbolic outbursts. Guilt-ridden by his continuing financial dependence on his father, he wrote: 'I could turn literary man, but repugnance to touching money with my pen is irresistible.' Journalism could in fact be quite lucrative: in 1875 Morley's annual income was about £1300, £800 of which was his editorial salary; when he later became editor of the *Pall Mall Gazette* his salary rose to £2000, and was further increased by his other literary activities (Harrison's income in 1875 was around £1200). But in the autumn of 1873, only a few months after expressing his repugnance, Harrison was ready to join Morley's 'party' – on his own terms: 'I henceforth cease to look upon the bar as my profession – that is now fixed. I am willing to give the FR what of my labour it will accept, and if I become professionally attached to it, I think I may fairly put myself upon its professional staff – it being of course understood that even you only invite me to write as a

friend on any subject, and do not order me to write on anything or at all.' Eager
to assist Morley in his 'splendid effort to put new life into politics,' Harrison undertook to write an article each month under the title 'Public Affairs.' He outlined to Morley his aims as a political journalist: 'I am at nothing above the opinion of the marketplace and the club and dislike everything subtle and original in
politics. The sole feature which can give any value to my political notes is that
the judgements are, I think, as a whole carefully balanced and grounded, though
the form of expressing them is often hot ... I am not ass enough to think there
is any Solomon about it, but I am vain enough to think that I can put the common opinions of the world into a solid whole that does and will bear trial.' Harrison was as good as his word; his articles were judicious, well written, and distinc-
tively conservative.[12]

    With an election in the offing, and 'the great sham Liberal party' apparently
on the verge of splitting between its radical and whig wings, there seemed a possibility that Morley's *Fortnightly* party might become the nucleus of a politically
viable radical third party. Harrison and his Comtist friends were at this time active members in the labour lobby against the Criminal Law Amendment Act of
1871 which vitiated much that the labour movement had gained from the Trade
Union Act of the same year (itself largely the result of Harrison's efforts on the
Royal Commission on Trade Unions). Morley was deep in the Education Question which he considered the crucial political issue of the day, an enthusiasm
which the Comtists did not particularly share, being suspicious of all forms of
state education as a potential barrier to the spread of their doctrines. In August
1873 Chamberlain, the practical politician of the *Fortnightly* party, produced a
'quadrilateral programme' – Free Church, Free Land, Free Schools, and Free Labour. Harrison thought it might serve as an effective platform for a third party
uniting the radical ranks, secularist, agrarian, trade unionist, and nonconformist.
Morley thought the platform too broad and vague, but Harrison argued that such
vagueness, while perhaps a liability to a party actually bidding for office, was an
advantage to a party in the process of formation. Harrison was even writing to
Morley about the possibilities of Parliament – a candidature *à la* Mill: 'As to the
House, it is possible that I might do some good there. If it came my way I do not
know that I should repel it, but I have no sense of call that impels me to struggle
towards it, and without such a struggle, and a very repulsive one in my case, it is
out of the question.' Harrison felt that he could do as well outside Parliament
what he could do in it, without feeling he had abandoned his principles. Morley
did not share Harrison's extreme distaste for the hustings, but lacked Harrison's
opportunities. He took soundings in Hastings as to the prospect for standing as a
National Education League candidate. Chamberlain, who was anxious to enter
Parliament himself, encouraged him. Morley wavered, wondering whether he

might be 'more useful as the literary spokesman of our cause.' Chamberlain assured him that, even if he lost, his candidature would increase the importance and readership of his literary work. But Morley was deterred by the election expenses.[13]

As the general elections drew nearer Harrison's commitment to the breakup of the Liberals, a central point of the *Fortnightly* party strategy, began to waver. Fear of a Tory victory made him grasp anxiously at any sign that the Liberals would adopt the reform of the labour laws as part of their programme. Since Harrison had been encouraging the working men to adopt independent candidates, labour leaders in Halifax pressed him to stand as their candidate against John Crossley, the carpet manufacturer and official Liberal candidate. But he backed out at the request of the nonconformist Liberation Society, who urged him not to split the Liberal vote. He remarked rather guiltily to Morley that the workmen 'feel, I fear, that I have run away from the very advice I gave them to make themselves felt.' On the eve of the 1874 election he delivered a very lukewarm charge to his congregation of *Bee-Hive* readers, diluting his remarks about the time being right for the creation of 'a real labour party' with stern warnings against letting any Tories get in and expressions of good will towards Gladstone and his colleagues. Harrison drew Morley's attention to this article:

In politics you cannot be too magnanimous, as I felt when I tried to shield Fawcett and help Hughes, neither of whom altogether deserves our help. You see the Government distinctly knock under to us, if not to you. We have won! and are therefore bound by all laws of politics to accept the offer. You will be furious to think of my helping Forster. Well I said nothing about the Bradford election. Let him fight that himself. But since he honestly adopts the Labour Programme, he ought to have the benefit of it ... There are no absolute tests and no irreconcilables in politics.[14]

Not long after this retreat from political activism Harrison also abandoned his role as political commentator for the *Fortnightly*. His relationship with Morley was becoming increasingly uncomfortable. Morley considered that Harrison's articles should be editorial, and that as editor he must have control. Harrison demanded that he be left 'as free to speak and as responsible for my opinion as a public man speaking on a platform who naturally takes care not to embarrass his party, but who utters his own views subject to previous consultation with the heads of his own side.' He was no hired journalist writing to order, and when Morley committed the 'outrage' of appending a dissenting note to one of his articles, thereby reducing him to 'the level of a hack,' he made it a cause for breaking off his arrangement. The incident illustrated another of the dilemmas of the journalistic profession. Morley wished to exercise the authority necessary to maintain a coherent doctrinal line in his journal. He was the professional journalist attempting to bring together the views of a number of self-consciously amateur gentlemen whose very individualism was advertised by the *Fortnightly*'s rule of signature. Frederic Harrison deeply resented any idea of editorial superiority as an intolerable affront both to his status as a gentleman and his principles as a Comtist.[15]

The strains of this journalistic connection unfortunately impaired the very warm friendship between the two men.* The problem was complicated by the fact that Harrison was a well-known spokesman of Comtism, and Morley had to contend with the real threat to his own intellectual and editorial independence posed by the public tendency to regard his review as an organ of Comtism. Naturally enough the Comtists were happy to avail themselves of his review and to take advantage of the public's assumptions, but Morley fought to avoid the Comtist grip, encouraging Huxley to controversy with them and even publishing a short article disclaiming the label for his review. Harrison felt with some justification that Morley was not quite candid about his debt to Comte. Comtist social formulas continued to play a considerable role in the economy of his mind. The Comtist dictum about the proletariat being not a class turned up time and again in Morley's rhetoric: thus in the late 1870s he could still proclaim that the workmen were 'not a class, but the great substance, bulk, body and reality of the nation.' Without the conviction and system of Comte behind it such a statement tended towards bombastic vacuity. Comtist tags and tatters clothed Morley's views on trade unionism, capitalism, and labour relations generally, serving as a substitute for reasoned analysis. Indeed, the Comtist formulation of the harmonious society provided a convenient conceptual skeleton for Morley's vague social ideas, thus relieving him from the need to occupy his mind with them and freeing his intellectual energies for the great moral, non-structural crusades that increasingly fascinated him in politics.[16]

If Harrison shrank from politics in 1874, Morley pressed on toward them, as Joseph Chamberlain increasingly took over Harrison's role as his confidant and in-

---

* Friendship with Morley was a strenuous and serious matter. In 1870 he abruptly broke off his close friendship with George Meredith, apparently because he found Meredith's levity on political matters unsettling to his own earnest quest for a political vocation. Meredith redeemed himself, however, by writing the excellent political novel *Beauchamp's Career* which Morley serialized in the *Fortnightly*. Its hero is an enthusiastic intellectual radical gentleman modelled on their mutual friend F.A. Maxse, a rather idiosyncratic gentry radical who twice stood unsuccessfully for Parliament. C.L. Cline, ed., *The Letters of George Meredith* (Oxford 1970), I, 443

spiration. From their first acquaintance Morley was awed by Chamberlain's superb political instincts and compelling self-confidence. In the ambitious mayor of Birmingham he saw a man of action of Carlylean dimensions. The masterful editor tended to belittle himself in his communications with Chamberlain. Pressing him to contribute a political article to the *Fortnightly*, Morley urged that the public would 'of course be impressed by anything from you, because you are in practical politics. They would be likely to think of my utterances on such matters as little better than literary declamation.' More than once he spoke of himself to Chamberlain as an 'academic politician.' Chamberlain, anxious to broaden his own somewhat provincial cultural frame of reference as a preparation for his intended role as a national statesman, treated Morley with respect. But Morley more than reciprocated with his humble avidity to learn the mysteries of practical politics at his feet. The partnership suited them both. Morley could proudly claim in 1873 that his journal had some 30,000 readers 'of the influential class,' whom he addressed 'seriously and steadily and conscientiously, knowing what we want and saying so'; its influence 'was very impalpable, very easy to sneer at, very hard to define, but still influence.' Inspired by the tactical dexterity of Chamberlain, the journalistic politician was even beginning to have second thoughts about the policy of signature that he had so bravely defended a few years earlier. In 1875 Morley wrote to Chamberlain about a projected controversial political article: 'My notion is to print an article unsigned. This fact alone will make it conspicuous in a signing review ... A mere literary shot would do no good unless it represents more than the words of an isolated writer. The authorship must be kept secret between you and me. It stirs controversy.' The cloak of anonymity had its political uses as Morley now appreciated. But so too had signature. A few months later he could give it as a reason against publishing a series of articles anonymously that 'as a militant party we shall have a great advantage if we are in a position to thunder against the men in masks.'[17]

The *Fortnightly* stirred up a good deal of excitement in the mid-1870s, when official Liberalism was at slack tide and the possibilities for its radicalization seemed promising. But the translation into political action – the test of the journalistic enterprise in Morley's eyes, was disappointing. This disappointment was evident in his 'Valedictory' as editor of the review in 1882 when he reviewed his record with justifiable pride but observed that 'the original scheme of the Review, even if there had been no other obstacle, prevented it from becoming the organ of a systematic policy.' He expressed his reservations about signed journalism even more strongly, noting the danger of readers being 'tempted to think more of the man who speaks than of the precise value of what he says' – the danger of 'lion-hunting' journalism as practiced so successfully by his rival James Knowles of the *Nineteenth Century*. It also tended to narrow the openings for the professional journalists who lacked a big name but who 'without being an expert will take the trouble to work up his subject, to learn what is said and thought about it, to penetrate to the real points, to get the same mastery over it as an advocate or a judge does over a patent case.' By the time he was writing this Morley does over a patent case.' By the time he was writing this Morley was editor of the prestigious *Pall Mall Gazette* (a post he took up in 1880 when Henry Yates Thompson, a founding member of the Century Club, became its owner). Here Morley was back in the world of anonymous journalism but firmly on the other side of the desk, with able and ambitious young journalists like W.T. Stead, E.T. Cook, and Alfred (later Lord) Milner obedient to his bidding. 'He believed in authority,' Stead recollected: 'No one ever took any liberties with Mr. Morley.' He was now free to use his journal as a pulpit, and did so. He had the ear of an audience that mattered even more than the *Fortnightly*'s – men of influence who took their politics into their libraries and into the lobbies, in clubland and at Westminster. And here at last politics and journalism merged when for a brief period, after finally entering Parliament early in 1883 as MP for Newcastle, Morley continued his editorship before finally relinquishing it for the life of 'real' politics.[18]

8

The Retreat into Politics: John Morley

I have known men who, with significant nods and the pitying contempt of smiles, have denied all influence to the corruptions of moral and political philosophy and with much solemnity have proceeded to solve the riddle of the French Revolution by anecdotes! Yet it would not be difficult, by an unbroken chain of historic facts, to demonstrate that the most important changes in the commercial relations of the world had their origin in the closets or lonely walks of disinterested theorists.

S.T. Coleridge, *The Statesman's Manual*

In the right understanding of this [the French Revolution] is involved all possible Knowledge for us, and yet at the present hour our ignorance of it in England is probably as bad as total ... To me it often seems as if the right *History* (that impossible thing I mean by history) of the French Revolution were the Grand Poem of our Time.

Thomas Carlyle to John Stuart Mill, 1833

In addition to his overtly political journalism, Morley was also engaged throughout the decade 1866-76 in a more rigorous search for a solution to the intellectual's perennial problem of defining his relationship with politics – determining how best his ideas can be translated into action. One of the shortcomings of Coleridge's clerisy ideal for academic radicals was that it offered no clear guidelines for the political functions of the intellectual, least of all in an age of mass politics. Coleridge's élitism took little account of democracy. Comte did, however. By means of his theory of the separation of the spiritual and temporal powers he quite explicitly defined and prohibited political activity by the intellectual élite, confining them to the realm of educating public opinion. Indeed, his technocratic, authoritarian conception of government in effect eliminated politics itself, thereby disposing of the whole problem of democracy, which he of course opposed. The young John Morley, with his attraction towards clear and compelling systems, was fascinated by Comte's sharply defined theory of the separation of powers, and apparently felt that he had come to terms with its implacable logic either by accepting or by overcoming it. Comte's whole theory of the functions of the intellectual was historical, as we have seen, and hinged especially upon his interpretation of the French Revolution. Embarking on the practice of externalizing and working out his own problems through historical and biographical studies, Morley commenced in the mid-1860s a series of studies of the background and events of the French Revolution. A number of his friends, particularly Mark Pattison (Lincoln was Morley's college) and Leslie Stephen, were students of the eighteenth century, and Morley was of course steeped in Carlyle's *The French Revolution*. But it was Comte, and more specifically Pierre Laffitte, who, as Morley admitted, provided the 'key and direction' to his studies. The attraction of Comte's theory of the French Revolution was its comprehensiveness and its emphasis on ideas as the chief cause of the revolution. What better way to study the role of ideas and men of ideas in history than through the eighteenth-century *philosophes*, and what more systematic guide than Comte? To study the revolution and its background was not only valuable to Morley as a means of working out the methods and possibilities for influence by the intellectual upon society, but he felt that a 'clear, definite and stable idea' of its meaning in the history of human progress was indispensable to his countrymen. He apparently intended eventually to write a history of the revolution but never did so; instead he left a series of biographical studies which may be regarded as contributions to such a history.[1]

The first of these was *Edmund Burke* (1867), followed by 'Joseph de Maistre' (1868). To approach the revolution through its most violent opponents was in keeping with the dialectical method of Comte, who greatly admired de Maistre, the ultimate exponent of 'order.' But it is Morley's study of Burke (whom Comte does not mention) that shows most strongly the Comtist influence. For Burke, like Comte and Coleridge, the French Revolution was a revolution of ideas, caused by men of ideas. The long shadow of Burke's *Reflections on the Revolution in France* fell over the work of all British students of the revolution. Until the end of the nineteenth century they approached it largely within the terms of reference laid down in this great polemic. But Burke particularly fascinated university radicals like Morley for being himself *par excellence* the intellectual in politics. Underlying his opposition to the revolution was his fear of the crude unbridled intellectualism which he saw at its root. Burke regarded it as the work of alienated, socially uprooted intellectuals and his perception of this phenomenon was all the sharper because he knew that he partook of it, that he was himself just such an intellectual in his own society. Burke's self-consciousness as an intellectual – his own struggle with the dilemma of thought versus action – informed practically all his political writings and largely account for their passionate intensity.[2]

Morley praised Burke for revivifying the 'dead Whig principles' of his time and for restoring ideas to the high place in practical politics which the intellectual sterility of eighteenth-century English politicians had denied them. The parallel with the politics of the Palmerstonian age was only too obvious to the intellectual radical. Matthew Arnold had noticed it three years earlier in calling attention to the fact that Burke 'almost alone in England ... brings thought to bear upon politics; he saturates politics with thought.' And although Burke was the great ideologist of party, Morley praised him for abandoning the Whig party over the issue of the revolution, an act of principle which confirmed Morley's own opposition to party politics as the enemy of principle. But Burke was also great in Morley's eyes for having avoided the obsessive concern with 'barren rights' and 'abstract truths' which was supposed to characterize the intellectual in politics. He rightly appreciated that duty and morality are the proper concerns of politics, rather than metaphysical notions (all of which soundly accorded with Comte). Morley suggested that Burke's political activities had enabled him to avoid that narrow utopianism which was the besetting vice of the closet philosopher, but conceded also that inevitably they had narrowed the range of his ideas. This perhaps accounted for Burke's hostility to the principles of the French Revolution.[3]

Morley was anxious to show that these principles were, contrary to Burke, 'in the main, true.' He therefore attempted to exorcise the revolution, and especially the notorious triad of 'Liberty, Equality, and Fraternity,' of the terrors which Burke attributed to it by means of judicious Comtist redefinition. Thus 'Liberty,' Morley explained, stripped of all the unfortunate metaphysical rhetoric of the ideologues which had discredited it, was essentially the doctrine of popular sovereignty, which could be justified by the soundly English criterion of the 'general happiness.' Citing his favourite Comtist formula, he pointed out that 'the multitude' – 'the only body whose real interests can never, like those of minor classes and special orders, possibly become anti-social' – was necessarily sovereign. Hence 'Liberty,' otherwise 'popular sovereignty,' stood revealed as nothing more fearsome than 'the national interest.' Similarly, 'Equality' was rescued from the obfuscations of metaphysical phraseology and shown to be nothing more than 'equality of external opportunity.' As for 'Fraternity,' Morley noted it was a central principle of Christianity. Significantly he hailed innocuous Fraternity, 'the generous and sublime sentiment of the brotherhood of man,' as the greatest of all revolutionary ideas. Certainly it was the most agreeable to the strategy of intellectual populism.[4]

Both Burke and Comte emphasized the intellectual nature of the revolution, and Comte, like Burke, was critical of the disorder which it brought about. These were the chief grounds for Morley's attempt to reconcile its two interpreters. The main difference between them was that Burke's catastrophic interpretation presented the revolution as a sudden and dramatic break with the past, a violation of the normal course of organic development which Burke considered the only legitimate type of historical change. He regarded it as not merely unhistorical but anti-historical – an arrogant, simplistic, and overly speculative repudiation of the accumulated experience and continuity of human society. Morley confronted this view with the Comtist interpretation of the revolution as no violent break with history, but only a phase, albeit a critical one, in a much larger historical movement. It was indeed an organic phenomenon and a continuing one. It had not yet ended because the ideas of this revolution of ideas had not yet been fully worked out. As a political event the French Revolution was a failure, Morley admitted. It had failed to translate its ideas into reality. But the reasons for this failure could be explained: Comte had done so with his doctrine of the two powers. The revolution was a political takeover by the men of ideas who, having developed their abstract social theories largely in political isolation throughout the eighteenth century, suddenly found themselves in possession of the levers of power, which they attempted to manipulate in accordance with their broad generalizations and speculative symmetries. Burke had correctly foreseen the tragic results that would issue from the 'rule of geometers.' Here again he agreed with Comte, for whom the revolution was the decisive historical lesson on 'the peril of confounding the two great functions of speculation and political action.' Indeed, the revolution posed on a gigantic scale the political dilemma which Burke felt acutely in his own situation as an intellectual in politics and from which he had intuitively extrapolated himself to predict its dire consequences. Yet the resolution to the problem was before his very eyes, had he but known it. For Adam Smith (another of Comte's heroes) provided the ideal example of the proper relationship between the philosopher and politics. Smith developed his ideas in 'serene and salutary tranquility, undisturbed by the harassing necessity of modifying them to meet particular political exigencies.' But it was William Pitt who having 'assimilated them with masterly comprehension, proceeded to apply them in limited and modified forms to the solution of actual problems.' Here, according to Morley, were embodied the correct roles of philosopher and statesman, of which the French Revolution had provided the negative example, but which the longer, as yet uncompleted European revolution would ultimately put into effect.[5]

Despite the intellectual assent which Morley yielded at the end of *Burke* to the Comtist division of powers, a sneaking preference for the politician over the intellectual pervades the book. The studies of Burke and de Maistre were followed by 'Condorcet' and 'Turgot' (1870) in which this preference becomes clearer. Morley slid away from the Comtist solution, though its clear-cut logicality continued to haunt him, in dealing with the two most illustrious French examples of the intellectual in politics. Rather than condemn them for engaging in politics, Morley if anything criticizes them for having been insufficiently political. Condorcet, who lived to participate in the revolution and to die one of its victims, was singled out by Burke as an arch-example of the intellectual catapulted into power and carried away by his ideas – 'of all men, the most dangerous.' But Comte, in contrast, had hailed as his own 'spiritual father' this man who during his last days, though a fugitive, could yet write a transcendantly optimistic outline of the progress of the human mind towards imminent perfection. As for Turgot, he had without bending in principle risen to the highest administrative position in the government of pre-revolutionary France where he attempted to institute the financial reforms necessary to the salvation of the old régime, only to be dismissed for his sound advice.[6]

Both men spoke to Morley as intellectuals who knew politics from the inside, and he explicitly judged them for their political performance and attitudes. Condorcet was a mathematician, an *Academicien* who became a member of the Paris municipal government, the Legislative Assembly, and the Convention, riding the revolutionary whirlwind for four years before falling prey to it. Morley praised his undisguised preference for 'active political labour' over mathematical problems, though admitting that Condorcet tended to bring to the forum methods better suited to the study. Morley yielded to Burke's assessment in describing him as the incarnation of the excessively 'geometrical' spirit of the revolution, remarking that 'there is no more fatal combination in politics than the deductive method worked by passion.' Yet he praised Condorcet for being 'no pedantic nor fastidious trifler,' for being 'never afraid of the spectre, as the incompetent revolutionist is,' even if on occasion he showed 'a certain want of eye for revolutionary methods.' Thus the radical young literary politician solemnly graded the revolutionary conduct of Condorcet.[7]

As an intellectual in politics Condorcet was flawed by his extremist faith in perfectibility. His friend and guide Turgot was the greater man for his realism, his sense of the limitations of politics. Morley saw Turgot as the paragon of the intellectual in politics (a view he shared with Mill and Matthew Arnold) and one of the few modern intellectuals who had successfully exercised real and substantial power. In a passage which he deleted from the republished version of his study, he even suggested that Turgot was the one man who might have saved France from the revolution if he had not been dismissed from his post: 'That

Turgot should have failed demonstrates the hopelessness of the situation, and assures us that the destinies of France had gone beyond the control of the one man who united profound self-abnegation and supreme zeal to the requisite administrative genius.' This observation illustrates one means by which Morley escaped from the uncomfortable logic of Comte's separation of the powers. Thought and action could perhaps be reconciled by greatness of character: 'There are crises when a character tells far more than an idea and is at once a saving opportunity and a decisive force,' Morley wrote. Turgot was such a character. The difficulty of this interpretation was that it smacked of the Carlylean doctrine of the hero to which Morley the undergraduate admirer of Cromwell had been drawn, but from the irrationalism of which Morley the mature rationalist recoiled. Yet if the great man could be demystified and shown to be no superhuman phenomenon, nor his qualities beyond the range of human effort, such lessons would surely be very salutary to mankind at large. This was to be the creed of Morley the biographer. Even Turgot had his flaws, however, for his stiffness, his austerity and unapproachability made him vulnerable to his opponents. Nor could Morley accept Turgot's rating the achievements of the study over those of 'practical work.' This was true only in exceptional cases, he noted severely: most literature, being 'subordinate and secondary,' served only to 'pass the time of the learned or cultured class.'[8]

Condorcet and Turgot were followed by Morley's three major eighteenth-century studies, *Voltaire* (1872), *Rousseau* (1873), and *Diderot* (1878), the *Philosophes* who, according to Comte, led the three major schools of thought which contributed decisively to the French Revolution. The sceptical school of Voltaire, with its emphasis on liberty, and the anarchistic school of Rousseau, bent on equality, were negative and destructive forces contributing to the break-up of the metaphysical stage of society, while the positive, organic school of Diderot alone contained constructive elements which, being historically premature, were not fully developed. These three thinkers had also been the subject of essays by Carlyle whose heavily moralistic and scornful attitude had contributed largely to the climate of hostility towards the eighteenth century that Morley was anxious to redress, the popular conception of Voltaire and Rousseau as devil-figures being in particular need of correction. The objective, scientific standpoint that Morley needed for dispassionate analysis of these thinkers was provided by Comte, whose basic theoretical and historical framework underlies each of these studies. Morley was evidently fascinated by Comte's tidy, intellectualist scheme which tied each man's influence to a specific stage of the revolution – Voltaire's culminating in the period of the bourgeois, libertarian Constituent Assembly, Diderot's in the heroic ascendancy of Danton (whom Comte regarded as the greatest revolutionary statesman), and Rousseau's in the doctrinaire dictatorship of Robespierre.[9]

While Morley generally accepted, at least as a starting point, Comte's determin-istic valuation of the historical function of each thinker, his own concerns in-creasingly obtrude and conflict with Comtist dogma, especially on the crucial issue of spiritual versus temporal power. The ambitious editor of the *Fortnightly* iden-tified strongly with Voltaire, virtually a one-man spiritual power who exerted a powerful and conspicuous authority in his time that was 'absolutely unofficial in its origin, and indebted to no system nor organization for its maintenance.' Yet as if to confirm Morley's own growing preference, this 'most puissant man of let-ters that ever lived' rated literature quite properly below action. Indeed, Morley criticized Voltaire for not being more politically active than he was. He also tried to make his hero more attractive to his readers by emphasizing how greatly Vol-taire's ideal of the man of letters' role in society was influenced by his admira-tion of England. Here, however, Morley again attempts to evade the horns of the Comtist dilemma. He grants the Comtist doctrine that 'the more closely literature approaches to being an organ of truly serious things, a truly spiritual power, the more danger there is likely to be in making it a path to temporal station or emolu-ment,' and he also concedes that the extraordinary influence of Voltaire set the pattern for the fatal predominance of the man of letters in France ever since. But, he suggests, there is in England a 'practical instinct which on some of its sides looks like a miraculously implanted substitute for intelligence' which has resisted any such similar predominance and in fact has 'led us almost too far in preserving this important separation of the new church from the functions and rewards of the state.' In other words, Comte generalized his doctrine of the separation of the powers in response to a uniquely French situation. In England the situation was precisely opposite; intellectuals if anything had too little influence in affairs.[10]

Morley also asserted his independence of Comte on another crucial point. Vol-taire might have been, as Comte claimed, an unsystematic and negative thinker without any new ideas of his own for the reconstruction of society, yet he was by virtue of his great character an emancipatory force whose example reminded Morley that the critical task was still uncompleted and that Comte's own author-itarian attempts at reconstruction were a premature synthesis. Morley thus de-clared his allegiance to the Millite ideal of open-ended, undetermined progress on the central point of difference between Comte and Mill.[11]

By contrast Rousseau attracted Morley neither as a thinker nor as an example of character and he was willing to acquiesce in the outlines of Comte's necessitar-ian interpretation. Within these outlines he wrote a judicious and at times even sympathetic study, particularly when examining Rousseau's religious and educa-tional ideas which, although reactionary, were for that very reason revolutionary within the Comtist dialectic. Unlike Voltaire, Rousseau did contribute new ideas, new in the sense that he galvanized certain existing notions with an emotional charge that attracted fervent discipleship and gave them new power. Once again Morley domesticates the fearsome doctrines associated with Rousseau – popular sovereignty and equality – by rephrasing them in Burkean terms, as if to provide a demonstration of how an emotive terminology can make a significant difference to the political quality of an idea. One of Rousseau's ideas that he does not attempt to domesticate, however, is the social contract. He resorts to the purest Comtist terminology to condemn it as a metaphysical idea which substituted 'retrograde aspiration for direction, and emotion for the discovery of law.' Here was the central political lesson to be drawn from Rousseau, for the social contract epitomized – in its blind abstraction, its utter lack of contact with any known social reality, and its explosive emotionalism – the dangers of hyper-intellectualism in the political realm. Those who play only with the simplicity of words, rather than handling the complexity of facts, Morley sternly warned, 'may advance with a speed, a precision, a consistency, a conclusiveness that has a magical potency over men who insist on having politics and theology drawn out in exact theorems like those of geometry.'[12]

By the time he had completed *Rousseau* early in 1873 Morley was already immersed in the 'complex facts' of practical politics – the National Education League, his exciting acquaintance with Chamberlain, the radical prospects opened by a declining Liberal government, and the coming general election. Morley could not resist the pull of politics, and even though he had freed himself from the doctrine of the two powers he still lacked a satisfactory framework within which to reconcile ideas and action. In *Voltaire* he had repudiated Comte's doctrine on the grounds of its inapplicability to England. Comte had universalized the peculiarly French problem of excessive intellectualization of politics. But the peculiarly English problem of the intellectual in relation to politics was the very opposite – the excessive politicization of thought. In the aftermath of the Liberal election defeat Morley determined, as he told Chamberlain, to rally the forces of true liberalism with 'three or four papers of a general kind about Compromise, in which I shall exalt the importance of Principles and show what a beggarly mood England is in because she has none.' Casting his thoughts into 'severe and philosophical shape,' he wrote a series of articles for the *Fortnightly* which, collected and expanded as *On Compromise*, now occupy a central place in the canon of nineteenth-century liberal thought.[13]

References to *On Compromise* commonly emphasize its rationalist character, for it is a rationalistic tract – manifesto, rather – to be classed with such contemporary works as Mill's *The Subjection of Women* and Leslie Stephen's *Essays on Freethinking and Plainspeaking*. Morley was a religious rationalist who wished also to be a political rationalist, and in *Compromise* he attempted to yoke these together, hoping to bring the bold blacks and whites in which he saw religious questions into the greyer realms of politics. But in its neglected political aspect the book can be regarded as a handbook for the intellectual in politics, and specifically an exercise in self-direction. It is a guide through the difficult frontier between speculation and action. In his book Morley tries to formulate certain principles of general application to the conduct of the intellectual by defining the straight and narrow path between the slough of political quietism on the one hand and the vanities of unprincipled activism on the other.[14]

On Compromise is unblushingly an élitist manifesto, originally addressed to the enlightened vanguard of *Fortnightly* readers: 'What is important is the mind and attitude, not of the ordinary man, but of those who should be extraordinary ... What are the best men in the country striving for?' The answer was discouraging. Morley saw all about him evidences of a cramped mentality, a low tone in national life. He attributed it partly to a sense of disillusionment over the outcome of the various causes which had been enthusiastically taken up by intellectuals over the previous forty years: parliamentary reform in England, the unification of Italy, emancipation in the United States – all had been achieved, but none had realized the high ideals which had been invested in them. The failures of 1848 had also discredited political theory and speculation, particularly in France where ideals had been perverted by the political immorality of the Second Empire.[15]

Morley detected a deeper reason for the enervating mental climate in the insidious spread of the 'Historical Method' beyond the bounds of scholarship and into everyday life. Virtually everything – physical, intellectual, and moral – was now being regarded from its evolutionary aspect. This tendency inevitably encouraged the suspension of judgment not only on the past but on the present which so clearly partook of the past. 'In the last century men asked of a belief or a story, Is it true? We now ask, How did men come to take it for true?' Thus confusion was growing between explanation and justification; relativity was becoming all-pervasive – every abuse could be shown to have a defensible origin, every error to have been true relative to a certain system of belief. The historical method was particularly prone to debasement at the hands of those lacking intellectual discipline into a 'slipshod preference of vague general forms over definite beliefs.' Worse still, it tainted the springs of action by its tendency to discount individual effort in accounting for change.[16]

Such speculative tendencies served only to strengthen a characteristic already endemic in Englishmen – their 'profound distrust of all general principles,' a distrust arising from their habit of regarding 'principle' and 'expediency' as necessarily antithetical. Morley proposed one of his judicious redefinitions to meet this difficulty, suggesting that principles were really nothing more than 'larger expediencies.' He was anxious to tighten his countrymen to the pitch of principle, but equally anxious to show that it was not beyond their range. Morley identified the newspaper press as one of the worst offenders against principle. By making a fetish of public opinion it catered to 'vulgar ways of looking at things and vulgar ways of speaking of them,' stereotyping and endlessly repeating them so as to deaden individual and private opinion. The press was particularly hostile to theory and principle and particularly given to improperly applying the political test, damping down speculation with cant about 'the limits of the practicable in politics.' A grotesque example of this was *The Times'* censuring Darwin for publishing his *Descent of Man* 'while the sky of Paris was red with the flames of the Commune.'[17]

The central theme of *Compromise* is the Comtist problem of the separation of the powers (though Morley nowhere mentions Comte in the book). *The Times'* reaction to Darwin was a case of the illegitimate application of the political test to non-political matters. If the intellectuals adopted this point of view, rejecting principle and worshipping instead practicality and narrow political expediency, than they were not only usurping the proper function of the politician, whose concern this was, but more importantly they were abandoning their own proper function, that of providing the unadulterated flow of higher ideas necessary to political and social progress. The politician was necessarily absorbed by immediate concerns and heedless of new ideas as yet outside the realm of practicality or public acceptance, but if the intellectuals acquiesced in the 'leaden tyranny of the man of the world' by politicizing their speculations and acting as their own censors, then they were removing the politician even further from the realm of pure ideas. Moreover, since their own ideas would still suffer modification at the hands of politicians regardless of their own politicizing efforts, these ideas would achieve realization, if at all, in an even more debased state than otherwise.[18]

Morley observed that it was indispensable to the social welfare of a nation that 'the divorce between political responsibility and intellectual responsibility ... should not be too complete and universal.' But he suggested that this divorce was in England largely the result of the intellectuals accepting, in public at least, the 'House of Commons view of life,' and thus depriving the populace of contact through them with ideas and the concern for truth. Morley was particularly concerned with the question of 'dual doctrine' – whether intellectuals should systematically keep their ideas to themselves and 'openly encourage a doctrine for the less enlightened classes which they do not believe to be true for themselves.' He cited its classic formulation in the bargain offered by Ernest Renan to the Catholic church: 'Do not meddle with what we teach or write, and then we will not dispute the common people with you.' Such a doctrine implies a hermetic ideal of an intellectual élite and an idea of knowledge as a rare and special commodity, to be preserved in its purity from the profane crowd. It also implies that truth can be dangerous in the hands of the uninitiated, as in the case of Hume's suggestion that the right of resistance to a tyrant, although a true doctrine, should be concealed from the populace.[19]

Morley dismissed such doctrines out of hand, for they were founded on a principle which he strenuously denied – that error might have social, political, or psychological utility. He devotes a chapter to demolishing this principle which had just received support from an unexpected quarter with the publication of Mill's posthumous essay on 'The Utility of Religion.' Here, to Morley's dismay, his master had suggested that religion might be 'morally useful' without being intellectually sustainable. The fervour of Morley's denial derived from his conviction of the indivisibility of truth – social, political, and psychological. Morley, the evangelical rationalist, fervently believed truth to be an independent, homogeneous, and eternal entity. He was able to do so because his definition of truth is essentially negative: it is the opposite of error, hence its clarity. This was closely tied to his negative conception of progress as the progressive repudiation of error. Truth is what remains after the obstructions of error, 'inevitable elements in human growth,' have been cleared away. This negative view of progress, which accounts for his un-Comtist sympathy for Voltaire, is readily apparent from Morley's remarks on the course of history. New ideas tend to be 'dissolvent ideas,' and history is 'for the most part, the history of insurrection.' 'To me at any rate,' Morley revealingly observed, 'the history of mankind is a huge *pis aller*, just as our present society is; a prodigious, wasteful experiment from which a certain number of results have been extracted.'[20]

Morley rejected the dual doctrine and the utility of error which implied an inherent conflict of interest between the intellectual élite and the populace because he saw the common people essentially as allies of the progressive élite against the privileged whose interests lay in preserving the status quo. Public opinion was the political lever of the intellectuals; therefore the masses who eventually sustained that opinion could not be ignored or sacrificed though there was obviously a great gap between the two groups.

It is this gap that creates difficulties for the intellectual élitist. How it is to be bridged, for bridged it must be, depends on how the élite's purpose is defined. Its two chief purposes are to maintain intellectual order and to ensure intellectual progress. Ultimately the two cannot by wholly reconciled, and the emphasis tends towards one or the other of these poles, one of which is essentially authoritarian, the other libertarian in spirit. Comte tried to reconcile order and progress by authoritatively defining the goal of progress – the positive social order whose integrity was to be maintained by a spiritual élite firmly in charge of the proletariat through their control of education. In this Comte came down decisively on the side of order and authority. It was essentially on this crucial point that Mill parted company with him (as did Morley), for Mill, by rejecting the possibility of authoritative blueprints for the ultimate society (in his own time at least), left progress an open question and committed himself to the free, continuing quest of the intellectual élite. The problem of the English Comtists as a proto-spiritual élite, as we have seen, was that of trying to accommodate themselves to conditions anterior to the realization of the society for which that élite was designed. It was their lot to live at a time when they were not yet fully in command, when 'progress' had not yet reached its destination and had still to be encouraged. The proletariat was on their side – the favourable experiences of the early 1860s had indicated this; Comte had confirmed and explained it. But again there was the dilemma: while the proletariat's support would be passive in the positive stage, rather more active support might be useful before the achievement of that stage to help bring it about, to give progress a push. How was this support to be mobilized without compromising the élite's intellectual authority and the proletariat's political purity? The problem for Mill, on the other hand, in opting for libertarian, undetermined progress, was that he continued to feel the need for some sort of organized authority among the intellectuals who were the sources of progress, to ensure that progress moved forward in an orderly, unimpeded manner, since he was not entirely sanguine about the reliability of the masses as supporters of progress. Hence Mill's attraction to Coleridge's clerisy and Comte's spiritual power as types of intellectual organization.

In defining his intellectual élite as the initiatory force on the side of progress, Morley rejected the traditional authoritarian conception in which the élite might be characterised as occupying the apex of an intellectual pyramid. Opposed to this static structural metaphor was Morley's dynamic temporal metaphor, in which the élite are seen as the leaders of a procession, the vanguard of progress. The idea of progress is essential to Morley's élitism. The common conception of a generation as a separate and homogeneous unit, Morley pointed out, does not conform to actuality; each generation has its leaders and laggards, as well as its vast inert bulk: only a small part of each generation 'can have nerve enough to grasp the banner of a new truth, and endurance enough to bear it along rugged and untrodden ways.' But in *Compromise* he tends to evade the important question of authority. Truth reveals itself to those whose minds are open to recognize it, minds in which, to use Morley's Arnoldian phrase, the 'free play and access of intellectual light' is unobstructed. Morley took it for granted that there would be a consensus among such minds as to what the truth was. His élite did not therefore act as guardians of received truth but as intellectual initiators in a world of change. 'Every age is in some sort an age of transition, but our own is characteristically and cardinally an epoch of transition in the very foundation of belief and conduct,' Morley noted. In turning from Comte back to Mill, he turned away from the question 'transition to what?' and confined his attention primarily to the fact of change itself, change as the condition of progress. Though Morley was a perfectibilist, the fulfilment of perfection could conveniently be projected sufficiently far into the future not to be a substantial issue. There was enough work combatting the obstacles of the present without being too concerned with the final goal, which would come of itself, provided the way was clear.[21]

Although Morley yoked the Millite ideal of a progressive libertarian élite to a Comtist faith in the amenability of the populace to authoritative direction, this faith was not wholly naïve. The dual doctrine does in fact slip into *Compromise* in a diluted form as the doctrine of 'reserve.' Without believing in the utility of error amongst the populace, Morley did recognize the necessity, especially in an age of transition, of some sort of system for keeping back or reserving from them incomplete or 'unripe' ideas. A believer in a fairly open intellectual market place, Morley was not, however, a believer in the 'plenary inspiration of majorities' as the sole means of judging ideas. Obviously the initiatory élite had certain duties in the preparation and release of ideas for the consumption of the wider populace, but he believed that these were quite limited. He was therefore anxious to establish clearly for the élite the correct boundaries separating 'wise suspense' from 'unavowed disingenuousness' in forming ideas, 'wise reserve' from 'voluntary dissimulation' in expressing ideas, and 'wise tardiness' from 'indolence and pusillanimity' in trying to realize ideas. In establishing these three apparently clear-cut divisions Morley hoped to overcome the English propensity for politicizing speculation by showing intellectuals that only in the third category, the realization of opinion, could political considerations be legitimately introduced. He was trying to provide a workable formula specifying the proper degree of separation between the powers, intellectual and political, while yet providing for a reasonable linkage between them.[22]

In the first category, the formation of opinion, Morley claimed that there were no grounds whatsoever for withholding ideas at least for the intelligent man (and it is always to be remembered that Morley's strenuous advice is aimed entirely at the élite). It was his 'duty' to progress to have clear ideas, if only provisional ones, upon all the most important questions, and deliberately to prefer these ideas to their opposites. The implication that all opinions have clear opposites is a reminder of Morley's tendency to see opinion in simple terms of truth and error. Progress comes through confrontation of opposites; one must either be a clear liberal or a clear conservative. Morley sternly prods his readers into making up their minds, avoiding 'flaccid' latitudinarianism or 'slovenly' suspension of opinion. 'There are too many giggling epigrams,' he remarks sharply. But instead of analyzing the critical problem of transition from tentative idea to firm opinion, he offers only a hectoring rhetoric.[23]

130 Brains and Numbers

'We see in solution an immense number of notions which people think it quite unnecessary to precipitate in the form of convictions,' Morley remarks. Yet it is one thing to speculate on the possible benefits of an idea and quite another to go further and decide that it is 'true' and therefore socially desirable – this is necessarily to introduce the political element, to consider feasibility and expediency. Morley's artificially compartmentalized model of intellectual progress evades the matter, however. According to his rather crude rationalist psychology, the man of intelligence who brings his intelligence firmly to bear on a question will find the view which commands his assent and belief. And because belief is independent of the will, the rational man will believe rationally (belief in superstition being of course the result of an 'irrational state of mind'). Yet, Morley claimed, a belief can be at the same time both firmly and yet provisionally held. Thus earnestness of conviction is quite compatible with a sense of liability to error; nor does belief in one's own infallibility necessarily entail intolerance.[24]

It might be protested that Morley's intellectual élite is composed of rational supermen, intellectual schizoids who can seize an idea, translate it into a personal conviction, expound it vigorously, and yet be ready at all times to recognize its falseness, if necessary, and to yield to a rationally superior opposing view. Morley admitted that this was not 'the actual frame of mind of the ordinary man,' but he believed it attainable even by persons of 'far lower than first-rate capacity.' In fact, the intellectual demands upon the rational man were not as severe as one might think, because Morley believed that rational men would generally agree, since in most cases the choice was a simple one between contradictory ideas – indeed, between true and false. It was also usually a choice between old and new; the old being generally obstructive or erroneous, the new necessarily progressive. 'In all cases,' Morley wrote, the possession of a new idea, whether practical or speculative, only raises into definite speech what others have needed without being able to make their need articulate [my italics]. Morley believed firmly that truth was the daughter of time.[25]

Just as in the formation of opinion, so in the expression of opinion Morley's confidence in the rationalism of the élite enabled him to deny the necessity of reserve. The only area in which he allowed limits to freedom of speech was, interestingly, in the area of religion, where the possibility of inflicting distress on close relatives made certain allowances permissible; yet he believed that the progress of popular opinion would make even this type of reserve increasingly unnecessary.*

---

* An example of Morley confronting a practical 'case of conscience' is provided by a letter to Huxley, urging him not to publish one of the papers which he had read before the Metaphysical Society on the 'Evidence of the Miracle of the Resurrection' (L. Huxley, *Life of T.H. Huxley* (London 1900), I, 319), on account of its highly controversial nature: 'On the whole, though I am strong for the liberty of prophesying in all its forms

In the sphere of politics, however, no such allowances were required: 'In politics no one seriously contends that respect for the feelings and prejudices of other people requires us to be silent about our opinions.' Morley could say this because he was confident that 'in every stable society ... incessant discussion of the theoretical bases of the social union is naturally considered worse than idle.' Of course even a republican was perfectly free to declare himself in England (as a few of the more daring radicals were doing in the early 1870s); indeed Morley himself cautiously demonstrated this freedom by directing a few criticisms against the institution of monarchy. It is apparent, however, that he expected no new ideas to be aired in the realm of politics that would be any more disturbing than this, no challenges to the political judgment of the rational man any sterner than this. Such enormous confidence was possible in England in 1874. Ironically, in the realm of political speculation, Morley unconsciously rested his optimism on the very politicization of thought in England which suppressed truly subversive political ideas and gave the country its political stability. This was the very 'House of Commons view of life' against which he protested so vigorously elsewhere.[26]

It was in the realization of opinion that Morley admitted the need to allow for the awkward realities of human existence: 'To insist on a whole community being made at once to submit to the reign of new practices and new ideas which have just begun to commend themselves to the most advanced speculative intelligence of the time' – this even if possible would do much to make life impractical and promote the breakdown of society. In his final chapter on the realization of opinion he leaves the realm of the élite, of strenuous rationalism, and descends to the realm of the people to speak in a Burkean vein of prejudices and customs which may no longer accord with reality but which must be respected nonetheless for their historicity and for their strong hold on common minds. Not for the masses the cold baths of intellectual rationalism, but rather judicious gradualism. The progressive intellectual élite must always be in advance of the people; the gap between the acceptance of a new idea by the élite and its realization in the lives of the people is inevitable. But at this crucial point Morley's formulation breaks

and degrees, I think it would be wiser for your own peace and freedom from vexations and interruption to let it alone. The publicity of the club is not so great, after all. It only means a little band of experts and initiated and the discussions, though extremely important, because these experts and initiated are leaders of opinion, still will not reach the ears of the wide general public and above all, will not *face* that noisy, abusive and irrelevant criticism from the press, of which you have had such abundant taste before. It is one thing to discuss such a thing at a semi-private table, and another to throw it down like a gauntlet to the profane crowd' (9 Jan 1876), Huxley Papers, Archives of the Imperial College of Science and Technology, London). To court notoriety was, after all, to endanger one's ability effectively to influence public opinion. Morley did not offer this advice without much consideration as to the line between caution and cowardice.

down and he is unable to define the boundary between 'wise tardiness' in the realization of opinion and unwise tardiness. He does not clearly indicate either how to determine when an idea is ready for realization or what the appropriate means of realization are. We have now passed over the uncertain boundary and into the realm of political judgment, where even the hard light of truth flickers. Here the intellectual élite are excluded and the best Morley can offer them is to observe somewhat lamely that time is always ripe at least for the 'expression of the necessity' of realizing a new idea. [23]

It is unfair to hold against Morley his failure to rationalize the process of translation from idea to political reality, since it lay, as he recognized, in the realm of political judgment and beyond the criteria of his élite. New ideas were to be strenuously canvassed by the intellectual until a sufficient public opinion was created to move the politician to take the idea in hand. Apparently the intellectual could do little more. But this was enough, Morley felt, given his happy confidence that the élite had only to convince the people of the necessity of new truths, and not to dissuade them from succumbing to new errors. He was writing for his own time, a time when he believed one of the greatest needs of the nation was a smooth and predictable dialectic of change as an alternative to the confused sequence of recoil, prejudice, and expedient with which his countrymen usually responded to the demands of progress. Discussion of any issue tended to be dismissed as premature and a waste of time until either some unforeseen crisis, or else the normal course of events, presented it forcibly for resolution, at which time the results of inadequate consideration of the issue and insufficient preparation of opinion showed up in a botched or hasty settlement. By recognizing and promoting the normal operation of change instead of wilfully disregarding and damming its potential only to be compelled by its pent-up force ultimately to submit willy-nilly with makeshifts, the nation would enjoy the full benefits of the disciplined influence of the national intelligence.

'Nearly every Englishman with any ambition is a parliamentary candidate, actual or potential,' Morley pronounced in *Compromise*. Certainly the dominant political note of his last chapter suggests the direction of his own ambitions, for here he almost impatiently sweeps away the unsolved problem of the political role of the intellectual. If the book begins with rational analysis of the activities and duties of the men of ideas, it ends as a profession of faith. Thus he charges those who are reluctant to allow free play to the expression of opinions with an 'irrational want of faith in the self-protective quality of a highly developed and healthy community'; in using the term 'irrational' he of course begs the question. But he then makes a significant statement on the role of ideas in history which marks a striking shift in the balance of his own views. 'Moral and intellectual conditions are not the only forces in a community, nor are they even the most decisive,' he declares. To illustrate this he cites the history of slavery, and declares that in no case has slavery ever been abolished on purely moral or intellectual grounds while the institution was still economically viable (a view that is still very much open to dispute among historians). Similarly, he contends, it is a mistake to believe that the destructive criticism of the French philosophers was 'the great operative cause of the catastrophe which befel the old regime.' In fact Morley seems to suggest that it would have happened even had Voltaire, Diderot, and Rousseau never lived. Morley no longer seems to be addressing the intellectual élite who form the audience for his first chapters. Now he speaks of 'mere opinion' and stresses the importance of circumstances. Having told the élite that the welfare of society depends upon their forming and expressing clear ideas, he turns to the 'men of the world' to tell them they have nothing to fear from the intellectuals. It is as if Morley is now addressing the House of Commons. His closing remarks, however, are addressed to the élite and form a curious contrast with the strenuous injunctions of the previous chapters: 'It is better to wait and to defer the realization of our ideas until we can realize them fully, than to defraud the future by truncating them, if truncate them we must, in order to secure a partial triumph for them in the immediate present.' Such advice to keep ideas pure at all costs underlines Morley's failure to resolve the dilemma of the two powers. He ultimately acquiesces in the inviolability of Comte's separate spheres. Translated into political terms Morley's advice is 'the better is the enemy of the best' – which leads to the sterile politics of postponement. [28]

'I care less for these abstract things than I used to do,' Morley significantly remarked in 1876 to Harrison on leaning of his own election to the Metaphysical Society. Certainly he never again 'cast his thoughts into severe and philosophical shape' for publication on the level of *Compromise*. It was in this year that he published the last of his eighteenth-century French studies, 'Robespierre,' a work which is almost entirely political in contrast to his earlier works. Like Condorcet, Robespierre was an arch-doctrinaire in politics, but where Morley was fairly indulgent towards Condorcet, he shows Robespierre little mercy. Morley shared the tendency of nineteenth-century liberals to cast him in the role of the villain of the revolution, the man who directed it into illegitimate channels. But his treatment goes beyond this and seems to become self-exorcism, a ritual of purification preparatory to his own political career. He so heaps his subject with pejorative epithets – 'priest,' 'pedant,' 'doctrinaire,' 'phrase-monger' – that the reader almost forgets that Robespierre even more successfully than Condorcet rode – indeed, directed – the revolutionary whirlwind and that he was an able politician with a very acute 'eye for revolutionary methods.' Morley refers to the principles of his master, Rousseau, 'ever pouring like thin smoke among his ideas and clouding his view of actual conditions,' without granting their central importance to the very aims of the revolution. 'The pedant, cursed with the ambition to be a ruler of men is a curious study,' he writes; 'suspecting himself to be a theorist, he hastens to clear his character as a man of practice.' This is an acute, but very ironic observation. Morley the intellectual was so intent on displaying a hardheaded analysis of the mechanics of the revolution that he grossly neglected the ideological impulse which Robespierre embodied, and which, one suspects, he would have appreciated more keenly ten years earlier.[29]

When the first volume of Hippolyte Taine's *Les Origines de la France contemporaine* appeared in 1876 it was immediately and widely reviewed in England as a book which developed most explicitly the argument that the source of the revolution lay in the ideas and intellectual habits of the French thinkers of the eighteenth century. Morley took advantage of the occasion to attempt once again to formulate satisfactorily his own position on this crucial matter. Taine claimed scientific sanction for his historical interpretation; Morley challenged not only his interpretation but his credentials as a scientific historian and pronounced him a man of letters. He then boldly laid down the proposition 'that no good social history has ever been written by a man who has not either taken a more or less active part in public affairs, or has been an habitual intimate of persons who were taking such a part on a considerable scale' – such an active part conveniently included membership of the 'executive committee of a Union or League' (such as the National Education League, which had recently brought Morley into habitual intimacy with Joseph Chamberlain). Morley granted that Taine was not writing history in the ordinary sense, but even as a sociologist Taine showed 'the characteristic weaknesses of the book-man dealing with the facts of concrete sociology.' Morley again emphasized the paramountcy of the social circumstances over the intellectual in eighteenth-century France – the agricultural, financial, and institutional difficulties which received much less attention in his own earlier studies but were becoming progressively more significant in his mind. Ideas were not negligible but 'books and ideas acquired a certain importance after other things had finally broken up the crumbling system. They supplied a formula for the accomplished fact.'* Yet another way of escaping Comte and the problem of the intellectual in politics was to devalue the role of ideas in history.[30]

That Morley himself felt that the two powers, spiritual and temporal, were

---

* Morley subsequently made Taine's acquaintance. In 1892 he was chiding Taine on his despondency about the state of democracy in France: 'I hinted delicately and respectfully, as well I might, that he was too fastidious, as a man of letters was to be excused for being; that the wise politician does not believe that every problem has a solution, that politics are a second best' (*Recollections*, I, 301). This latter significantly became one of Morley's favourite sayings. No doubt it comforted him.

separated by a gulf which defeated the attempts of theory to span it seems to be borne out by the way in which he turned his back on the first part of his career. His two-volume *Recollections* are quite unusually reticent about the first half of his life and they deal almost entirely with his second career, as a politician. It is as if Morley considered himself twice-born. The former apostle of signed journalism said nothing about his two volumes of reprinted *Saturday Review* essays. The 1867 study of Burke was never reprinted in Morley's lifetime. Instead, he wrote a second study of Burke which appeared in 1879, from which the strong Comtist influence, and the ventriloquial agonizing over thought versus action, were expunged. But in spite of the failure of *Compromise* to formulate a 'rational' (in Morley's sense of the word) connection between politics and the intellectual, it does go far to define the essential outline of Morley's subsequent career. If clear principles could not of themselves summon realization, they were at the root of 'coherency of character,' which could in itself be a very real political force. Morley was at least such a man of character in politics, and was deservedly respected for this. But he strove to maintain that coherency of character by limiting his choice of political issues to those in which clear principles were possible, the large issues in which there appeared to be a true and a false, a right and a wrong, such as the great Irish issue.[31]

9

The Retreat from Politics:
Frederic Harrison

These philosophers, in order to preserve that breadth and generality of view which is their principal intellectual characteristic, must abstain scrupulously from all regular participation in practical affairs and especially from political life, on the ground that its specializing influence would soon impair their speculative capacity.

Auguste Comte, *A General View of Positivism*

The modern rebel is at least half acquiescence. He has developed a historic sense.

John Morley, 'Byron'

Morley suggested in *On Compromise* that the tension between speculation and politics amounted to a problem in cultural history: 'a society is seldom at the same time successfully energetic both in temporals and spirituals; seldom prosperous alike in seeking abstract truth and in nursing the political spirit,' he contended, implying that in Victorian England the preponderance lay decisively on the temporal side. This in itself could be taken as justification for Morley's retreat into politics. None was more sensible of this national characteristic than Frederic Harrison. In 1875 he published *Order and Progress*, an unjustly forgotten book which also originated in the *Fortnightly Review*. It is in many respects similar, if superior, to Morley's work. Neither offers a convincing theoretical solution to the problem of politics and the intellectual. Harrison made his own peace by retreating into the intransigent categories of Comtism which Morley attempted unsuccessfully to evade. But Harrison's analysis of the problem is more subtle than Morley's, particularly in his greater sensitivity to the irrational factors in modern mass politics and their implications for the exercise of political authority by élites.[1]

Order and Progress consists of two parts: the first part, 'Thoughts on the

Theory of Government' (the title is revealingly tentative), was written specifically for the book; the second, 'Studies of Political Crises,' is a collection, revised and condensed, of a number of Harrison's *Fortnightly* articles written between 1867 and 1874, the years which tested the hopes of academic radicalism. These articles are interesting not only as political analysis, however, but also as intellectual autobiography, revealing changes in Harrison's own political attitudes which brought him to terms with the basic conservatism both of Comtism and his own personality.

Even among university radicals Harrison's radicalism was of a particularly intellectual kind; it was the radicalism of the offended intellect unwilling to accept the flaws and lacunae endemic in the social structure and affronted by the lack of correspondence between reality and a compelling ideal. Harrison had become a radical in the undergraduate world of Oxford. Knowledge of the ideal largely preceded knowledge of the disparate reality. The Comtist vision of social order which Harrison embraced was a deeply conservative one, appealing primarily to the conservative temperament and life-style with its instinctive taste for order, hierarchy, and the overt acknowledgement of spiritual values in social arrangements.

But prior to 1867 Harrison's conservatism was somewhat blurred by his rhetoric. His pre-1867 writings emphasized the necessity for change – the alterations needed to prepare society for the advent of the positive stage – and the language of change and of movement, certainly in mid-Victorian England, was the language of the left. In using this language Harrison seems at times to have lost his political and even his ideological identity, confusing himself with those towards whom he was opposed in spirit. He was constantly finding himself yoked by a common rhetoric with those whose attitude and aims were basically alien to him, for he sought the terminal change necessary to create a static, organic society, what might be termed 'prospective conservatism,' while radical liberalism was more concerned with change as an ongoing process of indefinite improvement in an individualistic society.

Another reason for Harrison's political displacement lies in the non-political nature of Comtism itself. Comte did not make it easy for his disciples to decide where they belonged within the conventional political spectrum. On the one hand he spoke in his *Appeal to the Conservatives* (1855) of the 'mass of conservatives or retrogrades' as the true centre of positivism, while on the other hand referring to the dictatorship of the proletariat, though followers of Comte would search the sacred texts in vain for a clear statement of the circumstances precipitating this dictatorship. (Indeed, they would find other passages suggesting that such a development was by no means inevitable or necessary.) At least the Marxist was given some indication that certain economic processes and signs would herald the new order. No such objective guideposts were provided by Comte, who cared no more for economics than politics in the practical and immediate sense. It was in the more shadowy realm of morality that watch was to be kept by the Comtist vanguard for the portents of change. But the paradox of progress coming from the retrogrades was somewhat opaque. Then too there was Comte's ambiguous concept of 'modifiable fatality,' according to which the greater the complexity of society, the greater the scope for the modification in degree (though not in kind) of individual constituent phenomena within the determined overall framework. Such a concept, while perhaps sensible, certainly left the door open to dispersion of political effort. Comte was of course an élitist, but this too is an essentially apolitical doctrine, despite the common tendency to classify it as part of the conservative nexus. There is the conserving élitism of order and the innovating élitism of progress; there is also the élitism of distrust, pessimism, and coercion and that of optimism and consensus. Comtism cut through these categories at an unusual angle. Such considerations help to explain the anomalies of Harrison's political behaviour. As a Comtist at least he was a man lacking bearings within the traditional political landscape.[2]

The fluid political situation of the 1850s and 1860s provided an appropriate climate for the adoption of an apolitical creed such as Comte's. The prospects of non-institutional political activity were artificially enhanced by the Palmerstonian interlude at Westminster, and the period of political instability between Palmerston's death and Gladstone's electoral triumph of 1868 created a climate of uncertainty in which both large hopes and large fears about the prospects of democracy could be entertained. After 1868, however, the political temperature was definitely lowered and a measure of stability returned with the restoration of a fairly clear party situation. The immediate results of reform fell short of expectations among both the extreme optimists and the extreme pessimists. Yet the settlement of 1867 was clearly no settlement in the sense that its full consequences were capable of prediction. Its open-endedness was evident to all and there could be no such talk of 'finality' as had followed 1832. The hopeful uncertainty which had immediately preceded 1867 was replaced by a larger, if less immediate uncertainty. Such circumstances are usually conducive to a recoil among intellectuals from idealism to realism, as Morley pointed out in *Compromise*. Harrison's attitudes illustrate Morley's point, for after 1868 his own temperamental conservatism seems increasingly to inform his political views. Moreover, a more intimate acquaintance with Comte's writings seems also to have led him to a fuller appreciation of the conservatism of their message, and particularly of the pervasive spirit of quietism which they exude.[3]

Central to this spirit of withdrawal was the Comtist doctrine of the provisional. In an age of transition, according to Comte, the most notable characteristic of institutions and practices is their temporariness. 'In politics now there is but one thing settled, that is the provisional character of everything,' Harrison wrote in 1873. They were makeshifts sustaining the social fabric while the inward moral transformation took place which was the necessary preliminary to the final outward and visible institution of the positive order. The collected political essays which constitute the second part of *Order and Progress* reveal Harrison coming down gently but firmly on the side of acquiescence, albeit of a very sophisticated kind, in this interim status quo, and of reluctance to contemplate any shaking of the temporal arrangements while the spiritual reconstruction went forward.[4]

An important aspect of Harrison's retreat into realism is the anti-intellectual note which became increasingly evident in his political responses. Here again one is dealing with a mixture of ideology and personality. The general term 'anti-intellectualism' embraces a variety of distinct but related attitudes. On the one hand it may be critical or suspicious of rational intellectual processes – a variety of irrationalism. While Comtism is not strictly anti-rational, Comte was very conscious of the limits of the rational: herein lay much of the subtlety of his analysis of political and social behaviour. His opposition to what he labelled the 'metaphysical' – his intellectual agnosticism – was a deprecation of excessive speculation among intellectuals, of their obsession with questions which were unfruitful or unanswerable. Comte's epistemology, which owed much to the practical realism of the eighteenth-century French sensationalists, as H.B. Acton has shown, stressed the value of common reason, popular good sense, and the 'spontaneous advance of public reason' against the absurdities of metaphysics which he claimed were due in large measure to the excessive introspection of isolated thinkers. For Comte 'a healthy philosophy ... combines its highest speculations with the most simple popular notions so as to build up ... a profound mental identity which no longer allows the contemplative class to remain in its habitual proud isolation from the active mass.' This sort of populist rationalism, implying that the average person is capable of the rational thought necessary for almost all intellectual purposes, dates back at least to Descartes in French thought.[5]

The other basic variety of anti-intellectualism is more a social phenomenon, directed against the intellectual as a social type rather than against the operations of the intellect. This is usually the anti-intellectualism of the non-intellectual, suspicious or resentful of the proud, often privileged isolation of the intellectual's role and life-style. It was Comte's awareness of this phenomenon which made him so anxious to stress the similarities between the life-style of his own spiritual power and that of the proletariat in the positive society. But there is also the anti-intellectualism of the intellectual himself, most commonly manifested by the intellectual who enters or attempts to enter politics and tends to overcompensate for the popular view of the impractical, idealistic intellectual by erecting a hard, man-of-action facade and flaunting the rhetoric of tough-mindedness, prag-matism, and expediency. (Morley's subsequent political career provides numer-ous examples of this syndrome.) In Harrison's case it served a different purpose, however. Since he was both temperamentally disinclined and ideologically dis-barred from practical politics (in spite of his periodic flirtations with them), poli-tical anti-intellectualism provided a justification for his own abstention.[6]

The basis of Comte's political anti-intellectualism is his distinction between the science and the complementary art. Thus physiology is the science of the hu-man body, and medicine the corresponding art of treating it. Sociology is the ra-tional science of society, and politics – the realm of feeling, will, and action – is the art. Harrison strongly emphasized this Comtist doctrine in *Order and Progress*, disparaging 'bare intellectual vision,' and asserting that 'in politics we must ever distrust logic.' 'Politicians owe no explanations to pedants,' he wrote to Morley, whom he particularly discomfited with his Comtist denials of the political claims of intelligence; this was another of Comte's doctrines from which Morley absorbed a great deal without fully admitting it. It was this political anti-intellectualism which aroused such suspicions among critics like Matthew Arnold and Lord Ar-thur Russell, who misinterpreted Harrison's and Beesly's deprecation of the ra-tional faculty in politics as a sort of base populism, pandering to the common people. It was very far from being this, however.[7]

Not surprisingly, John Stuart Mill provided the touchstone of Harrison's poli-tical anti-intellectualism. Claiming that Mill best represented the 'inherently meta-physical and impotent nature of modern Radicalism,' Harrison expanded in a let-ter to Morley on the political wrong-headedness of such intellectuals: 'You ought not to reason about politics. The part of the intelligence is very small. It is only to enable you to express articulately your passions. Politics is a matter of feeling. Right feeling, trained, intelligently trained feeling I grant, but not of syllogism. Mill teaches you all to chop logic in politics, very good logic no doubt, but you ought to feel with the mysterious force of nature.' He contended that Mill was to the present generation of radicals what Bentham had been to the previous; the un-happy result was 'the politics of Rights – wrong from top to bottom.' Instead of healthy instincts and sympathies, it offered only 'dry jargon ... everlastingly er-going round and round its strong circle – rights of women, rights of prostitutes, rights of every man to his own bit of ground, rights of everybody to get up his own god, rights of everybody to bring everything to the pint measure of his own private judgement.' Harrison thus attributed the predominance of the two social theories which he (and Comte) most abhorred, *laissez-faire* and individualism, to their espousal and introduction into politics by intellectuals – the philosophic radicals. Harrison's equation of the intellectual with excessive individualism, with selfish disregard for the higher needs of the community, was a common characteristic of the organicist frame of mind in the late nineteenth century which revealed itself most clearly in that *locus classicus* of anti-intellectualism amongst the intellectuals - the Dreyfus Affair. (Though not himself an anti-Dreyfusard, Harrison was to have some problems of conscience with the affair as a Francophile and devout believer in *La Grande Nation*).[8]

Mill, the great example of the intellectual in politics in nineteenth-century England, was also the positivist heresiarch, for he had been exposed to Comte's teachings and had largely rejected them. During the 1830s, the zenith of philosophic radicalism, Mill had on occasion expressed a desire to be in Parliament with Hume, Grote, Molesworth, and his other friends. Writing to Comte in 1842 he acknowledged that the doctrine of the separation of the powers offered a 'theoretically perfect' solution to the traditional dilemma of the intellectual, but claimed that political circumstances in England made Parliament, despite Comte's objections, 'the best chair of public instruction for a sociological philosopher, suitably circumstanced.' Mill was not then so circumstanced, however, and by 1842 philosophical radicalism as an organized political force had spent itself. So, Mill continued: 'I am entering a period in my life in which I will be so placed, for the first time, to know to what point purely philosophical activity, directed according to my opinions and to the extent of my capacities, is capable in our country of giving a real influence over the march of ideas, at least among advanced men.' The experiment proved extraordinarily successful. Rarely if ever has a philosopher enjoyed such widespread prestige and influence in his own lifetime as Mill did from 1845 to 1870. Mill rejected the Comtist spiritual power as an actual institution because he believed that it would inevitably exercise an intellectual tyranny, but he continued to believe in the ideal of the separation of powers - that the intellectual should not normally exercise temporal authority. He justified his own parliamentary ambitions by maintaining that a philosopher could legitimately sit in Parliament since deliberative assemblies were not properly law-making bodies, being really organs of public opinion and thus conforming with Comte's definition of the intellectual's role.[9]

By 1865, however, Mill was discussing the prospect of 'forming a real advanced liberal party; which I have long been convinced, cannot be done except in the House of Commons.' His 1865 candidature and election were models of philosophic integrity and were greeted with enthusiasm, as we have seen, but his three years in Parliament disappointed many observers, though for different reasons. The very extent of his participation in Parliament shocked some, who apparently expected him to serve merely as an intellectual ornament, intervening rarely in debates with a lofty and non-partisan appeal to philosophic ideals. On the contrary he spoke often and to the point on contentious issues such as the cattle plague and the Hyde Park Affair, and the *Saturday Review* sternly criticized him for bringing 'intellectual culture' into disrepute as its 'greatest living representative' by jeopardizing his great influence for the position of a 'second-rate Parliamentary Radical.'[10]

When Harrison learned the results of the general election of 1874 he wrote immediately to Morley assigning much of the blame for the Tory victory to the recently deceased Mill:

If I were asked who intellectually has brought about this conservative Reaction I should say Mill, with his fierce crudities and unearned increment and heroic remedies and other social solvents which have deeply alarmed the sober and comfortable mind. Many of them are quite right and just in the intellectual domain. But I am not sure that the intrusion of these necessarily absolute and revolutionary ideas into the world of practical politics – signified by and dating from Mill's advent to Parliament, was not the immediate cause of the insurrection of Timidity, Stupidity and Selfishness which we have all witnessed. All this may be matter for reflection for you and me and all of us of the speculative order.

This election, in which Harrison, like most other political observers, had expected a Liberal victory was a great shock to him; yet it confirmed his Comtist interpretation of politics by proving the 'hollowness of democracy and all the old radical nostra.' The election had not been a matter of rational political issues after all, but of moods and prejudices. 'The real truth,' he remarked perceptively, 'is that which leaders like G. [ladstone] (but perhaps not Dizzy), party men, whips, journalists, theorists and all of us, you and I even, in spite of our quiet convictions to the contrary, forget – we all forget that the political portion of the electors is in ordinary times but *one tenth*; the other nine tenths vote under odd local, personal, class, "interest" and prejudice.' Part of Mill's baneful influence was to create an intellectualist bias that distorted intelligent men's understanding of political processes by encouraging them to see politics in terms of the rational behaviour of a model 'political man' registering his considered political judgments in the electoral marketplace – a counterpart of the rational 'economic man' of the classical theorists, and equally misleading.[11]

The 1874 election result, according to Harrison's acute instant analysis, was the product of factors such as lower middle-class fears about the erosion of their social differential *vis-à-vis* the artisan class, fears of the wealthy classes lest Gladstone's legislative zeal be directed against them in any way, the abstentions of offended sectaries, and the superior political organization of the Conservative party. Ideal political principles such as 'conservatism' or 'liberalism' played little role in such considerations. The greatest shock of 1874, however, was the discovery of that 'residuum' whose existence the academic radicals, unlike Lowe, and even

Bright, had blithely ignored in the confident flush of the 1860s. Here apparently were working men voting for the Tories, not those idealistic, idea-moved workers whom the academic radicals extolled in 1867, but unskilled workers vulnerable to the pressures of the publican, the clergyman, the employer. The historian J.R. Green, who, though he shared the education and interest of academic radicals, had a real knowledge of the lowest social strata as curate of an East End parish, had remarked in his review of *Essays on Reform:* 'What strikes us most about these essays is the unconsciousness they show of the existence of a class beneath the artisan.' According to Green's own observation there was 'a marked rift on either side of the artisan class, and it is deeper below than above; the artisan is really more connected in feeling and interest with the small shopkeeper than he is with the unskilled.' Harrison came to a similar conclusion by deduction from the 1874 election. While in 1868 he had claimed that there was 'no greater gap in our class hierarchy than that between the lowest of the propertied classes and the highest of the non-propertied classes,' by 1874 he was writing that 'throughout all English society there is no break more marked than that which in cities divides the skilled from the unskilled workmen.' It was these unskilled workers, different in 'temper, interest and intelligence,' who were, according to Harrison, voting for the Conservatives. [12]

Harrison also argued that the Liberal defeat signified a recoil from the legislative frenzy of Gladstone's first government. In 1867 Harrison had vehemently criticized the legislative poverty of Parliament during the previous two decades, but by 1874 he was speaking in disenchanted tones of the very possibilities of 'heroic' legislation: 'Men must feel how little Acts of Parliament correspond to changes in the life of the nation,' he observed. Political intellectualism, with its mechanistic faith in the power of legislation, was insensitive to the 'infinitely subtle and complex character of society as an organism.' Social reconstruction was not to be wrought by 'sensational legislation.' Harrison's remarks did not imply adherence to *laissez-faire*, for he was no opponent of greater state activity. Rather, they reflected the Comtist strategy which assessed legislation in terms of its potential for promoting or thwarting the advent of the positive order. Defensive and regulatory legislation, such as the Trade Union Act of 1871, was acceptable, since trade unionism promoted desirable proletarian attitudes; but land reform, which was becoming an increasingly attractive issue amongst advanced radicals in the 1870s, had socialistic implications – extensive and potentially disruptive redistribution of property – which made it, at the very least, 'unripe' for the field of practical politics. On matters of social reform legislation Comtism preferred the known status quo to unknown alternatives. [13]

1874 seemed to vindicate Harrison's Comtist views on the irrationalism of politics and to provide a salutary warning to intellectuals who saw politics and government as open fields for theorizing. At the time Harrison was writing the dominant tendency in England was still to confine political theorizing to the realm of 'rational' behaviour. Theories of political irrationalism were still largely inarticulate, with the exception perhaps of Bagehot. Carlyle and Ruskin, two prophets of the irrational by whom Harrison was deeply influenced, tended to confirm this situation with their oracular and unsystematized mental dispepsia. Thus Harrison was quite self-consciously anti-theoretical in formulating his own 'thoughts on the theory' of government. Present, though not fully articulate, in his mind were intuitions about such evolving phenomena of mass politics as the swing vote, the floating vote, and the negative vote which he was among the earliest to recognize. The very apoliticality of Comtism gave Harrison certain advantages as a political analyst, and if his attempt to reconcile the realities of post-1867 English politics with the ideal techniques promulgated by Comte for the management of the positive polity was ultimately unsuccessful, it was fruitful of some quite penetrating insights.

Harrison, like Comte, was a republican on principle. When Bagehot's *English Constitution* first appeared (also in the *Fortnightly*), Harrison was incensed by his 'nonsense' and hotly urged Beesly to take up his pen and pitch into the ' "theatrical" theory of monarchy' and show why the 'Constitution figment' was so demoralizing to the political tone of the country. The mythology of British politics which so amused the somewhat cynical Bagehot was a deep affront to Harrison; yet *Order and Progress*, an an exercise in political demythologization, merits comparison with Bagehot's more famous work. Like Bagehot, Harrison was interested in revealing that the bourgeoisie, not the aristocracy, were the hegemonic force in British politics, despite the facade of aristocratic institutions which disguised this fact. The British political system was 'possibly a plutocracy, but it is certainly - thank Cromwell - not a real aristocracy.'[14]

Nor was Britain in reality a monarchy. Here again Harrison agreed with Bagehot. The country was already a republic, though a very imperfect one, the political role of the crown being largely vestigial. The tests of the republican system, Harrison claimed, were 'that power rests on fitness to rule, that its sole avowed object is the public good, and that it is maintained by public opinion and not by force.' Such was the generally accepted ideal of the British nation; but in practice it was vitiated by a monarchy whose continued existence served to encourage attitudes - such as respect for birth, wealth, idleness, and luxury - which tainted the ideals of true republicanism. Thus Harrison parted with Bagehot over the value of the monarchy, since he could not accept his pragmatic justification for its existence. Of the argument that the crown was a symbol, a rallying-point standing above the conflict of partisan feeling, he observed darkly: 'The danger of relying on fictions which all know to be fictions is that in times of excitement they are utterly vain.' Harrison could not regard the crown as a useful deception suited to the political simplicity of the populace. While the cautious Bagehot did not think it wholly desirable to expose them to the stark light of political reality, in view of their growing political power, the more optimistic Harrison felt that such illusions were harmful to the moral and political development of the people.[15]

When Harrison first published his remarks on the monarchy in the *Fortnightly* (not long after Dilke's famous House of Commons motion questioning the civil list, and particularly the dowries of Victoria's daughters), he expressed rather exaggerated fears to Morley about the social ostracism which his 'Figaro of the monarchy' might bring him, though he had characteristically diluted it with an almost Disraelian apostrophe to Queen Victoria. Harrison later assured his readers that he deprecated any 'crude propaganda against the Monarchy, a movement which would lead us far out of politics into the whirlpool of social recrimination and possible civil war, and for which it must be allowed few parts of English society have the requisite civic education.' Like the abolition of the second chamber, in short, the monarchy issue was to be indefinitely deferred.*[16]

Another of the shams which clouded the view of political realities was 'parliamentarism ... the whole code of rules, ideas and ways which bear no relation to the art of government whatever,' a political counterpart to the elaborate and artificial forms of the mediaeval tournament. Harrison was particularly anxious that the working classes should not be drawn into its corrupting delusions and urged newly enfranchised voters in 1868 to 'purge the country of this deep-seated disorder' (though hastening to add that no one should imagine him to mean by this 'anything so preposterous as the destruction of the power of the House of Commons') because he saw in it a threat to their pristine political virtue. But even more important than the demoralizing effect of 'parliamentarism' was its great functional inefficiency. Harrison stood Bagehot on his head, claiming that much of the inadequacy of the House of Commons stemmed from the fact that it had become, in effect, 'a huge floating cabinet'; it had transformed itself into an executive, and its proper consultative function was being submerged by the executive and administrative functions which it had usurped. Thus Bagehot's 'efficient secret' of the English Constitution, the cabinet, was nullified. The House of Commons, by interfering in the process of legislation and government not only to control and direct the actions of ministers but to spend inordinate amount of time and energy in debating trivial points of administrative routine or legal nicety, had created an artificial and wasteful system which made a mockery of the very

---

* Harrison was friendly with Henry Ponsonby, the Queen's private secretary, and when invited to dine with him at Windsor Castle Harrison exclaimed to Morley: 'Imagine Mazzini dining with the Pope's chamberlain,' adding, 'But then, I am not Mazzini' (25 June 1873).

idea of an executive and of Parliament's proper role as an organ of national opinion.[17]

As an advocate of 'efficiency' in government Harrison expounded the managerial style of government characteristic of Comte and Saint-Simon – government by experts. This accorded with his own experience and that of his friends, many of whom were legal technicians, like himself, or administrative technicians like Godfrey Lushington, who became permanent secretary of the Home Office. Parliamentarism meant the interference of the inexpert and untrained in the arcana of government. Harrison rather simplisticly compared the ordinary statute to a marriage deed: properly drawn up neither should give rise to any difference of interpretation. But the skilfully prepared bill almost inevitably left the draughtsman's hands to be mutilated and rendered incoherent by committees and divisions of Parliament. Harrison's narrow view of legislation was well illustrated by his own proposed bill for the protection of trade unions (the basis for subsequent legislation) which was regulatory in intent and strictly limited in scope. It did not basically alter social and economic relationships and it was not sectarian. Harrison believed that it struck the proper balance between labour and capital, and that it would be unnecessary to go beyond it. The Comtist managerial state was one which would of course require no constructive legislation, where the political function would be almost entirely administrative. For anything short of either perfection or stasis, however, the managerial ideal was in itself inadequate. Yet, Harrison's remarks had point: the roles of politician and administrator in mid-Victorian England were still somewhat confused; the higher permanent civil service was only just finding its bearings as a separate, functional, non-political entity and the House of Commons was still emerging from the private member mentality. In an increasingly complex industrial society clearer functional definitions in government were necessary and managerial values at least had their place.[18]

An even greater sham than parliamentarism, though increasingly related to it in nineteenth-century England, was democracy. But when Harrison spoke of 'the bitter cup of pure democracy,' he is to be understood again within the Comtist context. The positive polity was non-democratic in the literal sense of denying the possibility or desirability of direct popular participation (or 'interference,' in Harrison's negatively loaded phrase) in government. There was of course to be popular influence over government of a most pervasive kind, but not government by the people in the strict sense. He opposed what he considered the democratic fallacy, with its denial of the need for leadership from an élite. He felt that it encouraged people to believe, just because they chose their governors, that their governors were on a level with them and that anyone was capable of governing. Democracy encouraged its representatives to propagate this illusion – this crude flattery of the people: 'Of all quacks distrust most those who tell you that it is an easy thing to govern a country such as ours,' Harrison warned. On the contrary, government was 'the most difficult art of all,' demanding the rarest of talents, that of being able to comprehend the most generalized unit of human existence – society. Such abilities were to be found only in the very few, and even these few required special training.[19]

As a consequence of this illusion it was considered 'a kind of treason against the public that any man should pretend to a governing position,' and the governors pretended that they did not govern. This was a contract of mutual delusion between rulers and ruled based on the wilful repudiation of reality by all concerned. In the actual practice of government, however, this fiction was dropped by politicians, since the realities of politics were a standing denial of it. But Harrison did not doubt that 'the prevalence of this tone vitally affects the creative energy and leading power of our statesmen and makes the public suspicious of the slightest indication of gifts, which are simply the test qualities of the real ruler.' On all sides the meaningless phrase 'self-government' was bandied about and nobody would come forward and state that government necessarily meant 'the direction of the inferior by the superior.' As it was, the rhetoric of non-government, added to the sham of 'parliamentarism,' gave Britain inefficient, amateur government. Instead of professional government by a skilled élite, there had evolved in England a 'special profession called public life,' the arts of which were a barren dexterity in the manipulation of illusions. In *Compromise* Morley decried the unwillingness of the nation's intellectual élite to accept the duty of leadership and their tendency to acquiese in the dictation of majorities even in the realm of thought. In *Order and Progress* Harrison charged the nation's political élite with dereliction of duty in the political sphere, where he detected a similar denial of the realities of leadership and a slovenly acceptance of fallacies pandering to the ignorant conceit of the ruled. He argued that this was wholly unnecessary, at least in the case of the newly enfranchised working classes, who were much more ready to recognize and accept leadership than were the middle classes. Indeed, he perceptively remarked that democracy was an essentially middle-class creed, since it was intimately connected with the selfish doctrines of individualism.[20]

Harrison was anxious to remind his countrymen that the exercise of leadership was necessarily personal and could not be dissolved into vestries, boards, and committees – Bagehot's 'green baize tables' – despite the mythology of English politics. Behind the veil of convention was the reality of the man. 'The famous automaton chessman' of the British Constitution was not an ingenious mechanism, but only an elaborate disguise for the concealed player. The trick, he declared, had been exposed once and for all in 1867 by Disraeli's single-handed conversion of the Tory party to Reform. But to speak of leadership in mid-Victorian England was necessarily to summon thoughts of Carlyle, whose vehement rhetoric of authority and anti-sham Harrison echoed in *Order and Progress*. Although Harrison was ready to use Carlyle's rhetorical coat-tails to ease Comte's passage into the English mind, he took pains to distinguish between the unordered inspirations of the poet and the systematic thoughts of the philosopher, particularly to contrast the moderation and commonsense of Comte with the 'sardonic maxims about "thirty millions mostly fools," "whiffs of grape shot," and all the other apologies for self will, violence and personal ambition' characteristic of the Sage of Chelsea (and also with the 'communistic, subversive, terrorist ideal' of Karl Marx). But in his earnest efforts to allay any fears which his readers might entertain about the revolutionary implications of Comtism he came perilously near to explaining his master into insignificance with the ultimate reassurance that Comte's 'entire teaching remains in the sphere of counsel, and not of enterprise.'[21]

The most significant difference between the élitist authoritarianism of Carlyle and that of Comte was that the rule of the Carlylean hero was sanctioned by an unchallengeable, transcendant individual right, assisted by force, while the rule of the Comtist patrician was sanctioned by public opinion which was to mediate all the operations of government and ensure that no aberrations of the human will would vitiate the system by the abuse of concentrated power. The genealogist of fascism might claim that Comte's enthusiasm for Louis Napoleon, a pioneer in the modern techniques of manipulating public opinion for authoritarian purposes, indicated unhealthy tendencies. But while Harrison's 'minister of Public Opinion' might to our ears sound uncomfortably like 'minister of propaganda,' it should be noted that all the English Comtists, though theoretically illiberal, or anti-liberal in the strict sense, were in the context of their times very sound liberals indeed. Liberalism was their interim creed. If they rejected the literal principle of representative democracy as alien to the genius of Comtism, which rejected the notion of the inferior choosing the superior, they accepted it as realists of their time and place.

Harrison rejected democracy as a functional concept. As an effective mode of government, genuine rule by the people was impossible for him to conceive: it could not work. In this he was not perhaps so different from many Victorian liberals or radicals. Where he differed was in clear-sightedly recognizing and rejecting the deceptions – 'myths,' as Gaetano Mosca was later to call them – such as 'political equality' and 'majority rule,' by which the appearances of democracy would increasingly be sustained in a mass society in order to obscure the very different political realities. Thus Harrison avoided the casuistry of 'democratic élitism' which has since his time been incorporated into the 'science' of politics. The notion that mass apathy is desirable in a democratic system is a good contemporary example of what Morley referred to as 'dual doctrine.' Harrison's goals were similar to those of the modern democratic élitists – a system of political equilibrium, but he recognized that the rhetoric of democratic mythology could arouse dangerous expectations which political realities had no means of fulfilling. The Comtist motto 'live openly' enjoined frank élitism rather than the covert variety.[22]

But Harrison also had no use for the other interpretation of democracy, the normative, Millite interpretation which values it chiefly as a means of promoting the self-development of the citizen, as primarily an educational process which elevates and enhances the moral status of the individual. Comte's whole social organization, after all, was largely designed so as to achieve these desirable ends through other means, through the educational functions of the spiritual élite which did so on an organic rather than an individualistic basis. From the Comtist standpoint the Millite conception of democracy was basically flawed in confusing the spiritual function, education, with the temporal function, efficient government, which should be kept separate. And as for the democratic function of choosing between competing political élites, Comtism left no need for this, since it assumed a non-pluralistic society, with a single, unitary élite. Harrison was an anti-democrat, then, because he believed that Comte's system offered an ideally superior means of realizing through public opinion the ends which democracy sought through inefficient, inorganic, mechanical techniques. It was a commonplace of mid-Victorian politics that public opinion was of primary importance and that the function of Parliament was somehow both to mirror it in administration and to embody it into legislation. Intellectual radicals were its enthusiasts because they saw public opinion as a potential means of promoting their own national concerns. Yet public opinion remained largely in the realm of political mythology because it tended to be left unanalyzed and undefined. Among the most interesting and successful parts of *Order and Progress* are those where Harrison attempts to apply the Comtist ideal of public opinion to the mid-Victorian reality. Here the tension between the real and the ideal produces some very acute analysis.[23]

Harrison rejected the pretence that public opinion was reflected by Parliament, though he felt that Parliament could become a useful instrument for this purpose if it were to renounce its false claims to the executive function and return to 'its natural place as the Great Council of the nation.' In existing circumstances the public opinion which it purported to represent was in fact an artificial creation nurtured in the hermetic realm of Westminster and bearing little relation to the 'opinion of the country.' Even journalism, potentially 'the one organized spiritual power for counsel, progress and justice,' was in fact little more than an 'appendage of the Commons' because the leading journals identified themselves so closely with parliamentary parties and tended to propagate the false perspectives inherent in the parliamentary point of view. Harrison was perceptive in criticizing the tremendous hold that Parliament had over the political imagination in mid-Victorian England. The rapidly expanding press, still relatively unsophisticated in its appreciation of the nature of public opinion, and even less sophisticated in its ability to assess it, tended to focus attention on Parliament all the more, magnifying this national obsession and further limiting other political perspectives. Dismissing this crude Westminster-cum-Fleet Street notion of public opinion, Harrison offered instead a much more realistic approach in stressing its protean nature as 'a power which must be seen in many aspects and through a multitude of channels, which no single institution can exclusively express, and which is best felt by the instincts of a competent statesman, when brought face to face with it directly, and made responsible to it immediately.' Public opinion, 'the most subtle and elastic of all vital forces,' was necessarily vitiated and rendered lifeless by attempts to stereotype it, or to reflect it by mechanical means such as suffrage. Such methods were necessarily at odds with its organic nature. Thus Harrison objected to almost all theoretical plans for improving the suffrage 'because they inevitably erred in the assumption that the object is to get at the *independent* opinion of individual voters.' He rightly saw that the essential validity of the concept of mass public opinion lay in the wholeness which made it qualitatively different from the simple sum of its parts.[24]

Public opinion, because it had political relevance only insofar as it had this quality of coherence, had therefore to be made. It did not simply happen, as the popular democratic mythology tended to imply. 'There will, in fact, be nothing that can be really called opinion in the majority until combination and political agitation have begun, and have welded a more or less collective opinion,' Harrison stated. Herein lay the importance of leadership which the democratic mythology conspired to deny. On most questions the majority have no opinion, lacking the means to form one. But leadership could create opinion, not only through the process by which weak wills tend to gravitate towards stronger wills but also through the phenomenon of passive acceptance. Calling attention to the important distinction between what men do, or will allow others to do, and what they say should be done, Harrison discriminated between what he called 'the effective or real majority in force' and 'the numerical majority, or mere numbers,' in order to correct the common tendency to identify public opinion with crude enumeration. The effective majority he defined as 'that section of any community or social aggregate which for the matter in hand outweighs the remainder.' Influence, resources, and force of conviction, more than mere weight of numbers, were the sources of its preeminence. Practically all great achievements were the work of minorities who were able initially to lead the numerical majority in passive adhesion, but ultimately to convert that passive adhesion into reasoned concurrence. Thus, 'the keynote of an effective majority is that it is always becoming a numerical majority.'[25]

Harrison believed that one of the weaknesses of the existing political system was that it was founded upon a false identification of the suffrage with public opinion. This again was part of the fallacious rationalist-individualist view of political behaviour which assumed a sort of Arcadian polity of perfect individual representation. Voting was not the private intellectual operation of representational calculus that the Millites tended to assume. It was essentially a public act reflecting as much outside influences upon the individual, national moods, and the opinions of others, as it did personal opinions. It was in fact an act of acquiescence in one candidate or another, since so much of the political process, the power of formulation of issues, and selection of candidates lay outside the mechanism of the suffrage and hence the power of the voter. An election, even freed of all corrupt practice and electoral coercion, could never be an absolutely free expression of individual opinions since its most important features were decided 'not by those who give, but by those who take the vote.' Elections were not a means of determining public opinion but only a very crude register of public consent. Thus, what mattered most was not the actual election, Harrison argued, but the political campaign preceding it. Under the existing system it was 'that one feature, the agitation and the contest in the collective body, with its verdict of practical force, which gives to the voting process any reality at all.' Voting was mere head-counting; it was the campaign which gave power to the effective majorities, providing the real test of the balance of political forces which the vote merely registered.[26]

It is hardly surprising in the light of these views that Harrison vehemently repudiated the intellectualist ideal of minority representation, which tended to elevate voting into an entirely individual act with each voter acting as if he were the sole voter and the election depended upon his vote alone. Hare's elaborate scheme of multiple minority preferences, by removing elections to the realm of the study, repudiated the collective contest of forces which was the only true test of the effective balance of political forces. Highly intelligent voters, being much more likely to diverge in their opinions than the ordinary voters, were all the more in need of the discipline of collectivist tests. Proportional representation denied the organic nature of public opinion; it was the apothesis of the arithmetic, head-counting conception of public opinion. It followed that Harrison was no admirer of the secret ballot, because it too smacked of anti-organic individualism. He preferred the face-to-face confrontation of open voting where the vote of the man of intelligence and principle could attract others.[27]

Most thinking Victorians, even those of the liberal persuasion, were hostile to the idea of political campaigns, which they equated with the populist excesses of the United States. Harrison himself sensed the growing dangers of 'demonstrations' and deprecated the prevalence of 'idle crowding,' stimulated by the mass press which thrived on creating artificial mob enthusiasms. But this was not true public opinion. No political arguments could be drawn from such inorganic crowds. 'We might as well study the public opinion of sheep jamming through gates. Whole droves of these baa-lambs might be turned by two resolute men,' Harrison warned. Yet he claimed that many of the truths which he stated about political campaigns were already tacitly recognized by politicians, particularly by Disraeli. Party agents were increasingly winning elections in Britain rather than the candidates themselves. Paradoxically, Harrison argued that it was the election which corrupted the campaign rather than the campaign that corrupted the election. In the ideal polity there would be just the campaign, though refined and continuous in operation; its sole object would be to educate and crystallize public opinion, uncorrupted by the ambitions of politicians seeking to turn it to their own private ends. In the present reality, however, the election was an unfortunate necessity, and even the more 'vigorous' electoral techniques had a certain justification since they were valid evidence of political skill and force which, after all, it was the purpose of the election to register. Harrison believed that even the existing state would benefit from a clearing away of the individualist, intellectualist illusions, the debris of a pre-democratic era, which shrouded the realities of mass politics and mass public opinion.[28]

Significantly, it was Gladstone and the Irish disestablishment issue which Harrison cited to show the true manner in which public opinion becomes a political force in the hands of a genuine intuitive politician: 'Mr. Gladstone was but the nucleus of a floating body of opinion, long gathering and still to gather round such questions; the purpose which a generation or two had held in solution rapidly crystallized around the point presented by his initiative, and the whole movement followed, the national will taking form in the energy of one representative brain.' Mr Gladstone gave further point to Harrison's remarks about the primacy of the campaign in Midlothian, a few years later.[29]

Although both *Order and Progress* and *On Compromise* are élitist manifestoes, they reflect the differences in personality and circumstances of their authors. These differences show most clearly in their approaches to the problem of public opinion and change. Both Harrison and Morley saw in public opinion a force which could both facilitate and legitimize the leadership of the best men. Morley, however, was interested in public opinion as an agent of change under the existing political dispensation. He consequently attempted to formulate rules for its operation in order to point out how and where an intellectual élite could best exercise its leadership in order to bring about the alterations in national opinion which were the necessary preliminary to political change, and therefore to ordered and effective progress. Harrison, for all his perception and the subtlety of his analysis of public opinion, gave no such prescription for the process of change.

Thus the very title of his book (which was Comte's political motto) embodies the dilemma of his political philosophy. Between 'order' and 'progress' the neutral connective 'and' is merely a static link underlining his failure to achieve any successful interaction between the two desired ends. Harrison was capable of searching analysis of the realities of government as they existed in his own time, effectively pointing up the inadequacies of institutions and exposing the conventions and illusions which underlay them. As an iconoclast and élitist he offered a compelling critique of what, anticipating his present-day counterparts, he referred to as 'the system.' Yet, on closer examination, the alternatives continually dissolve into aspirations and one detects at a deeper level an implicit apology for the status quo.

Harrison's retreat into realism was a decision to come to terms with the disparity between the facts of politics as he so clearly recognized them and the ideal system which Comte held forth – a decision to recognize their irreconcilability and to acquiesce in a sort of dualistic viewpoint which involved on the one hand ideal criticism and on the other, effective acceptance. This sort of compartmentalization was the necessary consequence of adopting Comte's view of the intellectual's role and attempting to apply it to non-Comtist reality. In *Order and Progress* Harrison described his task as 'endeavouring from a basis of general principle to estimate the situation of the day.' This left him considerable scope for 'unaided judgment,' he claimed, and it was therefore not a 'hopeless or mistaken task' to attempt to examine and interpret public affairs from a Comtist viewpoint. Yet the view which he privately expressed to Morley in announcing his decision to discontinue his *Fortnightly* series reflected more accurately his real belief: 'Constant treating of politics from my point of view in our actual world is ... impossible.' He had decided henceforward to devote his attention to the study of Comte's writings. The publication of *Order and Progress* can therefore be seen as the seal upon a phase of Harrison's life.[30]

Comte's ability to deal systematically with contemporary political and social development, insofar as he dealt with them at all, was greatly enhanced by the regime of 'cerebral hygiene' which he practised during the second half of his life. He apparently did not open any political, or even scientific, journals of any kind, nor did he read books by contemporary writers (what reading he did was largely confined to the one hundred and fifty Great Books of Western Civilization which comprised his optimistically titled 'Proletarian Library,' a collection of works, literary, philosophical, historical, and scientific, providing the requisite background to the positive synthesis). He was not entirely cut off, for he had numerous informed correspondents, such as Mill, with whom he discussed contemporary affairs. However, the awkward task of aligning abstraction and actuality, particularly difficult given the political situation of France, doubtless went more smoothly in such relative freedom from distraction. This method of coping with his milieu emphasizes Comte's non-political nature. But Frederic Harrison was incapable of such prodigies of abstention, living very much in the world and being voracious of books and periodicals. He was compelled to take cognizance of the stubborn evidence of events, political and social, however inconvenient. The tactic of the provisional, and the related tactic of postponement (by which Harrison preserved his principles by projecting them into the indefinite future), were his chief means of doing this.

It is tempting to compare Comte with Marx in a number of ways, but one that seems particularly relevant here is their overmastering concern with the grand pattern, the larger dialectic extending over epochs, and their common impatience with the particulars of contemporary history. Marx, whose system required a dialectical unity of theory and practice, gave at least some attention to these particulars; Comte tended to ignore them. Marx's tactical contradictions are notorious, yet his ideology survives: Comte largely avoided such contradictions, yet his ideology is dead. Marx was of course extremely fortunate in having an intimate practical partner, as Theodor Schieder has remarked, who was much nearer than he to 'real events' and whose writings on tactics (notably the preface to *Class Struggles in France*) have had greater practical influence. One wonders what might have happened if Comte had had a Frederick Engels to improve his communications with the outside world – a Frederic Harrison perhaps.[31]

Epilogue: Innocence and Experience

The Lord Chancellor Bacon has told us that there is one and but one infallible source of political prophecy, the knowledge of the predominant opinions and speculative principles of men in general between the ages of twenty and thirty.

S.T. Coleridge, *Statesman's Manual*

Youth rules the world, but only when it is no longer young.

Randolph Bourne, *Youth and Life*

'In common language we speak of a generation as something possessed of a kind of exact unity with all its parts and members one and homogeneous. Yet very plainly, it is not this.' Each generation has its leaders, Morley claimed. The university radicals of the 1840s and 1850s saw themselves as just such leaders. They were a separate 'generation unit,' to use Mannheim's term, conscious of being in the van of their larger generation. Youth and political innocence were important sources of their identity and coherence. This study has attempted to describe the interaction between aspirations and realities that gave their creed of intellectual populism its distinctive flavour. It has dealt with a period of preparation and formulation of political responses, two of the most clearly defined being provided by Frederic Harrison and John Morley. The study ends, therefore, at the point where the preparation was effectively completed. One must necessarily be rather arbitrary in applying the historian's tourniquet in a study dealing with such intangibles as generation, aspiration, youth, and social and intellectual status. The careers of Harrison and Morley particularly justify the choice of the mid-1870s for this purpose. Yet the individuals lived on (a disproportionate number to a very old age), and something must therefore be said of the diaspora of their generation.

The precarious unity of the English Comtist movement was broken in 1878 by a split between the 'high' creed of Congreve and the 'broad creed' of Harrison, Beesly, and Bridges, the latter group being compelled to found a separate spiritual centre which they called Newton Hall, while Congreve, finally rid of the 'university coterie' who had long conspired, he believed, to thwart his authority, was able to give free rein to his sacerdotal pretensions. The unedifying circumstances which precipitated this schism have been well described by W.M. Simon; these, as well as the heroic task of translating the *Politique positive*, provided a considerable distraction from wider affairs for the Comtists. Harrison threw himself into the activities of Newton Hall, where he was much the most active lecturer among its members. The law was another continuing interest for Harrison; after ceasing to practise as a barrister he turned to teaching law and to the study, particularly, of Roman law (to which he had been introduced by Henry Maine). In 1873 he was selected as an examiner of Lincoln's Inn – professing surprise that his notoriety did not bar him from this responsible post. Four years later he became professor of jurisprudence and international law to the Inns of Courts.[1]

Harrison's interest in politics did not flag. Developments in trade unionism, the ascendancy of a new generation of labour leaders with whom the Comtists had few personal links, and changing attitudes (particularly towards socialism) within the labour movement with which the Comtists were increasingly out of sympathy placed Harrison more and more in the position of onlooker. Without the platform of the *Bee-Hive* his pronouncements on labour questions had to be confined to the heavy reviews and private pamphlets. It was, however, the imperial question, both in Ireland and overseas, that came to engross Harrison's attention most of all: the congruence of Comtism with anti-imperialism has already been noticed. The last quarter of the century provided causes and issues that matched the requirements of Harrison's political situation. They occupied that realm in which moral fervour could obscure the gap between the real and the ideal, and they were concerned with matters that did not threaten the line of advance towards the positive polity (unlike issues which touched on the structure of society: economic redistribution and other awkward matters) – they were national issues rather than class issues. Again the lectures and pamphlets of the Positivist Society were the organ of his views, in accordance with Comte's strictures on how to influence public opinion. But here he could also look to his extra-Comtist connections. Beatrice Webb referred to Harrison as 'a full-fledged member of political society,' who was much in evidence at the social functions of the Gladstone administration of 1880–6, particularly through his personal friendship with rising men like Morley, Dilke, and Chamberlain. Here perhaps was the real key to influencing events. Comte himself, after all, had only turned to the proletariat because the élite paid him no heed. When his friend Lord Lytton was viceroy of India from 1876 to 1880 Harrison had an ear for his anti-colonial views in the highest places. But an excerpt from one of Lytton's letters indicates the discouraging nature of the response:

There are only two conditions of power – action and criticism. Each has advantages and privileges peculiar to itself. There is a power in criticising the action of others, and a power in acting *maugre* the criticism of others ... those who have done nothing have the privilege of finding fault with all that has been done, a privilege I by no means despise, for it is sometimes useful and generally enjoyable. Every man's ideal 'Right' is somebody else's ideal 'Wrong,' and a hundred years hence which of us (I or my critics) will be the better for your Credo (if it be more than a Credo) in posthumous vicarious vitality? For my own part, I care not a damn.[2]

Harrison filled the role which the society he belonged to reserved for people like himself – not quite a full eccentric, perhaps, but a licensed irregular whose views were treated with the respect due to his sincerity, intelligence, and education, as well as his means and his numerous and important personal connections. One might compare him, for instance, with his friend Wilfrid Scawen Blunt, the knight-errant of anti-colonialism and gadfly of the Foreign Office. The two men largely agreed on foreign affairs until just before the First World War, when Harrison's Germanophobia brought him at last into agreement with popular sentiments. Harrison was not the man of action that Blunt was; unlike the latter, for instance, he never found himself imprisoned for his activities in opposition to government policies, whatever may have been his youthful fantasies. Nor was his social status quite on a par with Blunt's; yet both were dissenters who could still remain within the pale because it was recognized that they gave explicit acquiescence to the system. Harrison's politics were basically the politics of the major premise. Politicians deal with the minor – thus Harrison was, and was known to be, no serious politician. But he was by admission no revolutionary either: he was thus unobjectionable. Comtism no longer held any terrors for the press either. In 1877 the *Spectator* remarked that it united 'all the pleasures of aristocratic scepticism with all the pleasures of a glowing faith ... all the advantages of caste government with all the advantages of popular liberty.' This was indeed an acute analysis of Comtism's appeal to its English disciples.[3]

'I always feel myself a politician who occasionally takes up a pen for a purpose, and amongst you and your mates I instinctively feel myself an amateur amongst professionals,' Harrison wrote to Morley in 1873. In this same year he wrote in the *Fortnightly* a lofty dismissal of both politics and journalism remarking disdainfully *à propos* of political journalism: 'One must be to the manner born, one must be of the journalistic claque to follow with triumph or despair the move of every pawn on the board.' The *Spectator* picked up his point and flung it back at him, agreeing that Harrison was 'in no very serious sense a journalist ... Those who have done much of the steady pulling work of journalism, or have felt its grave responsibilities, outgrow that particular tone which makes a man an oracle among political undergraduates.' He was neither professional journalist nor politician. Yet organs like the *Spectator, Pall Mall Gazette, Times*, and *Saturday Review* tended generally, and increasingly, to treat him with genial (if slightly patronizing) respect. Thus the *Spectator* classed him with men like Froude, Arnold, and Carlyle, men whose work was that of the harrow, neither ploughing, sowing, nor reaping but helping to 'break up hard soil' - 'always read, and never followed,' fulfilling a social function nevertheless. The comparison with the harrow is apt, expressive at once of utility and sterility; the effect of such an implement is difficult to judge.[4]

From Harrison, as from Comte, little of apparent consequence sprang directly. In England the Comtist movement declined with its founders. Yet numerous and influential people came into contact with and were influenced by the English Comtists - Patrick Geddes, Charles Booth, Beatrice Webb, and Sydney Olivier among them. It is possible that the very limitations of the Comtists inspired many to try other avenues of approach to the problems of society. The politics of Comtism were walled-in behind an impractical vision of total change that effectively imposed upon them a policy of quietism. Fabianism, in contrast, was essentially an inversion of this attitude, making a virtue, almost, of its preoccupation with the minor premises of social change. Yet there was much in the Fabian style that was akin to that of the Comtists, particularly its confident, crypto-establishment manner and its tactical dexterity. The sociological dilettantism of the English Comtists may have inspired men like Booth and Geddes to more systematic and practical studies of social organization (although both went to extremes themselves, Booth choking on the sheer volume of factual information he collected and Geddes carried away with his obscure diagrams of social processes). But the unacademic, amateur character of the Comtists was probably one factor in the unduly prolonged non-professionalism of English sociology. Philip Abrams, who has remarked on this phenomenon, attributes considerable influence to Comte in the development of English sociology. That this influence has been underrated, and even denied, may paradoxically be partly due to the zeal of the Comtists, Harrison particularly, in detecting a Comtist *malgré lui* in practically every eminent late-Victorian thinker, thereby compelling many of them to issue sweeping denials lest they be suspected of sympathy for Comte's religious or political fantasies.[5]

At the age of eighty-six Harrison summed up his life for a lady correspondent:

'People here in Bath have no idea of what I am or have done or written ... I have tried every thing – have been an alderman, J.P., L.L.D., D.C.L., a horseman from boyhood, a swimmer, a mountaineer, a waltzer, a card player, a diner out, member of a dozen clubs, a man about town, a park revolutionary orator ... I have tried all these things in an amateurish way, and have been a failure in all, merely just trying them and turning to something else. Never succeeding in any one. Scholars call me a rank amateur, and politicians regard me as a rank outsider.' Whether from an excess of self-effacement or self-pity Harrison hardly did credit to his own achievements. Realist that he was, however, he did recognize the keynote of his career – amateurism. To summarize the second part of Harrison's long and varied life in a few words is difficult and almost necessarily does him injustice, even though these were not his years of achievement in the political sphere. Harrison was notably successful in arming himself with what David Riesman has called the 'nerve of failure' – that psychological mechanism which enables a man to face defeat and the loneliness of being in a minority without being destroyed by them. According to his son he kept the world at bay with a 'menacing optimism.' His friends marvelled at the fact that he never (so he claimed) had a pain or ache or sleepless night in his life – nor even dreamed! His determined personal conventionality in many areas of his life, and his ideological use of the tactic of postponement in saving his Comtist creed, were also a part of this mechanism. As a failure, at least, he was a marked success. Lytton was moved to verse by the 'high minded Harrison':

> Whose manners are mild as his pen is audacious,
> And whose wife is so pretty, so clever, so gracious,
> That were I in his place ('tis a figure of speech, Sir)
> I'd wish things to remain as they are.

Frederic Harrison deserved credit, in spite of all his advantages, for the considerable achievement of living a life that exemplified the individual integrity which was central to the Comtist prescription for social regeneration.[6]

Even to attempt to summarize the second part of Morley's life is impossible. The mid-1870s marked only the shift in the balance of his career from the literary to the political, yet even his political career cannot be comprehended unless one recognizes that the scales never settled decisively on the latter side. The element of tension remained to inform most of his political life. This element was to be found in the careers of practically all of the university radicals who went into Parliament. Morley was particularly sensitive to being regarded by other politicians as rather an exotic. Inevitably his stature as a man of letters, and particularly his

writings on eighteenth-century France, the age of ideologue, led to his being identified with the French 'man of letters in politics.' When G.J. Goschen (who as an
undergraduate had moved at the Oxford Union that the French Revolution had
'conferred the greatest benefits on mankind') referred to him in connection with
the Irish question as the 'Saint-Just of our Revolution,' Morley was quick to remark on the 'frivolity' and 'dilettantism' of comparisons between Ireland in 1888
and France in 1789. 'For the practical politician, his problem is always individual,'
Morley sternly pronounced. When Balfour chided him in a debating exchange in
the Commons, saying he preferred Morley when he was writing history rather
than making it, Morley replied that he had long known that three qualities were
essential to the politician - 'a strong heart, a cool head, and a thick skin.' Unfortunately he lacked the last of these and felt such barbs keenly.[7]

Morley strove to achieve the outward manner of the Carlylean man of action.
When Thomas Hardy asked him (by then Lord Morley) at a Downing Street party
what books he had been reading lately, he replied loftily, 'I never read anything.'
But between intervals in office he occupied himself in writing biographies of the
arch-politician, Walpole; the arch-man of action, Cromwell; and the man who synthesized the virtues of both (and added others) - Gladstone. Morley's own greatest opportunity for political achievement was his tenure of the India Office,
1906-10 (his three-and-a-half years' tenure of the Irish secretaryship under Gladstone and Rosebery being vitiated by the political impossibility of instituting
Home Rule at that time), and here he disappointed many who had expected
great reforms from him. Some felt that his very desire to live up to the man-of-
action ideal impaired him in his dealings with India. Yet it was almost inevitable
that his political career should be lamented as that of a fallen angel. The hopes
pinned to him by other intellectuals and reformers were perhaps excessive, and
the standards against which he was judged, both by his supporters and detractors,
were more rigorous than those applied to more 'normal' politicians. That this was
so was in a sense a compliment to him. Expectations apart, however, there is
something unsatisfactory about Morley's career - a certain dead-endedness. A
fervent exponent of the apostolic succession of generation-élites, he seems to have
had little to hand on to his successors except, like Harrison, his example.[8]

In a very real sense, however, the broad outlines of Morley's political career
took a fairly simple form. Like Harrison, he was a natural disciple. Harrison found
his master in Comte early in his career, a master who provided those larger verities that enabled him to move with a certain assurance through the uncertainties
- political, social, and intellectual - which cast shadows across the late-Victorian
landscape. Morley's search was not ended quite so soon. Carlyle, Comte, and
Mill, but also Chamberlain and Gladstone, were the great figures in his intellectual and political pantheon. He proclaimed in 1890: 'Two men made me - John

Stuart Mill and Mr. Gladstone,' thus citing a spiritual and a temporal master. By this time he had rejected the others – consciously, at least. Yet of the rejected prophets it was Comte who had provided the conceptual framework within which Morley had worked out his decision towards politics, and it was Chamberlain who initiated him in those mysteries of political instinct and intuition which according to Comte were beyond the apprehension of those belonging by nature to the 'spiritual power.' In a way Morley demonstrated the value of Comte's insight, since he was never really able to follow in the sinuous wake of Chamberlain's radicalism, a radicalism far from academic. The bold strokes of Chamberlain rather frightened Morley and it was with some relief that he took shelter under 'the Gladstone umbrella.' Here, in the mid-1880s, he found the combination that satisfied his needs, political, intellectual, and emotional: the one great man and the one great issue – Gladstone and Home Rule. Here were Morley's larger verities. Like Harrison, Morley found satisfaction in great national issues which filled the requirements of academic radicalism by transcending class interests and appealing to the higher morality of the nation. Such issues were the imperial issues. Despite their different paths, Harrison and Morley continued to share similar preoccupations.[9]

Morley saw his liberalism as an amalgam of Gladstone and Mill. But in Gladstone one sees not so much the temporal embodiment of the Millite ideal as that of the Comtist ideal for, without being in any conscious way a Comtist, Gladstone did in many respects fulfil the requirements of the Comtist formula for political leadership. Gladstone was the first great 'minister of public opinion.' At a time when Gladstone was himself only just becoming conscious of it, R.H. Hutton perceptively described his oratorical skill as an instinctive ability for 'returning to his audience in flood what he receives from them in vapour.' The metaphor is an apt one, for Gladatone's political method was founded on a certain faith in popular inspiration. He had a keen sense of timing and saw politics as a process in which matters reach a sort of critical point of saturation in the political atmosphere – a point which the politician must be able to detect, when his intervention can effect the crystallization of an issue in its politically viable form. The disestablishment of the Irish church provided one example of what Gladstone himself – echoing strikingly Harrison's earlier assessment – spoke of as his 'insight into the facts of particular eras and their relations to one another, which generates in the mind a conviction that the materials exist for forming a public opinion and directing it to a particular end'; Home Rule was another example. The issues suddenly became clear and their moral dimension became paramount and imperative. This was an aspect of Gladstone's leadership that appealed strongly to both Morley and Harrison (who also became a fervent Gladstonian). In the first place it *was* leadership; this was in itself important to the Morley of

On Compromise or the Harrison of *Order and Progress*. It was, in addition, moral leadership, publicly-inspired leadership. Those very qualities which led many to distrust Gladstone, particularly in traditional political circles, were his virtues to Harrison and Morley. Even the Midlothian campaign of 1880, which shocked so many traditionalists, could be seen as a verification of Harrison's views on the primacy of the political agitation in welding collective opinion.[10]

Gladstone was initially a source of unity but latterly of division to the university radicals. In the 1868 elections Gladstone himself had been largely the issue; certainly he seemed to embody their particular concerns. As MP for Oxford University he had been greatly respected by the university radicals, mainly as a Peelite double first, but their great enthusiasm for him dated from his defeat at Oxford, the inauguration of his second career in politics in the mid-1860s. Though the 1868 elections greatly disappointed the university radical candidates, they swept Gladstone triumphantly into office. Gladstone's first government proceeded to accomplish much, but a certain disillusionment appears to have set in during its closing years. Once out of office, however, Gladstone was again to provide a focal point during the Bulgarian Agitation of 1876.

R.T. Shannon has analyzed this *cause célèbre*, suggesting that the polarization of opinion among the intellectuals which it precipitated was one between exponents of the older tradition of optimistic, rationalistic, individualistic liberalism, who supported the agitation, and the critics of that tradition, representing the new idealistic, power-oriented imperialistic outlook, who opposed it. This does not altogether explain the position of the academic radicals, however. They were on the whole in the anti-Turk camp, but there were a number who were distinctly cool to the agitation, such as G.C. Brodrick, A.O. Rutson, Leslie Stephen, and Grant Duff. Morley remarked rather scornfully to Chamberlain on the self-importance of the 'London academic radicals,' and the absurdity of their calling a conference 'to settle the details of a government for Herzogovina.' The Comtists tended for doctrinal reasons to prefer the Turks to the Russians – the Moslem religion, Congreve observed, being 'nobler as a doctrine' than Christianity. Harrison was more moderately pro-Turk, but like the other Comtists diverted the argument by claiming that however bad the Turkish rule in Bulgaria was, England's conduct in India and Ireland gave her no right to moralize on the issue. Gladstone himself noted the parallel between Bulgaria and Ireland. Harrison seems to have felt that the Bulgarian agitation was an example of the wrong working of public opinion, particularly in the religious 'fanaticism' that it evoked, while Morley also suggested that the agitation lacked the proper coherence, complaining that Gladstone did not come forward sufficiently distinctly as its leader. At least among those university radicals of the 1840s and 1850s generation who were critical of the agitation there seems to be little evidence of any new 'imperial idea.' Of its supporters, most were indeed anti-imperialist, but they were by no means anti-idealist or rampantly individualistic in their political doctrines as Shannon's division suggests. Those on both sides of the issue felt they were serving the cause of 'the nation.' It is interesting, moreover, that a number of the university radicals who supported the agitation, F.H. Hill, R.H. Hutton, F.A. Maxse, Goldwin Smith, and Thomas Hughes among them, subsequently broke with Gladstone over Home Rule – another cause in which the 'national idea' and the 'imperial idea' were important strands – while Morley and the Comtists were to remain faithful.[11]

The university radicals were generally Gladstonian at the outset of the 1880s as Gladstone, reinvigorated by the Bulgarian agitation and Midlothian, prepared once more to take up his rightful position as prime minister. Almost immediately, however, the tone of this troubled decade was established – a new bitterness seemed to pervade politics as the inflamed Irish question injected its venom into English political life. Brodrick, defeated in his third attempt to enter Parliament, observed to C.H. Pearson in 1881: 'Assuredly if there ever as a year in which I could have wished to be out of Parliament, it has been this.' Grant Duff, justifying his acceptance of the governorship of Madras in the same year, remarked that 'the life of the House of Commons had become perfectly odious to me, thanks to the Irish – a mere ignoble grind.' C.S. Roundell, an Essay Society member elected to Parliament at last in 1880, commented on the falling of standards in the manners of public life, but still felt confident that 'if the upper classes, the possessors of cultivation and refinement, will do their duty and not abdicate it, the influence of the cultured classes which have naturally the leadership ought to do much to correct the rougher ways of the time to come.'[12]

But there was evidence of a swing to conservatism within the 'educated class' itself. Labelled by Mill the 'stupid party' a few decades earlier, the Tories, according to Lord Carnarvon in 1882, could claim the allegiance of three-quarters of the intellectually eminent. James Bryce remarked on this situation, hopefully attributing it partly to the fact that philosophers and historians tend to be in opposition to the prevailing political tendencies of the time and partly to intellectual caution at the prospect of increasing democracy: 'Those who are cautious, cool headed, averse to sentimental arguments, penetrated by a feeling of the difficulty which will attend the working of democratic institutions will tend towards Conservatism,' he remarked, while 'the man who is eager, hopeful, filled with sympathy for the humbler classes, persuaded that their impulses will generally be toward what is good, and that they may be therefore trusted to more power than they yet possess, will enlist on the liberal side.' The 'man of intellect and culture' could be either of these. Bryce's use of the plural for the conservative intellectuals, and the singular for the liberal intellectual, is perhaps unconsciously revealing. Liberalism was no longer the assumed creed of the intelligent and politically aware young university man as it had tended to be in his day.[13]

The Home Rule issue divided intellectuals in England far more dramatically than did the earlier Bulgarian and Governor Eyre agitations. The intensity of this division was equal to that caused in France by the Dreyfus Affair in the following decade. As G.M. Trevelyan observed in his father's biography: 'Many old friendships were being broken. The intellectual and literary society of London and the universities in which he had lived and moved all his life had been mainly Liberal: it now became mainly Unionist.' As in the case of the Bulgarian agitation, the characteristic concern of the university radicals for national unity provided justification to those on either side of the issue. Home Rule could be seen as the salvation of the unity of a nation too long distracted by the legitimate grievances of the Irish or as a dire threat to the security of the nation and a denial of an even wider ideal of national unity. Most of them had long been sympathetic to Ireland's plight and to Gladstone's attempts at legislative alleviation but many were appalled by his sudden and apparently reckless decision. A.V. Dicey was deeply concerned with the constitutional aspects of the Anglo-Irish difficulties and suggested a constitutional convention to consider the problem of union independently of politics: 'Many persons,' he wrote to Bryce, 'would be very fit members of such a convention who from one cause or another cannot be members of Parliament,' Sir Henry Maine, Frederic Harrison, and himself among them. On the Home Rule bill he thought there should be a plebiscite. Such radical ideas, strongly suggestive of the politics of the American union, indicate the strength of Dicey's concern over the British union. R.H. Hutton and F.H. Hill, the two most influential Liberal journalists in England, both reform essayists in 1867, both fervent Gladstonians until 1885, broke with their leader over Home Rule. Hill, editor of the *Daily News*, had called for justice to Ireland in *Questions for a Reformed Government.* Hutton's rejection of Gladstone's policy was said to have caused Gladstone the greatest pain, so high was his regard for Hutton's opinion. In 1869 Goldwin Smith wrote of Gladstone: 'He is serious and makes other people serious; government is not with him a game of chess or a harlequinade. His was the best figure on the whole to which you could turn the eyes of newly enfranchised working men.' After the betrayal of 1886, however, he became for Smith an 'unscrupulous demagogue,' appealing to ignorance against intelligence. Similarly Thomas Hughes became, in the words of Lionel Tollemache, 'anti-Gladstonian with that peculiar vehemence which is characteristic of the class which I would designate as the English "mugwumps" – those who, with full conviction and somewhat jauntily, followed the Radical leaders up to a certain point and then suddenly broke off with them.' Leslie Stephen could not follow Gladstone on Ireland either, nor could Brodrick, who became a violent opponent of Home Rule. The impact of the Home Rule crisis is suggested by the fact that Frederic Harrison, remaining firm in his Gladstonian allegiance, actually stood as a Home Rule candidate for the University of London in the parliamentary elections of 1886. (He did not seek the nomination, nor did he canvass or campaign in any way, and was defeated by a two-to-one margin.)[14]

Indeed, the most notable examples of the university radicals who stayed with Gladstone on the Home Rule issue were those actually in Parliament. Bryce entered Parliament in 1880 on the Gladstonian sweep, as also did Thorold Rogers, while Morley came in three years later. G.O. Trevelyan, an MP since 1865 but a rebel over the Education bill in Gladstone's first ministry, received his first major ministerial appointments in this second government (though he bolted at first over Home Rule, he subsequently returned rather sheepishly to the fold). C.S. Parker also remained a Gladstonian, if a rather lukewarm one: his political career was particularly disappointing, for his talents made virtually no impact on Parliament. Morley, Bryce, and Trevelyan, all of whom were born in 1838, were the three who went farthest in politics, though their careers all seem to be flawed in the same way, partly by their political personalities. Thus Bryce had an unfortunate lecture-room manner in the House of Commons which greatly diminished his effectiveness. Henry James remarked of him that he was torn by three conflicting dispositions – literature, law, and politics – adding that he was one of the 'young doctrinaire radicals (and they are growing old in it)' who were 'tainted with priggishness.' Trevelyan was also unsure of his political vocation and agonized to Henry Adams over Gladstone's offer of a parliamentary secretaryship in 1880: 'It is a terrible business to make such a serious decision as that which I have to make ... I do not feel as if one were living in a literary age or a literary century.' These three literary politicians also had the misfortune to be chief secretaries for Ireland; none was notably successful in that graveyard of political reputations (the fourth successive, and most successful, Liberal man-of-letters-in-Parliament to hold the post was Augustine Birrell). It was perhaps the mark of the 'genuine' politician to avoid this notorious office.[15]

Among the university radicals themselves many showed signs of growing pessimism, much of which seems not unconnected with personal disappointment. Brodrick, reluctantly accepting the wardenship of Merton, remarked that his tastes were not academical and his training was that of a statesman rather than a don: 'I must always feel that I have cast pearls (if they were pearls) before swine for the best twenty years of my life.' A sort of cosmic gloom seems to have settled over Charles Pearson, expending his refined talents in Australian politics and visualizing dark scenarios involving the triumph of the 'lower' races of the world over the 'higher'; while Goldwin Smith, after a short spell at the newly-founded Cornell University, made his home in Toronto, Canada, from which he wrote jeremiads to his English friends. Both Pearson and Smith seem to have been torn between a strong cultural attachment to England and an ideological commitment to the countries to which they emigrated. Both offered a great deal to their new countrymen, Pearson as minister of public instruction in Victoria where he contributed largely to the expansion and democratization of education, Smith as a brilliant independent journalist who introduced into Canada a standard of political writing and analysis still to be surpassed. Yet they gave offence by a somewhat aloof and critical attitude towards their new environment, a lack of the 'booster' spirit, and were regarded with a certain suspicion as over-refined aliens. Goldwin Smith, who attempted to recreate the life of an English country squire in his Toronto mansion, was particularly unpopular for his lucid and persistent advocacy of Canadian union with the United States. A.V. Dicey stayed in England to report his country's progress towards a collectivism that did not coincide with their youthful ideals. Writing from the perspective of old age to his friend Bryce, he reviewed the circumstances of their *Essays in Reform:* 'My thought on the whole is that we probably did no harm, and with equal probability did no good, but that we did the thing that was natural and right at our age and in our position.' The question at issue between the young essayists and those whose views were articulated by Robert Lowe was simply whether democracy involved dangers to the country: 'It seems to me that the youthful reformers, and some of them not quite so youthful, e.g. Goldwin Smith, did maintain that the advance towards democracy did not involve great danger and might produce great blessings, whilst Lowe and his friends with great vigour denounced possible and real peril which none the less existed because no human being whether Liberal or Conservative could foresee the form which those perils would take.' 'I do not,' he concluded, 'think hopefulness so indubitably good a characteristic as you do.'[16]

The aspirations of the university radicals as formulated in the 1850s and 1860s had lost much of their relevance by the 1880s and 1890s. The differences of circumstances between the two eras were substantial. The earlier period was one of general economic buoyancy and relative domestic content. Eric Hobsbawm has suggested that 'relatively speaking the position of the British artisan has never been higher than in the 1860s, nor his standard of living and access to education, culture and travel (by contemporary standards) so satisfactory nor the gap between him and the small local manufacturers who employed him so narrow, or that between him and the mass of "labour" so wide.' The legitimation of the trade unions which represented these artisans, sober and 'professional' in style, was a characteristic concern of the academic radicals, and one to which they contributed not a little. Another concern of the university radicals was the opening of the universities to dissenters; in this too they were successful. Their ideal of national unity could be seen primarily in terms of the introduction and integration into the Coleridgean 'nation' of the artisans and middle-class non-conformists, under the sponsorship of an élite of university-educated gentlemen. It was a process of bringing deserving social elements within the pale, a process of goodwill and fellowship in which the utilitarian crudities of 'class' language were deprecated even while the Coleridgean subtleties of status, both intellectual and social, remained quite implicit in their guiding assumptions and aspirations. All this became increasingly untenable in the face of subsequent developments. As the great body of the 'residuum' of the working class obtruded increasingly on the political scene, men were found who articulated its needs and demands in language and tone less familiar and less sympathetic to the ears of an aspiring clerisy. Economic and imperial complications brought out fault lines that cut through the social strata, creating tensions that did not conform to the élitist ideal of a hierarchical process of formation and transmission of public opinion, while the difficulties of consensus among the opinion-makers themselves became more apparent.[17]

Finally, the mid-century generation of university radicals of the 1840s and 50s lost its impetus in the normal process of dispersion and dilution as it moved further from the common grounds of its origin. Like other generations, it grew old.

Notes

PREFACE

1 Edward Shils, *The Intellectual and the Powers, and Other Essays* (Chicago 1972), 20, 105, 185
2 On generations, see Karl Mannheim, 'The Problem of Generations,' *Essays on the Sociology of Knowledge* (London 1952). Mannheim's term for the generation in the sense I use it is 'generation unit' (304ff). On Coleridge see the Introduction by John Barrell to Coleridge's *On the Constitution of Church and State According to the Idea of Each* (London 1972), xi-xii.
3 Since the completion of this book Christopher Harvie's *The Lights of Liberalism: University Liberals and the Challenge of Democracy* (London 1976) has appeared, in which may be found fuller detail on some of the material in Part I of the present work, particularly the university tests campaign of the 1860s. Harvie's book, based on a PH D thesis completed subsequently to my own, attempts other avenues of explanation for the activities of the group which I call university radicals and he calls university liberals. I am not persuaded by his dismissal of the Coleridge-Arnold-Maurice-Carlyle line of élitist thought and his heavy reliance on the attenuated Evangelical heritage in accounting for the phenomenon of university radicalism in the 1850s and 1860s. Nor do I think he does justice to the attempts of the English Comtists and their sympathizers to formulate the coherent ideology which the university men needed. It is an interesting work, however, and in many respects complementary to my own.

CHAPTER ONE

1 S.T. Coleridge, *On the Constitution of Church and State According to the Idea of Each*, ed. John Barrell (London 1972), 36

2 G. Hough, 'In Dark Times,' *Listener*, LXXIX, 15 May 1968, 661-3; Martin
  Malia, 'What is the Intelligentsia?' *Daedalus*, summer 1960, 441-58
3 G. Hough, 'Coleridge and the Victorians' in H.S. Davies and G. Watson, *The
  English Mind: Studies in the English Moralists presented to Basil Willey* (Cambridge 1964), 175-92; C.R. Sanders, *Coleridge and the Broad Church Movement* (Durham, NC 1942). The present study is primarily concerned with
  Oxford influences, but Coleridge's following was quite as great at Cambridge,
  particularly through Maurice (who was a student at both Oxford and Cambridge) and the Society of Apostles. An excellent study of the Cambridge
  milieu is Sheldon Rothblatt's *The Revolution of the Dons* (London 1968),
  143 and *passim*.
     On Rugby see A.G. Butler, *The Three Friends: A Story of Rugby in the
  1840s* (London 1900); A.H. Clough, *Correspondence*, ed. F.L. Mulhauser
  (Oxford 1957), I, 38-40, 45-8; W. Stebbing ed., *Memorials of C.H. Pearson*
  (London 1900), 19; A.W. Merivale, *Family Memorials* (Exeter 1884), 330.
  Interestingly, George Goschen while at Rugby used the 'élite,' remarking to
  his mother that 'the élite hardly considered me one of their number'; he was
  able to overcome this, however, and became head of the school. On Rugby's
  social tone, the fashionable hero of Disraeli's *Vivian Grey* (1826-7) was
  willing to go to Eton, Winchester, Harrow, or Westminster, but 'not Rugby,
  it was so devilish blackguard' (10). This was written shortly before Arnold
  became headmaster; the impious reference was deleted in later editions.
4 Congreve Papers, Bodleian Library, Oxford, MS Eng. Lett. c185, f 126,
  J.F.B. Blackett to Congreve, 1843; E.B. Greenberger, *Arthur Hugh Clough:
  The Growth of a Poet's Mind* (Cambridge, Mass. 1970), 68-70
5 A.H. Clough, *Poems and Prose Remains* (London 1869), I, 31; *Prose Remains*
  (London 1888), 295; *Selected Prose Works*, ed. B.B. Trawick (Alabama
  1964), 236; Rosslyn Wemyss, ed., *Memoirs of the Rt. Hon. Sir Robert Morier*
  (London 1911), I, 80
6 A.P. Stanley, *Life and Correspondence of Thomas Arnold* (London nd), 455,
  403; Vernon Lushington, 'Carlyle,' *Oxford and Cambridge Magazine*, 1856,
  193-211, 292-310, 336-52, 697-712, 743-70; Oxford Union *Proceedings*,
  27 Nov. 1854, 15 March, 1 Nov. 1858 (debates pertaining to Carlyle)
7 Selborne Papers, Lambeth Palace Library, MS 1861 f 192, Jowett to Roundell
  Palmer, 15 Nov. 1849. Stanley, *Arnold*, 108
8 D. Forbes, *The Liberal Anglican Idea of History* (Cambridge 1952), 31-50,
  111-18; T. Arnold, 'Rugby School,' *Quarterly Journal of Education*, VII,
  April 1834, 238.
9 Stanley, *Arnold*, 152, 372; Clough, *Correspondence*, I, 203-13; Palgrave Papers, V, BM Add.Mss 45738, ff 48-68 (Palgrave's account of the trip to Paris)

10 M. Arnold, 'England and the Italian Question,' *Prose Works of Matthew Arnold*, ed. R.H. Super (Ann Arbor 1960), I, 96, 81-2, 78

11 M. Pattison, 'Oxford Studies,' *Oxford Essays* (London 1855), 252, 254, 259

12 F.S. Taylor, 'The Teaching of Science at Oxford in the Nineteenth Century,' *Annals of Science*, VIII, 1, 1952, 88-9; E.C. Mack, *Public Schools and British Opinion, 1780-1860* (London 1938), 143-51; *University of Oxford, Report of Commissioners*, 1852, 'Evidence,' Part I, 212

13 M. Pattison, *Memoirs* (London 1885), 238 ff

14 H.H. Vaughan, *Oxford Reform and Oxford Professors* (London 1854), 18 *passim*; E.G.W. Bill, *University Reform in Nineteenth Century Oxford: A Study of Henry Halford Vaughan 1811-1885* (Oxford 1973), 96-116. Bonamy Price, *Suggestions for the Extension of Professorial Teaching in the University of Oxford* (London 1850), 12-17. Vaughan and Price were both staunch Arnoldians.

15 *Oxford Commission*, 'Evidence,' Part I, 45-6, 37

16 W.C. Lake, *Memorials*, ed K. Lake (London 1901), 79; *Oxford Commission*, 'Evidence,' Part I, 90; Mark Pattison, *Suggestions on Academical Organization* (Edinburgh 1868), 4

17 *Oxford Commission*, 'Evidence,' 34, 38; J.E.T. Rogers, *Education in Oxford* (London 1861), 170-1; *Special Report of the Select Committee on the Oxford and Cambridge Universities Education Bill* (1867), 40, 80

18 H.B. Thompson, *The Choice of a Profession* (London 1857), 322; *Oxford Commission*, 'Evidence,' Part I, 34; Rogers, *Education in Oxford*, 257

19 Thompson, *Choice of a Profession*, 46

20 Leslie Stephen, *Sketches of Cambridge by a Don* (London 1865), 38; Pattison, *Suggestions*, 59, 62

21 M. Pattison, 'Philosophy at Oxford,' *Mind*, I, 82; *Suggestions*, 294-5; Godfrey Lushington, 'Oxford,' *Oxford and Cambridge Magazine*, April 1856, 250; W. Stebbing, ed. *Memorials of C.H. Pearson* (London 1900), 51-2; W.B. Thomas, *The Story of the Spectator* (London 1928), 74; M. Francis, 'The Origins of *Essays and Reviews:* An Interpretation of Mark Pattison in the 1850s,' *Historical Journal*, XVII, 1974, 797-812

22 Smith, 'Oxford University Reform,' *Oxford Essays* (London 1855), 284, 276-7; *A Plea for the Abolition of Tests* (Oxford 1864), 40-1; *Oxford Commission*, 'Evidence,' 212

23 Rogers, *Education in Oxford*, 86-7, 91, 93, 103, 130; J. Roach, *Public Examinations in England, 1850-1900* (Cambridge 1971), 64-102

24 G.C. Brodrick, *Political Studies* (London 1879), 99-100, 103; Francis Galton, *Hereditary Genius* (Fontana ed. 1962), 61. One former Rugbeian, at least, was profoundly sceptical of the university radicals' enthusiasm: C.L. Dodgson

(Lewis Carroll) mocked them in a pamphlet which included the lines, 'Neglect the heart and cultivate the brain, Then this shall be the burden of our song: All change is good, whatever is, is wrong – Then intellect's proud flag shall be unfurled, And Brain, and Brain alone shall rule the world.' D. Roll-Hansen, *The Academy, 1869-1879: Victorian Intellectuals in Revolt* (Copenhagen 1957), 34

25 Pattison, *Suggestions*, 330; J.F. Stephen, 'Competitive Examinations,' *The Cornhill Magazine*, IV, (dec. 1861), 696, 704; Comte de Montalembert, *The Political Future of England* (London 1856), 75; M.C.M. Simpson, ed., *The Correspondence and Conversation of Alexis de Tocqueville with Nassau W. Senior* (London 1872), II, 86; Bernard Cracroft, *The Right Man in the Right Place* (Cambridge 1855), 34-5

26 R. Johnson, 'Administrators in Education Before 1870: Patronage, Social Position and Role,' in G. Sutherland, ed., *Studies in the Growth of Nineteenth-Century Government* (London 1972), 118-21, 126-30

27 Henry Parris, 'The Nineteenth-Century Revolution in Government: A Reappraisal Reappraised,' *Historical Journal*, III, 1960, 26

28 Alan Ryan, 'Utilitarianism and Bureaucracy: the Views of John Stuart Mill,' Sutherland, ed., *Studies*, 52-5; G.O. Trevelyan, *The Competition Wallah* (London 1864), 143; Pattison, *Suggestions*, 64; Rogers, *Education in Oxford*, 203; *Select Committee* (1867), 'Evidence,' 198-9

29 *Select Committee* (1867), 'Evidence,' 16, 76-7, 80; C.H. Pearson, *A Letter to the Provost of Oriel on a Scheme for Making Oxford More Accessible to Medical Students Generally* (London 1858)

30 *Special Report of the Select Committee on the Oxford and Cambridge Universities Education Bill* (1867), 'Evidence,' 76-7; Goldwin Smith, *The Reorganization of the University of Oxford* (London 1868), 28; James Bryce, 'The Organization of a Legal Department of Government,' *Fortnightly Review*, XIX, 1873, 316 ff

31 H. Sidgwick, 'Idle Fellowships,' *Contemporary Review*, XXVII, April 1876, 679-80, 684; Brodrick, *Political Studies*, 561

CHAPTER TWO

1 G.C. Brodrick, *Memories and Impressions* (London 1900), 86-9; G.D. Boyle, *Recollections* (London 1895), 154-7; Melvin Richter, *The Politics of Conscience: T.H. Green and his Age* (London 1964), 75-7; P. Grosskurth, *John Addington Symonds* (London 1964), 56-7

2 F. Harrison, *Autobiographic Memoirs* (London 1911), I, 100-2; F. Harrison Papers, London School of Economics Library, box IV, G.J. Goschen to

Harrison, 'May 1863'; C.H. Pearson Papers, Bodleian Library MS Eng. Misc. c386, ff 2-3, 'Covenant of Tugend Bund'; 'The Old Mortality Register,' Bodleian MS Top. Oxon. d242.

3 H.A. Morrah, *The Oxford Union, 1823-1923* (London 1923), 110-65; C. Hollis, *The Oxford Union* (London 1965), 94-102, 242-7

4 J.R. Green, 'Oxford As It Is,' *Oxford Studies* (London 1901), 265; J. Morley, *Life of Gladstone* (New York 1904), I, 327-36

5 T. Carlyle, *Life of John Sterling* (Oxford 1907), 67; H.R. Rudman, *Italian Nationalism and English Letters* (London 1940), 220-36. Congreve Papers, Bodleian MS Eng. Lett. c185, f 155 (J.B. Blackett to Congreve, 22 Aug. 1849)

6 E. Ions, *James Bryce and American Democracy* (London 1968), 28; *Proceedings of the Oxford Union*, 17 Nov. 1856; Harrison Papers, box I, Harrison to Beesly, '1859'; M. Arnold, *England and the Italian Quesion*, 81-2, 96

7 Richter, *Politics of Conscience*, 93-4; Brodrick, *Memories*, 135; Mary Ellison, *Support for Secession: Lancashire and the American Civil War* (Chicago 1972), 199-219; Harrison Papers, box I, Harrison to Fanny Hadwen, 25 Oct. 1861, 24 July 1863

8 B. Semmel, *The Governor Eyre Controversy* (London 1962), *passim.*

9 H.G. Hanbury, *The Vinerian Chair and Legal Education* (Oxford 1958), 98

10 *Proceedings of the Oxford Union*, 30 Jan. 1854, 15 Nov. 1858; T. Carlyle, *Past and Present* (Oxford 1926), 201

11 Harrison Papers, box I, Harrison to Beesly, '1858'; J. McCarthy, *Reminiscences* (London 1899), I, 71-4, 86

12 E.A. Freeman, *Parliamentary Reform: A Letter* (Cardiff 1859), 6; Cobden Papers, box VI, BM Add. Mss 43652, f 42; Bright Papers, Bright to his wife, 11 June 1866 (University College, London)

13 W.R. Ward, *Victorian Oxford* (London 1965), 244-61; Cobden Papers, Add. Mss 43665, f 220, Smith to Cobden, 11 March 1864; Thorold Rogers Papers, Magdalen College, Oxford, f 234, Cobden to Rogers, 30 April 1864

14 G.C. Brodrick, ed., *Abolition of Tests at the Universities of Oxford and Cambridge* (London 1866), 14, 19, 70

15 *General Reports of Assistant Commissioners to the Schools Inquiry Commission* (Taunton Commission), 1868, VIII, 134; IX, 679, 784, 786-7; M.E. Grant Duff, *Elgin Speeches: 1860-1870* (Edinburgh 1871), 55

16 [A.V. Dicey] 'John Bright,' *The Nation* (New York), 31 Aug. 1882, 180; Thomas Hughes, 'To Mr. Cobden and Other Public Men in Search of Work,' *Macmillan's Magazine*, IV, Aug. 1861, 331; Cobden Papers, Add Mss 43669, ff 105-11, Arnold to Cobden, 30 Jan., 1, 3 Feb. 1864

17 Congreve Collection, Eng. Lett. e69, f 186; c186, f 178; Bright Papers, Bright to his wife, 22 June 1863; *Hansard*, CLXXVI, 26 March 1867, 636-7

18 [Cornell Price], 'Lancashire and Mary Barton,' *Oxford and Cambridge Magazine* (July 1856), 441-51; J.F. Stephen, 'The Relation of Novels to Life,' *Cambridge Essays* (Cambridge 1855), 184

19 D. Read, *Cobden and Bright* (London 1967), 165, 210-14; Hughes, 'To Mr. Cobden ... ' 330; Harrison Papers, box I, Harrison to Beesly, '1856'

20 M. Arnold, *Culture and Anarchy* (Cambridge 1935), 211

21 F. Harrison, 'The Century Club,' *Cornhill Magazine*, NS XV, 1903, 314-19; R. Harrison, *Before the Socialists* (London 1965), 147; L. Oliphant, *Picadilly* (London 1928), 135. L. Stephen, 'The Mausoleum Book,' BM Add. Mss 57920, f 6

22 Bryce Papers, Bodleian Library, IX, ff 72, 76; J. Vincent, *The Formation of the Liberal Party* (London 1966), 184, 192-5; A. Briggs, *The Age of Improvement* (London 1959), 496; George Howell Papers, Bishopsgate Institute, London, E.S. Beesly to Howell, 18 Oct. 1865, Frederic Harrison to Howell, 5 Sept. 1866, Goldwin Smith to Howell, 14 Jan. 1866

CHAPTER THREE

1 Bernard Cracroft, *Essays, Political and Miscellaneous* (London 1868), I, 158-9; *Essays on Reform* (London 1867), v

2 Brief biographical details of the essayists have been appended to an abridged version of the two volumes of reform essays edited by W.L. Guttsman, *A Plea for Democracy* (London 1967). The network of associations, journalistic and social, linking the essayists gives some notion of the extent to which the university radicals generally continued to maintain close contact through the 1860s and beyond. Meredith Townsend and R.H. Hutton were joint editors of the strongly pro-Northern *Spectator*, to which George Hooper, A.V. Dicey, C.H. Pearson, and Bernard Cracroft contributed regularly. Pearson had been co-editor with Hutton and Walter Bagehot of the *National Review*. J.M. Ludlow was the first editor, and Lloyd Jones (the one essayist of working-class origins) a sub-editor of the short-lived Mauricean intellectual review the *Reader*, to which Frederic Harrison, Leslie Stephen, Thorold Rogers, Dicey, Townsend, and Hutton contributed. F.H. Hill was assistant editor of the liberal pro-Northern *Daily News*, for which J.B. Kinnear was a leader writer. A.O. Rutson, James Bryce, Goldwin Smith, G.C. Brodrick, Hutton, Pearson, Stephen, and Hill had been *Saturday Review* contributors. Godfrey Lushington, W.L. Newman, C.S. Parker, Brodrick, Bryce, Dicey, Harrison, and Rutson were Essay Society members. Pearson, Parker, Ludlow, Harrison, Lloyd Jones, and Lushington were connected with F.D. Maurice's Working Men's College. Lord Houghton was a member of the Cambridge Society of Apostles

with Maurice. Bryce, Lushington, Goldwin Smith, Stephen, and Sir George
Young were early members of the Ad Eundem Club, a dining society founded
in 1864 to bring together academic radicals from Oxford and Cambridge.
Brodrick, Bryce, Hill, Houghton, Hutton, Lushington, Rogers, Rutson, and
Stephen were among the earliest members of the New Club (the present
Savile Club), established in mid-1868 as a London social centre for young
intellectual gentleman journalists, most of whom were university reformers.
Brodrick, Bryce, Dicey, Harrison, Hill, Houghton, Lushington, Rogers, Rut-
son, Stephen, and Young belonged to the Century Club.

3 Lowe appropriately reviewed the reform essays in the *Quarterly Review*,
   CXXIII, July 1867, 244-77; R. Lowe, *Speeches and Letters on Reform* (London 1867), 130. A. Briggs, *Victorian People* (Chicago 1955), 232, 247, 248
4 *Essays on Reform*, 16, 7, 9
5 Ibid., 253, 274-8
6 Ibid., 29-30, 33, 36, 41, 42, 94, 100
7 Ibid., 117-20; H. Adams, *The Education of Henry Adams* (New York 1931)
   33; E. Samuels, *The Young Henry Adams* (Cambridge, Mass. 1948), 145-6
8 Cobden Papers, West Sussex Record Office, 39, Smith to Cobden, 14 and 19
   Sept. 1864; E. Wallace, *Goldwin Smith: Victorian Liberal* (Toronto 1957),
   34; BM Add. Mss 43665, f 251; *Essays on Reform*, 218, 223, 236-7
9 Lowe, *Speeches*, 37; *Essays on Reform*, 200-5, 209, 215
10 *Questions for a Reformed Parliament* (London 1867), 126; [Goldwin Smith]
   'The Philosophy of the Cave,' *Macmillan's Magazine*, XIV, June 1866, 82
11 *Essays on Reform*, 278, 69, 82, 120, 123
12 H. Perkin, *The Origins of Modern English Society, 1780-1870* (London 1969),
   252-70; M. Arnold, *Culture and Anarchy* (Cambridge 1935), 109. In his
   essay, 'Numbers, or the Majority and the Remnant,' *Discourses in America*
   (London 1896), Arnold's term the 'remnant' seems to be a collective term
   for all the 'aliens' in a society.
13 Arnold, *Mixed Essays, Irish Essays* (New York 1896), 45, 110-11; cf Lord
   Houghton, 'On the Present Social Results of a Classical Education,' *Essays on
   a Liberal Education*, ed. F.W. Farrar (London 1868), 377; Bryce Papers, Bodleian Library MS IX, ff 58-9; G.M. Young, *Victorian England: Portrait of an
   Age* (London 1960), 71. *Questions for a Reformed Parliament*, 217. Leslie
   Stephen, 'The Political Situation in England,' *North American Review*,
   Oct. 1868, 566
14 Arnold, *Mixed Essays*, 109; *Culture and Anarchy*, 99; Joan Thirsk, 'Younger
   Sons in the Seventeenth Century,' *History*, LIV, Oct. 1969, 358-77; A.G.
   Gardiner, *Life of Sir William Harcourt* (London 1923), I, 152; *Questions for
   a Reformed Parliament*, 120-1, 126

15 Noel Annan's brilliant *tour de force*, 'The Intellectual Aristocracy,' *Studies in Social History*, ed. J.H. Plumb (London 1955), attributes the absence of a disaffected English intelligentsia largely to this intermarriage. Arnold, *Mixed Essays*, 66

16 *Essays on Reform*, 117, 120

17 *Questions for a Reformed Parliament*, 75, 55; cf [James MacDonnell] 'Trades Unionism in the City and May Fair,' *Fraser's Magazine*, LXXVIII, Aug., Oct. 1868, 159-74, 433-60. R.H. Tawney, *The Acquisitive Society* (Fontana Edition 1961), 88-96

18 J.S. Mill, *Representative Government* (Everyman's Edition 1910), 265, 285-6, 328-9

19 T. Hare, 'Suggestions for the Improvement of our Representative System,' *Macmillan's Magazine*, V, Jan. 1862, 295ff; J.E.T. Rogers, *Cobden and Modern Political Opinion* (London 1873), 295-301; D.A. Hamer, *John Morley* (Oxford 1968), 386-7; G.O. Trevelyan, 'A Few Remarks on Mr. Hare's Scheme of Representation,' *Macmillan's Magazine*, V, April 1862, 484; B. Cracroft, *Essays, Political and Miscellaneous* (London 1868), I, 33

20 F.D. Maurice, *The Workman and the Franchise* (London 1866), 222-35

21 J.S. Mill, *Principles of Political Economy* (London 1891), 498-510

22 J.S. Mill, *Letters*, ed. II, H. Elliot, 44-5

23 W. Bagehot, *The English Constitution, Collected Works*, ed. Norman St John Stevas (London 1965), V, 166

24 'Mr. Mill for Westminster,' *Pall Mall Gazette*, 25 March 1865; 'The Lesson of the Metropolitan Elections,' ibid., 12 July 1865

25 *Brighton Election Reporter*, 13 Feb. 1864; M.S. Packe, *Life of John Stuart Mill* (London 1954), 449-50; J.S. Mill, *Autobiography* (Worlds' Classics 1924), 241

26 H.J. Hanham, *Elections and Party Management* (London 1959), ix; J. Morley, *Life of Gladstone* (London 1904), II, 126; Goldwin Smith Papers, Cornell University Library, box 1, Smith to C.E. Norton, 26 July 1865; J. Vincent, *The Formation of the Liberal Party* (London 1966), 213-17, 231-5

27 Harrison Papers, London School of Economics Library, box 1, Harrison to Beesly, 24 Sept. 1867; G. Smith, *Correspondence* (London nd), 13; A. Swinburne, *Letters*, ed. C.Y. Lang (New Haven 1959-62), I, 306-7

28 Green Papers, Balliol College, Oxford, MS, Nettleship Notebooks, 31 Oct. 1868; *The Times*, 10 Oct. 1868, 5e; 29 Oct. 1868, 7e; 7 Nov. 1868, 7d; 14 Nov. 1868, 4e; 27 Nov. 1868, 5e; Bryce Papers, IX, Bryce to Freeman, 30 Nov. 1868; *Spectator*, 28 Nov. 1868, 1394-5; Gladstone Papers, BM Add. Mss 44416, f 86; Hodder, *Morley*, 267-8; L. Stephen, 'England,' *The Nation*, VI, 8 Oct. 1868, 289; 3 *Hansard*, CLXXXV, 240; *Saturday Review*, 31 Oct. 1868, 584-5

29 Green Papers, Nettleship Notebooks, 29 Nov. 1868; Dilke Papers, BM Add.
Mss 43901, f 140; L. Stephen, *Life of Henry Fawcett* (London 1885), 241;
J. Morley, 'The Chamber of Mediocrity,' *Fortnightly*, X, Dec. 1868, 692,
681; 'Politics as a Profession,' *Quarterly Review*, CXXVI, Jan. 1869, 273, 278,
281-2. (See also [Lord Robert Cecil] 'The House of Commons,' *Quarterly
Review*, CXVI, July 1864, 273-4; W. Bagehot, 'Politics as a Profession' [1865],
Collected Works, VI, 130-4; 'The Use of Goldwin Smiths in Parliament,'
Spectator, 11 Jan. 1868; 'Political Life as a Profession,' ibid., 22 Aug. 1868;
'The Decline of Parliamentary Talent,' ibid., 11 Feb. 1871.) W. Bagehot,
'Lord Althorp and the Reform Act of 1832,' *Collected Works*, ed. Mrs R.
Barrington (London 1915), III, 227; *Tomahawk*, 5 Dec. 1868 (the 'swart
mechanic' refers to the handful of working-class candidates who ran as
Liberals in 1868, with even less success than the intellectuals; see R. Harrison,
Before the Socialists (London 1965), 137-209).
30 Hanham, *Elections and Party Management*, ix
31 G.M. Young, *Victorian Essays* (London 1962), 135

CHAPTER FOUR

1 *Edinburgh Review*, LXVII, 1838, 278
2 A.T. Kitchel, *George Lewes and George Eliot* (New York 1933), 36-46;
J.S. Mill, *Auguste Comte and Positivism* (Ann Arbor 1965), 125
3 R.K. Biswas, *Arthur Hugh Clough* (Oxford 1972), 139; Positivist Papers,
British Museum Add. Mss 45259, f 2; E.G. Sanford, ed., *Frederick Temple*
(London 1907), 300; G. Faber, *Jowett* (London 1957), 184. D. Forbes in
his useful *Liberal Anglican Idea of History* (Cambridge 1952) misunderstands
Comte's historical theories and their influence in England in suggesting that
an unbridgeable gap separated them from those of the Liberal Anglicans (15).
He wrongly equates Comte's theories with those of the utilitarian historians
like Macaulay, though he apparently unwittingly quotes an English historian
of Comte's school as a major critic of Macaulay (127). Although the Liberal
Anglican and the Comtist approaches were not congruent, they did share
significant common ground, as Broad Church interest in Comtism would
suggest. A good example of Broad Church history overlapping Comtist
ground is Frederick Temple's 'The Education of the World' in *Essays and
Reviews* (1860), which Frederic Harrison labelled 'sham positivism.'
4 Congreve Collection, Bodleian Library, Oxford, Eng. Lett. c 181, ff 13, 60,
71; 84-5; Positivist Papers, Add. Mss 45259 f 2; Tait Papers, Lambeth Palace
Library, 107, ff 219-20; E.H. Coleridge, *Life and Correspondence of Lord
Coleridge* (London 1904), 344; W. Stebbing, ed. *Memorials of C.H. Pearson*
(London 1900) 18; F.J. Woodward, *The Doctor's Disciples* (London 1954), 32

5 Congreve Collection, MS Eng. Lett. c181, ff 5-10; c186, f 99; Jowett Papers, Balliol College, box E, X, Congreve to Louis Campbell, 1 April 1897; Harrison Papers, Library of the London School of Economics and Political Science, box I, Harrison to Mrs Hadwen, 27 May 1861, Harrison to Beesly 'Trouville, 1855'

6 M.A. Bridges, *Recollections of J.H. Bridges* (1908), 72; Harrison Papers, box I, Harrison to Beesly '1856, 1853'; Harrison to Mrs Hadwen, 22 May 1861, 'Feb. 1861,' 'March 1861'; F. Harrison, *Autobiographical Memoirs* (London 1911), I, 97; F. Harrison, *Creed of a Layman* (London 1907), 14, 17-18, 28.

7 The best extended analysis of Comte's social thought is Paul Arbousse-Bastide, *La doctrine de l'education universelle dans la philosophie d'Auguste Comte*, 2 Vol. (Paris 1957). The standard biographies are Henri Gouhier, *La vie d'Auguste Comte* (Paris 1965) and *La Jeunesse d'Auguste Comte et la formation du positivisme*, 3 vols. (Paris 1933-41). The best English analysis is Edward Caird, *The Social Philosophy and Religion of Comte* (London 1885). Raymond Aron provides a good introduction to Comte's social thought in his *Main Currents in Sociological Thought*, I (Penguin 1968). Two interesting analyses of Comte from the Marxist point of view are Lucy Prenant, 'Marx et Comte,' and Paul Labérenne, 'Efficacité politique et sociale du positivisme et du marxisme' in *A la Lumière du marxisme*, II (Paris 1937), 19-76, 77-124. Also of interest is Herbert Marcuse, *Reason and Revolution* (London 1955), 340-60.

8 A. Comte, *Lettres à divers* (Paris 1902), I (1), 545; I (2), 92, 128. I am grateful to Professor W.M. Simon for the use of material collected by him pertaining to the occupations of French and British Comtists and their sympathizers. While these lists, to which I have made some additions of my own, are not exhaustive, they do suggest relative proportions. Of 88 British Comtists, there were 13 academics, 13 lawyers (all but one a barrister), 13 in business, 10 higher civil servants. Of the 19 of undetermined occupations, the majority were clearly men of leisure. At least half of the 88 listed here were university men. By contrast, Simon tabulated 198 French Comtists of whom 51 were 'proletarians,' 49 doctors, 26 civil servants, 23 army officers, 20 lawyers, 17 engineers, and 12 teachers. Of the French total, at least 11 were *Polytechniciens*. It is striking how many more men of scientific education there were among the French than the British Comtists, although this becomes less surprising when one appreciates Oxford's role in the development of the movement in England.

On the English Comtists Royden Harrison, *Before the Socialists* (London 1965), is valuable, especially for the working-class milieu with which they were involved in the 1860s and 1870s. J.E. McGee, *Crusade for Humanity*

(London 1931) contains considerable information on the organization of the English movement, as does W.M. Simon, *European Positivism in the Nineteenth Century* (Ithaca 1963) and Simon's articles cited in the Bibliography of this work. H.W. McCready's unpublished Harvard PhD thesis (1952), 'Frederic Harrison and the British Working Class,' is soundly based on the Harrison Papers, and is very full on Harrison's activities on behalf of the organized labour movement. McCready's published articles on this subject are cited in the Bibliography. S. Eisen's unpublished PhD thesis, 'Frederic Harrison: The Life and Thought of an English Positivist' (Johns Hopkins 1957) deals particularly with Harrison's religious and philosophical ideas. A full-scale biography of Frederic Harrison by Martha S. Vogeler is expected shortly.

9 H.B. Acton, 'Comte's Positivism and the Science of Society,' *Philosophy*, XXVI, 1951, 297-302

10 See James Clerk-Maxwell to Mark Pattison, Pattison Papers, Bodleian Library, 54, f 442; T.H. Huxley, 'On the Physical Basis of Life,' *Fortnightly Review*, V, Jan., 1866, 141, and 'Scientific Aspects of Positivism,' ibid., V, April 1866, 407-8; Prenant, 'Marx et Comte,' 22, 23, 63; A. Comte, *Positive Polity* (London 1875), I, 412

11 Harrison Papers, box I, Harrison to Beesly, 29 Aug. 1866

12 Harrison, *Autobiographical Memoirs*, I, 205-6; F. Harrison, 'Neo-Christianity,' *Westminster Review*, NS XVIII, Oct 1860, 331-2

13 C.E. Osborne, *Christian Ideas in Political History* (London 1929), 263; *Tracts For Priests and People*, I, vii, 1861, 'Two Lay Dialogues by J.M. Ludlow between Smith, an Enlightened man [Godfrey Lushington] and Williams, a Plain Speaking man [Ludlow]'; Harrison Papers, box IV, F.D. Maurice to Harrison, 27 Feb. [1861]; C.R. Sanders, 'Stephen, Coleridge, and the Two Coleridgeans,' *Publications of the Modern Language Institute of America*, LV, Sept. 1940, 797; Harrison Papers, box I, Harrison to Beesly, '1859'

14 Harrison Papers, box I, Harrison to Beesly, '1857,' '1858,' '1862'; Harrison to Mrs Hadwen, 3 April 1862; Congreve Collection, MS Eng. Lett. c185, f 18, Congreve to Beesly, 1860

15 A. Comte, *Positive Philosophy*, ed. H. Martineau (London 1853), II, 166, 240-67

16 Ibid., 303, 314, 353

17 Harrison Papers, box I, Harrison to Beesly, '1856'; A. Comte, *Lettres à divers*, I, 1 (Paris 1902), 514; A.P. Stanley, *Life and Correspondence of Thomas Arnold* (London nd), 402; G. Eliot, *Letters*, ed. G.S. Haight (New Haven 1954-5), IV, 216

18 Harrison Papers, box I, Harrison to Beesly, '1859,' '1857,' '1855,' '1856';

S. Liveing, *A Nineteenth Century Teacher: John Henry Bridges* (London 1926), 121
19 See my 'Higher Journalism and the mid-Victorian Clerisy,' *Victorian Studies*, XIII, Dec. 1969, 181-98.
20 Comte, *Positive Polity*, IV, liii, 332-3, 400; Harrison Papers, box I, Harrison to Beesly, '1856'; C.H. Sanders, *Coleridge and the Broad Church Movement* (Durham, NC 1942) 63, 93; T. Hughes, 'Anonymous Journalism,' *Macmillan's Magazine*, V, Dec. 1861, 158

CHAPTER FIVE

1 Harrison Papers, Library of the London School of Economics and Political Science, box I, Harrison to Mrs Hadwen, 3 April 1862; F. Harrison, *Order and Progress* (London 1875), 151; Congreve Collection, Bodleian Library, Oxford, MS Eng. Lett. c183, ff 5-6
2 P. Arbousse-Bastide, *La Doctrine de l'education universelle dans la philosophie d'Auguste Comte* (Paris 1957), I, 225-8
3 A. Comte, *Positive Polity* (London 1875), I, 144
4 Harrison Papers, box I, Harrison to Beesly, '1853'; J. Saville, 'The Christian Socialists of 1848,' J. Saville, ed. *Democracy and the Labour Movement* (London 1954); Harrison Papers, box I, Harrison to Beesly, '1856'
5 J.F.C. Harrison, *A History of the Working Men's College, 1854-1954* (London 1954), 29; Harrison Papers, box I, Harrison to Beesly, '1860'; ibid., Harrison to Mrs Hadwen, 10 Dec. 1861
6 *Working Men's College Magazine*, II, 1860, 61, 71, 93
7 F. Harrison, *The Creed of a Layman* (London 1907), 47; Harrison Papers, box I, Harrison to Beesly, '1860,' '1862'; Harrison to Mrs Hadwen, 3 Feb., 3 April 1862; F. Harrison, *The Meaning of History* (London 1862), 12, 22; F. Harrison, *Autobiographical Memoirs* (London 1911), I, 248
8 R. Congreve, *Essays, Political, Social and Religious*, I (London 1874), 108-10; Harrison Papers, box I, Harrison to Mrs Hadwen, 3 Sept. 1861; Harrison to Beesly, '1861'; *The Times*, 15 April 1861, 6; 22 July 1861, 10; Harrison Papers, box I, Harrison to Mrs Hadwen, 22 May, 29 June 1861; 29 Oct. 1860; A. Comte, *Lettres à divers* (Paris 1902), I (2), 261
9 T.W. Reid, *Life of W.E. Forster* (London 1888), I, 285; Harrison Papers, box I, Harrison to Beesly, '1861'; VIII, 'Diary of a Lancashire Visit of 1863,' 6 April 1863
10 Harrison Papers, box I, Harrison to Mrs Hadwen, 8 Oct. 1861; V, Holyoake to Harrison, 31 March 1863; 'Diary,' 23 April, 1 April, 21 March 1863; F. Harrison, 'Industrial Cooperation,' *Fortnightly Review*, III, Jan. 1866, 502

11 Harrison Papers, box I, Harrison to Mrs Hadwen, 'Summer, 1862', 3 Sept.
   1861, 26 Nov. 1863; S. Coltham, 'George Potter, the Junta and the *Bee-Hive*,'
   International Review of Social History, IX, X, 1964-5
12 *Commonwealth*, 19 May 1866; Harrison Papers, box I, Harrison to Beesly,
   15 Jan. 1864, 8 Dec. 1865, 29 Aug. 1865
13 Harrison Papers, box I, Harrison to Beesly, (March) '1866,' '1866' (different);
   Harrison to Mrs Hadwen, 3 March 1866; *Saturday Review*, 27 Oct. 1866,
   509-10
14 *Commonwealth*, 10 March 1866
15 Harrison Papers, box I, Harrison to Beesly, (April) '1864,' (May) '1864';
   F.E. Gillespie, *Labour and Politics in England 1850-67* (Durham, NC 1927),
   219; Howell Papers, Bishopsgate Institute, London, Harrison to Howell, 5
   Sept. 1866
16 Harrison Papers, box I, Harrison to Beesly, 20, 25 July 1868; 3 Nov. 1870
17 F. Harrison, 'The Good and Evil of Trade Unions,' *Fortnightly Review*, III,
   Nov. 1865, 53
18 *Fortnightly Review*, III, Jan. 1866, 480
19 Harrison Papers, box I, Harrison to Beesly, 26 Aug. 1862; '1864'
20 Royden Harrison, *Before the Socialists* (London 1965), 322-9; Asa Briggs,
   Victorian People (New York 1963), 173-7
21 Henry Pelling, *A History of British Trade Unionism* (Pelican 1963), 64-8;
   J.B. Jeffreys, ed., *Labour's Formative Years* (London 1948), 104-5 (contains
   part of Beesly's speech); H.W. McCready, 'British Labour and the Royal
   Commission on Trades Unions 1867-69,' *University of Toronto Quarterly*,
   XXIV, July 1955, 390-409
22 Comte, *Positive Polity*, I, 115, IV, 306; Christopher Kent, 'The Whittington
   Club: A Bohemian Experiment in Middle Class Social Reform,' *Victorian
   Studies*, XVIII, Sept. 1974, 31-55

CHAPTER SIX

1 *Politique d'Auguste Comte*, ed. Pierre Arnaud (Paris 1965), 269; Sir E. Perry,
   'A Morning with Auguste Comte,' *Nineteenth Century*, II, 1877, 626-7; A.
   Comte, *Positive Polity* (London 1875), III, xxiv, xii, IV, 427-8; R. Aron,
   Comte et Tocqueville, juges de l'Angleterre (Oxford 1965), 5-10
2 Harrison Papers, Library of the London School of Economics and Political
   Science, box I, Harrison to Beesly, '1865'
3 On Comte and industrial society see Raymond Aron, *Main Currents in Sociological Thought*, I (Penguin 1968), 72-86; P. Arbousse-Bastide, *La Doctrine
   de l'education universelle dans la philosophie d'Auguste Comte* (Paris 1957),

II, 569-72, *passim*; David Cohen, 'Comte's Changing Sociology,' *American Journal of Sociology*, LXXI (Sept. 1965), 168-77.

4 Frederic Harrison, *John Ruskin* (London 1903), 91; A. Comte, *Lettres à divers, 1850-57*, I, part 2 (Paris 1902), 291; Harrison Papers, V, file 76, Ruskin to Harrison, 12 Dec. 1865; *Fortnightly Review*, III, 45, XVIII, 280; cf J. Ruskin, *Unto this Last, Works*, XVII, (London 1905), 20-1

5 F. Harrison, 'The Good and Evil of Trade Unions,' *Fortnightly Review*, III, Nov. 1865, 52; cf Ruskin, *Unto this Last*, 39-42; Harrison, 'Industrial Cooperation,' *Fortnightly*, III, Jan. 1866, 488, 491, 496; - 'Mr. Brassey on Work and Wages,' *Fortnightly*, XVIII, Sept. 1872, 286; Harrison Papers, box I, Harrison to Beesly, 1 Sept. 1865

6 Comte, *Positive Polity*, IV, 430; Harrison Papers, box I, Harrison to Mrs Hadwen, 3 Feb. 1862; Harrison to Beesly, 13 Jan. 1858; F. Harrison, 'The Destruction of Kagoshima,' *National Review*, XXXV, Jan. 1864; *International Policy* (London 1866) contains essays by Harrison, Bridges, Congreve, Beesly, Henry Dix Hutton, C.A. Cookson, and E.H. Pember; *Saturday Review*, 11 Aug. 1866, 177

7 Harrison Papers, box I, 'Summer, 1864', 28 Aug. (1864), '1864,' '1865'; F. Harrison, *Autobiographic Memoirs* (London 1911), II, 80-96; A.W. Brown, *The Metaphysical Society* (New York 1947), 33

8 H.W. McCready, 'British Labour's Lobby 1867-75,' *Canadian Journal of Economics and Political Science*, XXII, May 1956, 141-60

9 G.C. Brodrick, *Memories and Impressions* (London 1900), 90-2; Congreve Collection, Bodleian Library, Oxford, MS Eng. Lett. c183, ff 10, 43

10 Beesly Papers, Library of University College, London, II, 19 July 1867; Harrison Papers, box I, Harrison to Mrs Hadwen, 'Dec., 1863'; V, Jowett to Harrison, nd (1861); I, Harrison to Mrs Hadwen, 22 May 1861

11 Harrison Papers, box I, Harrison to Beesly, '1864'

12 Beesly Papers, II, Beesly to H. Crompton, 14 July 1867, 17 March 1866; Harrison Papers, box I, Harrison to Mrs Hadwen, 3 March 1864; Harrison to Beesly, 24 Sept. 1867, 17 March 1866; R. Congreve, *Essays, Political, Social and Religious* (London 1874), I, 213-15; Justin McCarthy, 'The English Positivists,' *Galaxy*, VII, March 1869, 380

13 W.M. Simon, *European Positivism in the Nineteenth Century* (Ithaca 1963), 40; Congreve Collection, MS Eng. Lett. e69, f 12, Congreve to Beesly (11 Nov. 1860)

14 Congreve Collection, MS Eng. Lett. e69, f 37; c183, ff 56, 91, 122; G. Eliot, *The George Eliot Letters*, ed. G.S. Haight (New Haven 1954), III, 293, IV, 363; M.E.G. Duff, *Notes from a Diary* (London 1897), II, 109

15 Positivist Papers, Add. Mss 45227, f 119-20; Congreve Collection, c183,

f 161; Archives Positivistes, Musée Auguste Comte, Paris, Congreve-Laffitte, 7 July 1873

16 Harrison Papers, box I, Harrison to Beesly, 28 Feb. 1870; Congreve, *Essays*, I, 296

17 Harrison, *Order and Progress* (London 1875) 150; M. Arnold, *Culture and Anarchy* (Cambridge 1935), 65-6; Pollock, *For My Grandson: Remembrances of an Ancient Victorian* (London 1933), 100

18 F. Harrison, *Tennyson, Ruskin, Mill and Other Literary Estimates* (London 1899), 132; W. Bagehot, *Physics and Politics* (London 1900), 58; M.S. Vogeler, 'Matthew Arnold and Frederic Harrison: The Prophet of Culture and Prophet of Positivism,' *Studies in English Literature*, II, 1962, 441-62

19 Arnold, *Culture and Anarchy*, 117; *Pall Mall Gazette*, 22 April 1867

20 Congreve Collection, c183, f 285; Austin Harrison, *Frederic Harrison: Thoughts and Memories* (London 1926), 103; F. Harrison, 'Bismarckism,' *Fortnightly*, XIV, Dec. 1870, 644, 647; Harrison Papers, box II, Harrison to Morley, 11 Jan. 1871; R. Harrison, 'Professor Beesly and the Working Class,' in A. Briggs and J. Saville, eds., *Essays in Labour History* (London 1960), 233; R. Harrison, *Before the Socialists* (London 1965), 229-38. R. Harrison, ed., *The English Defence of the Commune* (London 1871), reprints a number of articles by the English Comtists supporting the Commune.

21 Harrison Papers, box II, Harrison to Morley, 8 Feb., 24 April, 21 June 1871, 11 Jan. 1872; *Fortnightly*, XIV, Dec. 1870, 644, 647

22 Royden Harrison, 'E.S. Beesly and Karl Marx,' *International Review of Social History*, IV, 1959, 212; Labérenne, 'Efficacité politique et sociale du positivisme et du marxisme,' *A la lumière du marxisme*, 98; Harrison Papers, box II, Harrison to Morley, 22 June, 4 May 1871

23 Bertrand and Patricia Russell, *The Amberley Papers* (London 1937), II, 462, 473, 466; Harrison Papers, box II, Harrison to Morley, 13 Jan. 1870; *Pall Mall Gazette*, 15 April 1871; E.S. Beesly, 'Workmen and Non-Workmen,' *Letters to the Working Classes* (London 1870), 5; J.S. Mill, *Letters*, ed. H. Elliot, II, 347; M. Arnold, 'The Function of Criticism at the Present Time,' *Essays in Criticism* (London nd), 15; E. Alexander, *Matthew Arnold and John Stuart Mill* (London 1965), 62-3; E.S. Beesly, *Bee-Hive*, 7 March 1863

24 Theodore Schieder, *The State and Society in our Times* (London 1962), 36, n81; A. Comte, *Lettres à divers*, I (1), 313; Congreve Collection, MS Eng. Mis. d485, 1 ff; Hedva Ben-Israel, *English Historians and the French Revolution* (Cambridge 1968), 263

25 Harrison Papers, box I, Harrison to Beesly, 30 July 1870; C.M. Davies, *Heterodox London* (London 1874), 11

26 Harrison Papers, box I, Harrison to Beesly, 6 July 1870; F. Harrison, 'Newton Hall,' *Nineteenth Century*, LI, May 1902, 822
27 *Fortnightly Review*, XXIV, July 1875, 74
28 M. Quin, *Memoirs of a Positivist* (London 1924), 110, 115, 118; A. Harrison,
   Frederic Harrison, 42-3; Harrison Papers, box I, Harrison to Beesly, 18 June
   1869

CHAPTER SEVEN

 1 C.A. Kent, 'Higher Journalism and the Mid-Victorian Clerisy,' *Victorian
   Studies*, XIII, Dec. 1969, 183
 2 F.W. Hirst, *In the Golden Days* (London 1947), 165; T. Carlyle, *Sartor Resartus*, *Works* (London 1897), I, 35; J. Morley, 'Anonymous Journalism,'
   Fortnightly Review, VIII, Aug. 1867, 292; J. Morley, *Recollections* (London
   1917), I, 117; L. Stephen, 'Some Early Recollections – Journalism,' *National
   Review*, XLII, Nov. 1903, 432
 3 F.W. Hirst, *Early Life and Letters of John Morley* (London 1927), I, 138;
   [J. Morley] *Modern Characteristics* (London 1865), 135, 239, 244, 247
 4 *Macmillan's Magazine Review*, VII, Jan. 1863, 243; J. Morley, 'Political Prelude,' *Fortnightly Review*, X (July 1868), 107; see also Leslie Stephen, 'The
   Value of Political Machinery,' ibid XXIV, Dec. 1875, 845
 5 J. Morley, 'Young England and the Political Future,' ibid., VII, April 1867,
   365; Macmillan Papers, BM Add. Mss 55055, ff 6-14, Morley to Macmillan,
   30 Oct., 3 Nov. 1867, 17 May 1868; Hirst, *Early Life*, I, 154-7
 6 J. Morley, 'Liberal Programme,' *Fortnightly Review*, VIII, Sept. 1867, 359,
   362-3, 365; Morley, 'Political Prelude,' 113-19
 7 Harrison Papers, Library of the London School of Economics and Political
   Science, box III, Morley to Harrison, 19 Feb. 1873
 8 *Modern Characteristics*, 10, 193-4; 'On Popular Culture,' *Miscellanies*, III, 27;
   Modern Characteristics, 278, 282; 'An Address to Some Miners,' *Fortnightly
   Review*, XXVII, March 1877, 392-3
 9 'A Note to Col. Chesney's Letter,' *Fortnightly Review*, XIV, Nov. 1870, 591;
   'England and the War,' ibid., 482, 479; [J. Morley] *Studies in Conduct* (London 1867), 266, 273; 'Chamber of Mediocrity,' *Fortnightly*, X, Dec. 1868,
   692, 690
10 J. Morley, *Diderot and the Encyclopaedists* (London 1886), I, 9, 18; A.
   Comte, *Positive Polity* (London 1877), III, 497-502; J. Morley, *Studies in
   Literature* (London 1890), 287, 305
11 J. Morley, 'England and the War,' *Fortnightly Review*, XIV, Oct. 1870, 480;
   J. Morley, 'Old Parties and New Policy,' X, Sep. 1868, 324, 330-2, 335-6;

J. Morley, 'The Chamber of Mediocrity,' ibid., X, Dec. 1868, 693-4; J. Morley, 'The Struggle for National Education,' ibid., XX, Aug., Sept., Oct., 1873; J. Morley, *Recollections*, I, 148; J. Morley, 'Review,' *Fortnightly Review*, X, Nov. 1868, 584

12 Harrison Papers, box II, Harrison to Morley, 21 June, 22 May 1870; 24 April 1871; 11 Jan. 1872; 6 Sept., 8 Sept., 12 Dec. 1873

13 H.W. McCready, 'The British General Election of 1874: Frederic Harrison and the Liberal Labour Dilemma,' *Canadian Journal of Economics and Political Science*, XX, May 1954, 166-75; Harrison Papers, box II, Harrison to Morley, 4 Aug., 21 Aug., 27 Aug., 8 Sept. 1874; Chamberlain Papers, Library of the University of Birmingham, I, Morley to Chamberlain, 15 July, 6 Aug. 1873

14 Harrison Papers, II, Harrison to Morley, 29 Jan. 1874; 8 Sept. 1873; 12 Dec. 1873, 30 Jan. 1874; F. Harrison, 'Workmen and the Election,' *Bee-Hive*, 31 Jan. 1874

15 Harrison Papers, box II, Harrison to Morley, 8 Dec. 1873, 24, 28 April 1874

16 J. Morley, 'The *Fortnightly Review* and Positivism, A Note,' *Fortnightly Review*, July 1870; Harrison Papers, box II, Harrison to Morley, 11 Jan. 1874; 'Lancashire,' *Fortnightly Review*, July 1878; D.A. Hamer, *John Morley: Liberal Intellectual in Politics* (Oxford 1968), 16-33

17 Chamberlain Papers, I, Morley to Chamberlain, 5 Dec. 1875, 31 Jan. 1876, 11 Aug. 1873, 18 Jan. 1875, 29 Aug. 1875; Harrison Papers, box III, Morley to Harrison, 9 Sept. 1873

18 Morley, *Studies in Literature*, 346-7, 331; Hirst, *Early Life*, II, 97

CHAPTER EIGHT

1 J. Morley, *Recollections* (London 1917), I, 69; Chamberlain Papers, Library of the University of Birmingham, I, Morley to Chamberlain, 5 May 1877

2 J. Morley, *Burke: A Historical Study* (London 1867), 248; H. Ben-Israel, *English Historians and the French Revolution* (Cambridge 1968), 10

3 Morley, *Burke*, 27, 33, 146; M. Arnold, 'The Function of Criticism at the Present Time,' in *Mixed Essays* ... (New York 1896), 10

4 Morley, *Burke*, 241-3, 310

5 Ibid., 231-3, 282-7; A. Comte, *Positive Polity* (London 1877), IV, 632

6 T. Burke, *Reflections on the French Revolution* (Everyman's edition 1910), 316; Comte, *Positive Polity*, III, xviii

7 J. Morley, 'Condorcet,' *Miscellanies*, II, 170, 181, 195-6, 199

8 J. Morley, 'The Life of Turgot,' *Fortnightly*, XIV, Aug. 1870, 160-2; D.A. Hamer, *John Morley: Intellectual in Politics* (London 1968), 40-3; 'Turgot,' *Miscellanies*, II, 75, 148, 154-7

9 Comte, *Positive Polity*, III, 509-17; *Cours de philosophie positive*, V, 396-410
10 'Condorcet,' 171; J. Morley, *Voltaire* (London 1885), 18, 59-61, 177-80, 29
11 Ibid., 37-9
12 J. Morley, *Rousseau* (London 1886), I, 2; II, 120, 134-8, 156-7, 192-4
13 Chamberlain Papers, I, Morley to Chamberlain, 12, 15 March 1874
14 J. Morley, *On Compromise* (London 1886), 4, 2
15 Ibid., 9-14, 28, 23
16 Ibid., 29-32
17 Ibid., 33-5, 6, 144, 16-17
18 Ibid., 117, 98, 118
19 Ibid., 109, 117, 44-6, 144
20 Ibid., 83, 258, 226, 80
21 Ibid., 202-3, 42, 36
22 Ibid., 118, 4
23 Ibid., 95, 222, 127, 135, 130
24 Ibid., 151, 243-5, 151
25 Ibid., 244, 217
26 Ibid., 143-4, 223-4
27 Ibid., 201-3, 217
28 Ibid., 126, 254, 257-9, 261-2, 265, 230
29 J. Morley, 'Robespierre,' *Miscellanies*, I, 55-7
30 J. Morley, 'M. Taine's New Work,' *Fortnightly*, XXV, March 1876
31 Morley, *On Compromise*, 121

CHAPTER NINE

1 J. Morley, *On Compromise* (London 1886), 108
2 P. Arnaud, *Politique d'Auguste Comte* (Paris 1965), 266-70, 283; R. Aron, *Main Currents in Sociological Thought* (London 1968), 66; P. Arbousse-Bastide, *La Doctrine de l'éducation universal dans la philosophie d'Auguste Comte* (Paris 1957), II, 629-41
3 Morley, *Compromise*, 13-14
4 F. Harrison, 'Public Affairs,' *Fortnightly*, XX, Oct. 1873, 551
5 H.B. Acton, 'Comte's Positivism and the Science of Society,' *Philosophy*, XXVI, 1951, 296-7
6 Two useful books treating the subject of anti-intellectualism (albeit in an American context) are R. Hofstadter *Anti-Intellectualism in American Life* (New York 1966), espec. 24-55, 393-433; and C. Lasch, *The New Radicalism in America* (New York 1967), espec. 286-349.
7 Frederic Harrison, *Order and Progress* (London 1875), 61. A new edition of this scarce book, edited by Martha S. Vogeler, has recently been published.

8 Ibid., 61, 89, 98; Harrison Papers, Library of the London School of Economics and Political Science, box II, Harrison to Morley, 31 March 1874; 20 Feb. 1871; Steven Lukes, 'Durkheim's "Individualism and the Intellectuals," ' *Political Studies*, XVII, 1969, 14-30

9 J.S. Mill, *Earlier Letters, 1812-1848*, ed. F. Mineka (Toronto 1963), II, 324, 503; J.S. Mill, *Letters*, ed. H. Elliot (London 1910), I, 253; J.S. Mill, *Autobiography* (Oxford 1924), 166-7

10 M.S. Packe, *Life of John Stuart Mill* (London 1954), 447; Harrison Papers, box I, Harrison to Beesly, 28 Aug. 1865; *Saturday Review*, 11 Aug. 1866, 167-9

11 Harrison Papers, box II, Harrison to Morley, 10 Feb. 1874

12 Frederic Harrison, *Order and Progress* (London 1875), 268-81, 171, 273; *Saturday Review*, 6 April 1867

13 Harrison, *Order and Progress*, 141-2, 251-2, 256-8; cf Morley, *On Compromise*, 229-31

14 Harrison Papers, box I, Harrison to Beesly, '1866'; Harrison, *Order and Progress*, 311, 313

15 Harrison, ibid., 301-3 (cf W. Bagehot, *English Constitution* (New York 1963), 262, 307, 346, 327

16 Harrison Papers, box II, Harrison to Morley, 10 May 1872, and Morley's reply, 13 May 1872; Bagehot, *Order and Progress*, 29

17 Harrison, *Order and Progress*, 14, 216-17, 21, 7, 261 (cf Bagehot, *English Constitution*, 65)

18 Harrison, *Order and Progress*, 227, 251; H.W. McCready, 'The British Labour Lobby 1867-75,' *Canadian Journal of Economics and Political Science*, XXII, May 1956, 141-59; F. Harrison, 'The New Labour Laws,' *Bee-Hive*, 7 Aug. 1875; cf 'The New School of Radicals,' *Spectator*, 25 April 1868

19 Harrison, *Order and Progress*, 227-9, 353, 357-8

20 Ibid., 108-9, 355-6, 217, 195

21 Ibid., 179, 34-9; W. Bagehot, 'Average Government,' *Works* (London 1915), VI, 86

22 James H. Meisel, *The Myth of the Ruling Class: Gaetano Mosca and the Elite* (Ann Arbor 1962), 54-61, 348-53; Peter Bachrach, *The Theory of Democratic Elitism: A Critique* (Boston 1967), *passim*.

23 Harrison, *Order and Progress*, 104-33; S. Lukes and G. Duncan, 'The New Democracy,' *Political Studies*, XII, 1963, 156-77

24 Ibid., 30, 101-6, 98-9

25 Ibid., 96-7, 99

26 Ibid., 159-60, 77, 71, 74-5

27 Ibid., 75-8

28 Ibid., 336-8, 234, 82-3

29 Ibid., 69
30 Ibid., 40; Harrison Papers, box II, Harrison to Morley, 8 June 1874
31 T. Schieder, *The State and Society in our Times* (London 1962), 18-19

EPILOGUE

1 W.M. Simon, 'Auguste Comte's English Disciples,' *Victorian Studies*, VII, Oct. 1964, 161-72; *Reports of the London Positivist Committee* (Newton Hall 1881-90); Harrison Papers, Library of the London School of Economics and Political Science, box II, Harrison to Morley, 8 June 1874
2 R. Harrison, *Before the Socialists* (London 1965), 326-33; *Positivist Comments on Public Affairs: Occasional Papers issued by the London Positivist Society, 1878-92* (London 1896), and *Positivist Review*, 1893-1925 (the bibliography provided in F. Harrison's *Autobiographic Memoirs* (London 1911), II, 342-5, includes a list of his contributions to this periodical up to 1911); B. Webb, *My Apprenticeship* (London 1929), 125; Robert, 1st Earl of Lytton, *Letters*, ed. Balfour (London 1906), II, 99
3 *Spectator*, 17 Nov. 1877, 1429
4 Harrison Papers, box II, Harrison to Morley, 25 June 1873; 'Public Affairs,' *Fortnightly*, XVIII, Nov. 1873, 685; *Spectator*, 8 Nov. 1873, 1403-4; 10 Dec. 1870, 1494
5 W.M. Simon, *European Positivism* (Ithaca 1963), 222-3, 234-6; Philip Abrams, *The Origins of British Sociology* (Chicago 1968), 55-67
6 Edmund Gosse Collection, Brotherton Library, University of Leeds, Harrison to Mrs Betham Edwards, 1 Oct. 1918; D. Riesman, *Selected Essays from Individualism Reconsidered* (New York 1955), 48-66; A. Harrison, *Frederic Harrison: Thoughts and Memories* (London 1926), 192, W.S. Blunt, *Diaries* (London 1932), 233; C.E. Norton, *Letters* (Boston 1915), I, 446; Lord Lytton, *Personal and Literary Letters* (London 1906), I, 325
7 D.A. Hamer, *John Morley: Liberal Intellectual in Politics* (Oxford 1968), *passim*; A. Filon, *Profils anglais* (Paris 1893), xx; J. Morley, 'A Few Words on French Models,' *Studies in Literature*, 1890, 182-6
8 J. Morgan, *John, Viscount Morley* (London 1924), 29; Sir H. Cotton, *Indian and Home Memories* (London 1911), 304 ff; but cf R.J. Moore, *Liberalism and Indian Politics* (London 1966), and S.A. Wolpert, *Morley and India 1906-1910* (Berkeley and Los Angeles 1967), which show Morley's Indian policies in a more favourable light.
9 Filon, *Profils anglais*, 129; Hamer, *Morley*, 162-82
10 R.H. Hutton, *Studies in Politics* (London 1866), 18; J. Morley, *Life of Gladstone* (New York 1904), II, 241; R.T. Shannon, *Gladstone and the Bulgarian*

Agitation (London 1963), III; on Gladstone's Midlothian campaigns see G.W. Smalley, *London Letters* (London 1890), I, 413-527.

11 Shannon, *Gladstone and the Bulgarian Agitation*, 203, *passim*; G.C. Brodrick, *Memories and Impressions* (London 1900), 239; Chamberlain Papers, Library of the University of Birmingham, Morley to Chamberlain, 28 Nov. 1876; A.O. Rutson, 'Turkey in Europe,' *Fortnightly*, XXVI, Sept. 1876; F. Harrison, 'England and Turkey,' ibid., Oct. 1876; R. Congreve, 'Cross and Crescent,' ibid., Nov. 1876

12 Pearson Papers, Bodleian Library, Oxford, MS Eng. Lett. d186, f 165; ibid., d187, f 117; Selborne Papers, Lambeth Palace Library, MS 1868, f 210

13 James Bryce, 'Intellect and Education in English Politics,' *Nation*, XXXVI, 25 Jan. 1885, 76

14 G.M. Trevelyan, *Sir George Otto Trevelyan* (London 1932), 124; Bryce Papers, Bodleian Library, Oxford, box II, 68, 82; 'Letters of Goldwin Smith to C.E. Norton,' *Massachusetts Historical Society Proceedings*, XLIX (Boston 1916), 145; Selborne Papers, 1877, f 156; Goldwin Smith, *My Memories of Gladstone* (London 1904), 71; [L.A. Tollemache] *Essays, Mock Essays and Character Sketches* (London, nd), 254; Earl of Midleton, *Records and Reactions* (London 1939), 14-15; F.W. Maitland, *Life and Letters of Leslie Stephen* (London 1906), 388-9

15 Leon Edel, *Henry James: The Conquest of London 1870-1883* (London 1962), 336; E. Samuels, *Henry Adams: The Middle Years* (Cambridge, Mass. 1958), 123

16 John Tregenza, *Professor of Democracy: The Life of Charles Henry Pearson, 1830-1894* (Melbourne 1968), 226-36; Pearson Papers, d186, f 165; E. Wallace, *Goldwin Smith: Victorian Liberal* (Toronto 1957), 253; Bryce Papers, box II, ff 265-70

17 E.J. Hobsbawm, *Labouring Men: Studies in the History of Labour* (New York 1967), 381

Bibliography

I MANUSCRIPT COLLECTIONS

The E.S. Beesly Papers in the Library of University College, London
The John Bright Papers in the Library of University College, London, and the
   British Museum
The James Bryce Papers in the Bodleian Library, Oxford
The Joseph Chamberlain Papers in the Library of the University of Birmingham
The A.H. Clough Papers in the Bodleian Library
The Richard Cobden Papers in the British Library and the West Sussex County
   Record Office, Chichester
The Richard Congreve Papers in the Bodleian Library
The Sir Charles Dilke Papers in the British Library
The T.H.S. Escott Papers in the Senate House, University of London
The W.E. Gladstone Papers in the British Library
The T.H. Green Papers in the Balliol College Library, Oxford
The Edmund Gosse Papers in the Brotherton Library, The University of Leeds
The Frederic Harrison Papers in the British Library of Political and Economic
   Science
The George Howell Papers in the Bishopsgate Institute, London
The T.H. Huxley Papers in the Archives of the Imperial College of Science and
   Technology, London
The Benjamin Jowett Papers in the Balliol College Library
The Macmillan Company Papers in the British Library
The Max Muller Papers in the Bodleian Library
The Francis Palgrave Papers in the British Library
The Mark Pattison Papers in the Bodleian Library
The C.H. Pearson Papers in the Bodleian Library

The Positivist Papers in the British Library
Archives Positivistes in La Maison d'Auguste Comte, Paris
The James E. Thorold Rogers Papers in Magdalen College, Oxford
The Selborne Papers in Lambeth Palace Library, London
The Goldwin Smith Papers in the Cornell University Library, Ithaca, New York
The Archbishop Tait Papers in Lambeth Palace Library
The Archives of the Working Men's College, Crowndale Road, London

II PARLIAMENTARY PAPERS

University of Oxford, Report of Commissioners, etc. (1852)
Report on the Reorganization of the Civil Service, etc. (1854)
Report on H.M. Commissioners Appointed to Enquire into the Revenues and Management of Certain Schools, etc. ('Clarendon Commission'), (1864)
Special Report of the Select Committee on the Oxford and Cambridge Universities Education Bill (1867)
General Reports of Assistant Commissioners of the Schools Enquiry Commission ('Taunton Commission'), (1868)

III PERIODICALS (published in London unless otherwise indicated)

Academy
Annual Register
Bee-Hive
Commonwealth
Contemporary Review
Cornhill Magazine
Daily News
Fraser's Magazine
Leader
Macmillan's Magazine
Morning Star
Nation (New York)
National Review
North American Review (Boston)
Nineteenth Century
Pall Mall Gazette
Politics for the People
Positivist Review
Proceedings of the Oxford University Union Society (Oxford)

Reader
Transactions of the National Association for the Promotion of Social Science
Revue des deux mondes (Paris)
Saturday Review
Spectator
Saint Paul's Magazine
The Times
Westminster Review
Working Men's College Magazine

IV BOOKS

Abbott, E. and L. Campbell. *The Life and Letters of Benjamin Jowett.* London 1897
Abrams, P. *The Origins of British Sociology.* Chicago 1968
Adams, H. *The Education of Henry Adams.* New York 1933
Alexander, E. *John Morley.* New York 1972
- *Matthew Arnold and John Stuart Mill.* London 1965
Annan, N. *Leslie Stephen.* London 1951
Arnold, M. *Prose Works*, ed. R.H. Super. Ann Arbor 1960-
Arnold, T. *Miscellaneous Works.* London 1845
Aron, R. *Main Currents in Sociological Thought, I.* London 1845
- *Auguste Comte et Alexis de Tocqueville: Juges de l'Angleterre.* Oxford 1965
Bachrach, P. *The Theory of Democratic Elitism: A Critique.* Boston 1967
Bagehot, W. *Works and Life*, ed. Mrs Barrington. London 1915
Bastide, P. Arbousse-. *La Doctrine de l'education universelle dans la philosophie d'Auguste Comte.* Paris 1957
Besant, W. *Autobiography.* London 1902
Bevington, M.M. *The Saturday Review: 1855-1868.* New York 1941
Bill, E.G.W. *University Reform in Nineteenth Century Oxford: A Study of Henry Halford Vaughan 1811-1885.* Oxford 1973
- and J.F.A. Mason. *Christ Church and Reform.* Oxford 1970
Blunt, W.S. *Diaries.* London 1932
Bottomore, T.B. *Elites and Society.* London 1966
Bridges, M.A. *Recollections of J.H. Bridges.* 1908
Briggs, A. *Victorian People.* New York 1963
- and J. Saville, eds. *Essays in Labour History.* London 1960
Bright, John. *Diaries.* London 1930
Brodrick, G.C. *The Abolition of Tests at the Universities of Oxford and Cambridge.* London 1866

- *Memories and Impressions.* London 1900
- *Political Studies.* London 1879

Brown, A.W. *The Metaphysical Society: Victorian Minds in Crisis.* New York 1947

Caird, E. *The Social Philosophy and Religion of Comte.* London 1885

Calleo, D. *Coleridge and the Idea of the Modern State.* New Haven 1966

Cambridge Essays. Cambridge 1858

Campbell, L. *The Nationalization of the Old English Universities.* London 1901

Carlyle, T. *Works.* London 1897

Christenson, T. *The Origins and History of Christian Socialism 1848-1854.* Aarhus 1962

Clarke, M.L. *Classical Education in Britain 1500-1900.* Cambridge 1959

Clough, A.H. *Correspondence,* ed. F.L. Mulhauser. Oxford 1957

Coleridge, E.H. *Life and Correspondence of Lord Coleridge.* London 1904

Coleridge, S.T. *On the Constitution of Church and State According to the Idea of Each.* London 1972

Colmer, J. *Coleridge, Critic of Society.* Oxford 1959

Comte, A. *Appeal to Conservatives.* London 1889
- *Catechisme positive.* Paris 1966
- *Eight Circulars.* London 1882
- *Lettres d'Auguste Comte à divers.* Paris 1902-5
- *Politiquè d'Auguste Comte,* ed. P. Arnaud. Paris 1965
- *The Positive Philosophy of Auguste Comte,* ed. H. Martineau. London 1875
- *The Positive Polity.* London 1875-77

Congreve, R. *Essays: Political, Social and Religious.* London 1874-1900

Connel, W.F. *The Educational Thought and Influence of Matthew Arnold.* London 1950

Cotton, H. *Indian and Home Memories.* London 1911

Cowling, M. *1867: Disraeli, Gladstone and Revolution.* Cambridge 1967
- *Mill and Liberalism.* Cambridge 1963

Cracroft, B. *Essays Political and Miscellaneous.* London 1868

Cunningham, H.S. *Lord Bowen.* 1896

Davies, H.S. and G. Watson, eds. *The English Mind.* Cambridge 1964

Duff, M.E. Grant *Elgin Speeches.* Edinburgh 1867
- *Political and Social Survey.* Edinburgh 1867

Duncan, G. *Marx and Mill: Two Views of Social Conflict and Social Harmony.* Cambridge 1973

Eliot, G. *Letters,* ed. G. Haight. New Haven 1954-5

Essays on the Endowment of Research by Various Writers. London 1876

Essays on Reform. London 1867

Everett, E.M. *The Party of Humanity: The Fortnightly Review and Its Contributors, 1865-1874.* Chapel Hill 1939

Farrar, F.W. ed. *Essays on a Liberal Education.* London 1867

Feaver, G. *From Status to Contract: A Biography of Sir Henry Maine.* London 1969

Filon, A. *Profils anglais.* Paris 1893

Fisher, H.A.L. *James Bryce.* London 1927

Forbes, D. *The Liberal Anglican Idea of History.* Cambridge 1952

Fraser, W.H. *Trade Unions and Society.* London 1974

Gardner, A.G. *Life of Sir William Harcourt.* London 1923

Garvin, J.L. *Life of Joseph Chamberlain,* Vols. I and II. London 1932-3

Gillespie, F.E. *Labour and Politics in England 1850-1867.* Durham, NC 1927

Glaisher, J.W.L., ed. *The Collected Mathematical Papers of H.J.S. Smith.* Oxford 1894

Green, V.H.H. *Oxford Common Room: A Study of Lincoln College and Mark Pattison.* London 1957

Greenberger, E.B. *Arthur Hugh Clough: The Growth of a Poet's Mind.* Cambridge, Mass. 1970

Godkin, R. *Life and Letters of Edward Laurence Godkin.* New York 1907

Gooch, G.P. *Life of Lord Courtney.* London 1920

Gouhier, H. *La Vie d'Auguste Comte.* Paris 1965

- *La Jeunesse d'Auguste Comte et la formation du positivisme.* Paris 1933-41

Gould, F.J. *The Life Story of a Humanist.* London 1923

Gross, J. *The Rise and Fall of the Man of Letters.* London 1969

Grosskurth, P. *John Addington Symonds.* London 1964

Guttsman, W.L. *The British Political Elite.* London 1963

Gwynn S. and G. Tuckwell. *The Life of Sir Charles Dilke.* London 1918

Haight, G. *George Eliot.* Oxford 1968

Hamburger, J. *Intellectuals in Politics: John Stuart Mill and the Philosophic Radicals.* New Haven 1965

Hamer, D.A. *John Morley: Liberal Intellectual in Politics.* Oxford 1968

Hansen, D. Roll *The Academy, 1869-1879: Victorian Intellectuals in Revolt, Anglistica, VIII.* Copenhagen 1957

Harris, S.H. *Auberon Herbert, Crusader for Liberty.* London 1943

Harrison, A. *Frederic Harrison: Thoughts and Memories.* London 1926

Harrison, F. *Autobiographic Memoirs.* London 1911

- *The Creed of a Layman.* London 1907

- *The Choice of Books.* London 1886

- *The Meaning of History.* London 1862

- *Memories and Thoughts.* London 1906

- *Oliver Cromwell.* London 1888
- *Order and Progress.* London 1875
- *Realities and Ideals.* London 1908
- *Studies in Early Victorian Literature.* London 1895
- *Tennyson, Ruskin and Mill, and Other Literary Estimates.* London 1905
- *John Ruskin.* London 1902

Harrison, J.F.C. *A History of the Working Men's College 1854-1954.* London 1954

Harrison, R. *Before the Socialists: Studies in Labour and Politics 1861-1881.* London 1965
- *The English Defence of the Commune, 1871.* London 1971

Himmelfarb, G. *Victorian Minds.* New York 1968

Hirst, F.W. *The Early Life and Letters of John Morley.* London 1927
- *In the Golden Days.* London 1947

Hobsbawm, E.J. *Labouring Men: Studies in the History of Labour.* New York 1967

Hofstadter, R. *Anti-Intellectualism in American Life.* New York 1966

Hollis, C. *The Oxford Union.* London 1965

Hort, A.F. *The Life and Letters of F.J.A. Hort.* London 1896

Humberstone, T.L. *University Representation.* London 1951

Hutton, R.H. *Studies in Parliament.* London 1866

Huxley, L. *The Life and Thought of T.H. Huxley.* London 1900

Israel, H. Ben- *English Historians and the French Revolution.* Cambridge 1968

J[ackson], H., and A. S[idgwick]. *Ad Eundem Club.* 1925

Jackson, W.W. *Ingram Bywater: Memoirs of an Oxford Scholar.* Oxford 1919

Johnston, W. *England as it is.* London 1851

Kennedy, W.F. *Humanist versus Economist: The Economic Thought of Samuel Taylor Coleridge.* Berkeley and Los Angeles 1958

Kingsley, C. *Letters and Memories,* ed. F.E.K. London 1894

Kinnear, J.B. *Principles of Reform, Political and Religious.* London 1865

Knickerbocker, F.W. *Free Minds: John Morley and His Friends.* Cambridge, Mass. 1943

Knight, R. *Illiberal Liberal: Robert Lowe in New South Wales 1842-1850.* Melbourne 1966

Knight, W. *Principal Shairp and His Friends.* London 1888

Kolakowski, L. *Positivist Philosophy from Hume to the Vienna Circle.* London 1972

Lake, W.C. *Memorials,* ed. K. Lake. London 1901

Leventhal, F.M. *Respectable Radical: George Howell and the Victorian Working Class.* London 1971

Lichtheim, G. *The Concept of Ideology and Other Essays.* New York 1967
Liveing, S. *A Nineteenth Century Teacher: John Henry Bridges.* London 1926
Lowe, R. *Speeches and Letters on Reform.* London 1867
Ludlow, J.M. and L. Jones. *The Progress of the Working Class.* London 1867
Lytton, Robert, Lord *Personal and Literary Letters*, ed. B. Balfour. London
   1906
McCarthy, J. *Portraits of the Sixties.* New York and London 1903
- *Reminiscences.* London 1899
McCarthy, P.J. *Matthew Arnold and the Three Classes.* New York 1964
Mack, E.C. *Public Schools and British Opinion, 1780-1860.* London 1938
Maitland, F.W. *Life of Leslie Stephen* London 1906
Mallet, C. *A History of Oxford.* London 1927
Mannheim, K. *Essays on the Sociology of Knowledge*, ed. P. Kecksmeti. London
   1957
- *Essays on Sociology and Social Psychology*, ed. P. Kecksmeti. London 1953
Marshall, T.H. *Class, Citizenship and Social Development.* New York 1965
Martin, A.P. *The Life and Letters of the Rt. Hon. Robert Lowe, Viscount
   Sherbrooke.* London 1893
Martineau, J. *Essays, Reviews and Addresses.* London 1891
Masterman, N.C. *J.M. Ludlow.* Cambridge 1963
Maurice, F. *Life and Letters of F.D. Maurice.* London 1885
Maurice, F.D. *On the Reformation of Society and How All Classes Contribute
   to It.* Southampton 1851
- *The Workman and the Franchise: Chapters from English History on the
   Representation and Education of the People.* London 1866
Meredith, G. *Letters*, ed. C.L. Cline. Oxford 1970
Mill, J.S. *Auguste Comte and Positivism.* Ann Arbor 1965
- *Autobiography.* Oxford 1924
- *Earlier Letters 1812-1848*, ed. F.E. Mineka. Toronto 1963
- *Essays in Politics and Culture*, ed. G. Himmelfarb. New York 1965
- *Later Letters 1849-1873*, ed. F.E. Mineka. Toronto 1972
- *Letters*, ed. H. Elliot. London 1910
- *Principles of Political Economy.* London 1909
Montalembert, Comte de. *The Political Future of England.* London 1856
Montgomery, R.J. *Examinations: An Account of their Evolution as an Adminis-
   trative Device in England.* London 1964
Morgan, J. *John, Viscount Morley.* London 1924
Morley, J. *Burke, A Historical Study.* London 1867
- *Cromwell.* London 1904
- *Diderot and the Encyclopaedists.* London 1886

- *Life of Richard Cobden.* London 1906
- *Life of W.E. Gladstone.* London 1904
- *Miscellanies.* London 1886
- *Modern Characteristics.* London 1865
- *On Compromise.* London 1886
- *Oracles on Man and Government.* London 1923
- *Politics and History.* London 1923
- *Rousseau.* London 1886
- *The Struggle for National Education.* London 1875
- *Studies in Conduct.* London 1867
- *Studies in Literature.* London 1890
- *Voltaire.* London 1885
- *Walpole.* London 1890

Morrah, H.A. *The Oxford Union: 1823-1923.* London 1923

Newsome, D. *Two Classes of Men: Platonism and English Romantic Thought.* London 1974

Nicoll, W.R. *James MacDonnell, Journalist.* London 1890

Osborne, C.E. *Christian Ideals in Political History.* London 1929

Oxford Essays: By Members of the University. London 1855-8

Packe, M.S. *Life of John Stuart Mill.* London 1954

Pankhurst, R.K. *The Saint Simonians, Mill and Carlyle.* London 1957

Papers Published by the Tutors' Association. Oxford 1854

Pattison, M. *Memoirs.* London 1885
- *Suggestions on Academical Organisation.* Edinburgh 1868

Perkin, H. *The Origins of Modern English Society, 1780-1880.* London 1969

Plumb, J.H., ed. *Studies in Social History: A Tribute to G.M. Trevelyan.* London 1955

Quin, M. *Memoirs of a Positivist.* London 1924

Rait, R.S., ed. *Memorials of A.V. Dicey.* London 1925

Reader, W.J. *Professional Men.* London 1966

Reynolds, J.S. *The Evangelicals at Oxford.* Oxford 1953

Richter, M. *The Politics of Conscience: T.H. Green and His Age.* London 1964

Roach, J. *Public Examinations in England, 1850-1900.* Cambridge 1971

Rogers, J.E.T. *Cobden and Modern Political Opinion.* London 1873
- *Education in Oxford: Its Methods, Its Aids and Its Rewards.* London 1861

Rothblatt, S. *The Revolution of the Dons: Cambridge and Society in Victorian England.* London 1968

Royle, E. *Victorian Infidels.* Manchester 1974

Rudman, H.W. *Italian Nationalism and English Letters.* London 1940

Runciman, W.G. *Relative Deprivation and Social Justice.* Berkeley and Los Angeles 1966

- *Social Science and Political Theory.* Cambridge 1965
Ruskin, J. *Works,* eds. Cook and Wedderburn. London 1905
Russell, B. and P., eds. *The Amberley Papers.* London 1937
Sanders, C.R. *Coleridge and the Broad Church Movement.* London 1954
Sandford, E.G. *Frederick Temple, by Seven Friends.* London 1907
Saville, J., ed. *Democracy and the Labour Movement.* London 1954
Saville, J. and J. Bellamy, eds. *Dictionary of Labour Biography.* London 1972–
Sayce, A.H. *Reminiscences.* London 1923
Scott, J.W.R. *The Life and Death of a Newspaper.* London 1962
Semmel, B. *The Governor Eyre Controversy.* London 1962
Senior, N.W. *Correspondence and Conversation of Alexis de Tocqueville with Nassau W. Senior,* ed. M.C.M. Simpson. London 1872
Shils, E. *The Intellectual and the Powers, and Other Essays.* Chicago 1972
Sidgwick, A. and E.M. *Henry Sidgwick: A Memoir.* London 1906
Simon, W.M. *European Positivism in the Nineteenth Century.*
Smith, F.B. *The Making of the Second Reform Bill.* Cambridge 1966
Smith, Goldwin *Correspondence,* ed. A. Haultain. London 1913
- *Empire: A Series of Letters Published in the Daily News.* Oxford 1863
- *Lectures on the Study of History.* New York 1866
- *My Memory of Gladstone.* London 1904
- *A Plea for the Abolition of Tests.* Oxford 1864
- *Reminiscences,* ed. A. Haultain. London 1910
- *The Reorganization of the University of Oxford.* Oxford 1868
Sparrow, J. *Mark Pattison and the Idea of a University.* Cambridge 1966
Stanley, A.P. *Life and Correspondence of Thomas Arnold.* London 1844
Stebbing, W. *Memorials of C.H. Pearson.* London 1900
Stephen, Sir Herbert. *The Savile Club.* Edinburgh 1923
Stephen, L. *Life of Henry Fawcett.* London 1885
- *Life of Sir James Fitzjames Stephen.* London 1895
- *Sketches of Cambridge by a Don.* London 1865
- *Some Early Impressions.* London 1924
Sutherland, G., ed. *Studies in the Growth of Nineteenth Century Government.* London 1972
Swinburne, A.C. *Letters,* ed. C.Y. Lang. New Haven 1959–62
Taylor, A.J.P. *The Trouble Makers: Dissent over Foreign Policy 1792–1939.* London 1957
Thompson, H.B. *The Choice of a Profession.* London 1857
Tillotson, G. and K. *Mid-Victorian Studies.* London 1965
Tollemache, L. *Old and Odd Memories.* London 1908
Tregenza, J. *Professor of Democracy: The Life of Charles Henry Pearson 1830–1894.* Melbourne 1968

Trevelyan, G.M. *Sir G.O. Trevelyan.* London 1932
Trilling, L. *Matthew Arnold.* New York 1955
Vaughan, H.H. *Two General Lectures on Modern History.* Oxford 1849
- *Oxford Reform and Oxford Professors.* London 1854
Vidler, A. *F.D. Maurice and Company.* London 1966
Vincent, J. *The Formation of the Liberal Party.* London 1966
Wallace, E. *Goldwin Smith, Victorian Liberal.* Toronto 1957
Ward, W. *Ten Personal Studies.* London 1908
Ward, W.R. *Victorian Oxford.* London 1965
Weber, M. *From Max Weber: Essays in Sociology*, eds. H.H. Gerth and C. Wright Mills. London 1948
Wemyss, Mrs R. *Memoir of the Rt. Hon. Sir Robert Morier.* London 1911
Winter, J. *Robert Lowe.* Toronto 1976
Woodward, F.J. *The Doctor's Disciples: A Study of Four Pupils of Arnold of Rugby: Stanley, Gell, Clough, W. Arnold.* Oxford 1954
Young, G.M. *Portrait of an Age.* Oxford 1960
- *Victorian Essays.* London 1962

V ARTICLES

Adelman, P. 'Frederic Harrison and the "Positivist" Attack on Orthodox Political Economy.' *History of Political Economy*, III, spring 1971, 170-89
Acton, H.B. 'Comte's Positivism and the Science of Society.' *Philosophy*, VI, 1951, 291-310
Arnold, T. 'Rugby School.' *The Quarterly Journal of Education*, VII, April 1834
Bamford, T.W. 'Public Schools and Social Class 1801-1850.' *British Journal of Sociology*, XII, 3, 1961, 224-35
Coats, A.W. 'The Historicist Reaction in English Political Economy, 1870-90.' *Economica*, May 1954, 143-53
Compton, J.M. 'Open Competition and the I.C.S., 1854-76.' *English Historical Review*, LXXXIII, April 1968
De Laura, D.J. 'Arnold and Carlyle,' PMLA, LXXIX, March 1964, 104-29
Eisen, S. 'Huxley and the Positivists,' *Victorian Studies*, VII, June 1964, 337-58
Francis, M. 'The Origins of *Essays and Reviews*: An Interpretation of Mark Pattison in the 1850s.' *The Historical Journal*, XVII, 1974, 797-812
Farmer, M.E. 'The Positivist Movement and the Development of English Sociology.' *Sociological Review*, XV, 1, 1967, 5-20
Frye, N. 'The Problem of Spiritual Authority in the Nineteenth Century.' C. Camden, ed., *Literary Views: Critical and Historical Essays.* Chicago 1964, 145-58

Hughes, E. 'Sir Charles Trevelyan and Civil Service Reform.' *English Historical Review*, LXIV, 1949, 53-88, 206-34
Jex-Blake, T.W. 'Rugby Memories of Three Eminent Rugbeians.' *National Review*, XLIX, April 1907, 232-6
Kent, C.A. 'Higher Journalism and the Mid-Victorian Clerisy.' *Victorian Studies*, XIII, Dec. 1969, 181-98
Lukes, S. and G. Duncan. 'The New Democracy.' *Political Studies*, XII, 1963, 156-77
McCready, H.W. 'The British Elections of 1874; Frederic Harrison and the Liberal-Labour Dilemma.' *Canadian Journal of Economics and Political Science*, XX, May 1954, 166-75
- 'British Labour's Lobby, 1867-75.' Ibid. XXII, May 1956, 141-60
- 'British Labour and the Royal Commission on Trade Unions, 1867-1869.' *University of Toronto Quarterly*, XXIV, July 1955, 390-409
Moore, R.J. 'The Abolition of Patronage in the India Civil Service and the Closure of Haileybury College.' *Historical Journal*, VII, 1964, 246-67
Musgrave, F. 'Middle Class Education and Employment in the Nineteenth Century.' *Economic History Review*, XII, 1, 1959, 99-111
- 'Middle Class Education and Employment in the Nineteenth Century: A Rejoinder.' Ibid., XIV, 2, 1961, 321-9
Nettl, J.P. 'Ideas, Intellectuals and Structures of Dissent.' P. Rieff, ed. *On Intellectuals*. New York 1970, 57-136
Nisbet, R.A. 'Conservatism and Sociology.' *American Journal of Sociology*, LVIII, Sept. 1952, 167-75
Pattison, M. 'Philosophy at Oxford.' *Mind*, I, Jan. 1876, 82-93
Perkin, H.J. 'Middle Class Education and Employment in the Nineteenth Century: A Critical Note.' *Economic History Review*, XIV, 1, 1961, 122-30
Richter, M. 'Intellectual and Class Alienation: Oxford Idealist Diagnoses and Prescriptions.' *Archives européenes de sociologie*, VII, 1966, 1-26
Roach, J. 'Liberalism and the Victorian Intelligentsia.' *Cambridge Historical Journal*, XIII, 1, 1957, 58-81
- 'Victorian Universities and the National Intelligentsia.' *Victorian Studies*, III, Dec. 1959, 131-50
See, H. 'Auguste Comte et la vie politique et sociale de son temps.' *Revue d'histoire moderne*, II, 1927, 412-21
Simon, W.H. 'Auguste Comte's English Disciples.' *Victorian Studies*, VII, Dec. 1965, 161-72
- 'Comte's Orthodox Disciples: The Rise and Fall of a Cenacle.' *French Historical Studies*, IV, 1, 1965, 42-62
Taylor, F.S. 'The Teaching of Science at Oxford in the Nineteenth Century.'

Annals of Science, VIII, 1, 1952, 82-112
Vogeler, M.S. 'Matthew Arnold and Frederic Harrison, the Prophet of Culture and the Prophet of Positivism.' *Studies in English Literature*, II, 1962, 141-62
Winter, J. 'English Democracy and the Example of Australia.' *Pacific Historical Review*, XXXV, 1966, 67-80

VI THESES

Brick, A.R. 'The *Leader*; Organ of Radicalism.' Yale University PHD, 1957
Byrne, J.F. 'The *Reader*: A Review of Literature, Science and the Arts 1863-67.' Northwestern University PHD, 1964
Eisen, S. 'Frederic Harrison: The Life and Thought of an English Positivist.' Johns Hopkins PHD, 1957
McCready, H.W. 'Frederic Harrison and the British Working Class.' Harvard PHD, 1952

Index

Lawyers 66, 67-8, 89
Leader 74
Lewes, G.H. 56, 85, 108
Liberal Anglicanism 57; *see also*
　Broad Church
Liberal party 20, 48
Liberalism 49-50, 163
Liberation Society 113
Life Peerages 22, 44
Lincoln College 118
Lincoln's Inn 31, 67, 156
Lloyd's Weekly London Newspaper
　24, 75
London Positivist Society 91, 93
London Trades Council ('Junta') 81;
　see also trade unions
Lowe, Robert 35-6, 38, 40, 110, 142,
　166
Lowell, James R. 38
Ludlow, J.M. 63
Lushington, Godfrey 22, 25, 26, 31,
　43, 72, 73, 74, 146; *Times* leader
　writer 27; parliamentary candidate
　48-9; conversion to Comtism 58;
　senior civil servant 90, 102
Lushington, Vernon 31, 89
Lytton, 2nd Earl 157, 159

McCarthy, Justin 91
McLaren, Duncan 47
Macmillan, Alexander 107
Maine, H. 66, 94, 156, 164
Maistre, J. de 118
Manchester 6, 25, 29, 33, 41, 73
Mannheim, K. 155
Manning, Cardinal 89
Marlborough College 67
Martineau, Harriet 56
Marx, K. 59, 62, 84, 97, 137-8, 148,
　154

Maurice, F.D. 5, 7, 21, 37, 58, 63,
　71-2
Maxse, F.A. 48, 114n, 163
Mazzini, G. 23, 49, 145n
Meredith, George 114n
Metaphysical Society 89, 130n, 133
Miall, Edward 26, 29
Michelet, Jules 8
Middle Class: and the universities 29;
　and university radicals 40-2; and
　Comtism 59, 65, 70, 75, 80, 98,
　147; and 1874 elections 142
Midland Institute (Birmingham and
　Midland Institute) 162
Midlothian campaign 162
Mignet, F.A.M. 8
Mill, J.S. 9, 26, 124, 163; as intellec-
　tual in politics 37, 46-7, 49-50, 51,
　121, 141-2; inspires university radi-
　cals 44-7; and Comte 56, 127-8,
　140, 141-2; and John Morley 105,
　106, 127-8, 160, 161
Milner, Alfred 116
Milton, John 99
Miner and Workman's Advocate 75
Miners' Council 81
Minority representation 44, 151
Molesworth, Sir W. 141
Montalembert, Comte de 16
Morgan, G.O. 48, 50
Morier, Robert 8
Morison, J.C. 107, 108
Morley, John 33, 34, 96, 97, 104, 136,
　142, 153, 155, 156; parliamentary
　candidate 48, 50, 52, 112, 116;
　journalist 105-7, 110, 111-16; uses
　of Comtism to 108-10, 118-24; and
　Chamberlain 111-13, 161; ambiva-
　lence towards Comtism 114; *Burke*
　118-20, 135; 'Condorcet,' 'Turgot'